THE MODERNIST MOVEMENT
IN THE ROMAN CHURCH
ITS ORIGINS & OUTCOME

LONDON
Cambridge University Press
FETTER LANE

NEW YORK · TORONTO
BOMBAY · CALCUTTA · MADRAS
Macmillan

TOKYO
Maruzen Company Ltd

THE MODERNIST MOVEMENT
IN THE ROMAN CHURCH
ITS ORIGINS & OUTCOME

BEING THE NORRISIAN PRIZE ESSAY
IN THE UNIVERSITY OF CAMBRIDGE
FOR THE YEAR 1933

by

ALEC R. VIDLER, M.A.

Priest of the Oratory of the Good Shepherd
Formerly Exhibitioner of Selwyn College

CAMBRIDGE
AT THE UNIVERSITY PRESS
1934

To

W. L. K.

CONTENTS

PART III

TYRRELL

PART IV

OTHER MODERNISTS: OTHER MODERNISMS

Contents

PART V

THE OUTCOME OF THE MODERNIST MOVEMENT

PREFACE

The words 'modernism' and 'modernist' are used throughout this essay with exclusive reference to the movement which is its subject, *i.e.* to the movement in the Roman Catholic Church which began about 1890, was condemned in the encyclical *Pascendi* in 1907, and lasted till about 1910. This usage is determined by considerations of convenience, and it is not intended to deny the propriety of giving to these words that much wider application which is now current especially in England and America. They were indeed originally applied[1] to the movement with which we are here concerned, and it is permissible to regret their application to other movements and to other groups of persons, which, however similar in some respects, have in view a different, and even a directly opposite, aim. Such regrets have been expressed by more than one English writer.[2] They are however idle. The wider and more comprehensive usage is now securely established among us; both its existence and its legitimacy were in fact acknowledged by Tyrrell as early as 1909.[3] Nevertheless, since I need here some single term to denote the particular movement and group of persons which form the subject of my essay, I restrict myself to the original, narrower usage, which still retains its ascendancy in France.

[1] This statement requires qualification if the occasional use of the words by earlier writers is taken into account; see Appendix I, p. 270 below.

[2] *E.g.* by A. Fawkes in a letter to *The Times*, February 19th, 1914 (quoted by M. D. Petre, *Modernism*, p. 101), by W. R. Matthews, *Studies in Christian philosophy*, p. 16, and by J. N. Figgis, *The fellowship of the mystery*, p. 265. Cp. C. W. Emmet, *Journal of Religion* (November, 1922), p. 562; S. C. Carpenter, *Church and people 1789–1889* (1933), pp. 143, 578; J. S. Bezzant, *Theology* (August, 1933), p. 100; *The Times Literary Supplement* (October 12th, 1933), p. 680.

[3] *Christianity at the cross roads*, p. 3; cp. *Medievalism*, pp. 143 ff.

Perhaps a yet further restriction ought also to be mentioned. Modernism in the Roman Catholic Church was not a single, unified movement, but a complex of movements. They fall into two main divisions, for doctrinal modernism was largely separate, and is in any case easily separable, from sociological modernism.[1] The 'Christian democrat' movements in France and Italy, whose course was more or less contemporaneous with that of doctrinal modernism, were not condemned by the pope in the encyclical *Pascendi*, but on other occasions. This in itself explains their exclusion from the scope of this essay; if they enter into it at all, they do so only indirectly.

Its prescribed subject was 'The origins and outcome of the modernist movement condemned by the encyclical *Pascendi gregis*'. The greater part of my essay consists of an investigation of the course of the movement itself, rather than specifically of its origins and outcome. The reasons for this method of treating the subject are readily explained. It is impossible to take for granted any definition or description of what the movement was, or of what were its principles or doctrines. The whole subject is one about which widely different opinions are held. It would be futile to try to trace the ancestry of, and the influences which moulded, a character in history, or the outcome of his activity, unless his identity and the distinguishing features of his life were evident. *A fortiori* this applies to a movement in which many different persons were engaged, and of which the characteristics were anything but simple and coherent. It is therefore necessary to investigate and to understand the character of the movement itself in order to appreciate in what sense, and to what extent, it had, or could be expected to have, any specific origins and outcome. Moreover, to follow the course of the movement, and in particular the careers of the two most prominent figures who took part in it, is to go a

[1] Cp. E. Buonaiuti, *Le modernisme catholique*, pp. 98 f.

long way towards discovering the nature of its origins and outcome.

I do not know of any book that covers the same ground or that is constructed on the same plan as the present essay. In the bibliography (see pp. 274–9 below) I have marked with an asterisk those books to which I am consciously most indebted. In the text or in the notes I have tried to acknowledge as fully as possible the sources from which I have derived particular pieces of information, and also to make clear where I have depended at all closely on the work of others.

While in connexion with each part of the essay I have carried my investigations and verifications as far as time and opportunity permitted, the subject is so vast and so varied that I cannot claim to have produced more than a general introduction to it. There does not exist such an introduction in English. The books of Archdeacon Lilley and Miss Petre, both of which bear the title *Modernism*, valuable as they are, are more restricted in their scope. The two best studies of the movement as a whole, those in French by Houtin and Rivière, are written on plans which have not suited my purpose, within limits which I have had to exceed, and from points of view neither of which is my own.

A. R. V.

The Oratory House
Cambridge
February 1934

INTRODUCTION

If the encyclical *Pascendi* (September 8th, 1907)[1] were by itself a reliable introduction to the subject of this essay, we should begin our inquiry into the origins and outcome of the modernist movement with certain clear suppositions. It would lead us to suppose that there had been actively at work in the Roman Catholic Church, for at least some years previous to the date of the encyclical, a 'school' of thinkers and writers, both priests and laymen, whose object was to achieve a complete *bouleversement* of Catholicism in its traditional form. If the doctrines of this school had seemed to lack 'order and systematic arrangement', this was due to a 'clever device'. In reality, the 'modernist system' was a coherent whole; the connexion between its various parts could be clearly distinguished. The system proceeded from a philosophical foundation, viz. 'agnosticism', according to which 'human reason is confined entirely within the field of *phenomena*', to a doctrine of 'vital immanence', according to which the explanation of religion 'must certainly be found in the life of man'. From these premises the theology, the history, the criticism and the apologetics of the modernist school followed in a strict and logical sequence. 'Their historico-critical conclusions are the natural outcome of their philosophical principles.' 'Their system does not consist in scattered and unconnected theories, but, as it were, in a closely connected whole, so that it is not possible to admit one without admitting all.'[2]

If these suppositions were accepted as a working hypothesis, the method of our inquiry would be plainly indicated. First, we should study the works of the modernists, in order

[1] References are to the Eng. trans. of the encyclical in Paul Sabatier's *Modernism* (1908), pp. 231–346.

[2] *Op. cit.* pp. 288, 309.

to test and amplify the account of their system which is contained in the encyclical. Next, we should investigate the process by which the system was developed, and the special contribution to its development of the various members of the school. Thence, we should try to trace back its central ideas and principles to their ultimate origins. As for the outcome of the movement, we should examine the effects of its condemnation within the Roman Church, and seek to discover what influence, since it was condemned there, the modernist system has had elsewhere.

If, however, we did adopt this procedure, we should quickly discover that the encyclical is not a reliable introduction to our subject, and that to accept its account of the character of the movement, even as a working hypothesis, would be extremely misleading. For it would become evident that those, who by common admission were the most prominent modernists, unite in testifying that there was no 'modernist system', that their thought had no strict or logical coherence, and in fact that there was no such thing as a 'modernist school'. Nor is there any reason to suppose that this lack of 'order and systematic arrangement' was due to a 'clever device', or that the modernists 'deliberately and advisedly' advocated doctrines, contrary one to another, so as to give a false impression of their attitude.[1] Not only does a perusal of their writings contradict the supposition that what we have to do with is the system of a school, but in particular it contradicts, what is a leading contention of the encyclical, that the historico-critical methods and conclusions of the modernists were consequent upon, and derived from, preconceived philosophical principles.

It should be observed that we have not to consider whether it is *possible* out of the writings of the modernists to construct a logically coherent system. By a sufficiently ingenious process of selection and abstraction it would be possible to

[1] *Op. cit.* p. 262.

construct such a system out of much more disparate material. We have to ask (*a*) whether a system was implicit—obviously none was explicit—in their works, and (*b*) whether the system of the encyclical has a *prima facie* claim to be regarded as a true representation. Now the modernists themselves, if they agree about nothing else, agree that both these questions, and especially the latter, must be answered in the negative.

The so-called modernists (wrote M. Loisy in 1908) are not a homogeneous and united group, as one would suppose if one consulted the papal encyclical, but a quite limited number of persons, who share the desire to adapt the Catholic religion to the intellectual, moral, and social needs of the present time....

The pope's exposition of the modernist doctrines is practically a fantasy of the theological imagination, whereas he has ignored what is the most important, one might say the only essential, question....Pius X attributes to (the modernists) a system conceived after the manner of the scholastic theories, where not one of them will recognize himself, and he condemns them *en bloc* in the name of his own system....The fact is that they have never formed in the Church a sect nor a party, nor even a school; that they have worked on very diverse fields...and that, if they have found themselves in agreement on certain points, and in the first instance on the necessity of a reform of Catholic teaching, it is because they have entered by different routes into the current of contemporary thought, and that, through varied experiences, they have reached the same conclusion....This state of things is misconceived from the beginning to the end of the papal encyclical.[1]

What M. Loisy said then, he has reiterated since.[2] Indeed he had in effect said as much as early as 1903 in the introduction to *Autour d'un petit livre*.[3]

Not less emphatically did Tyrrell, who of other modernists

[1] *Simples réflexions*, pp. 14f., 149–52; cp. pp. 18ff., 117, 155, 188, 245, 269f.
[2] *Mémoires*, I, 477, 535, II, 22, 565–70, III, 71, *et passim*.
[3] Pp. xviiif.

is acknowledged to have been the most prominent, protest
that the encyclical travestied the movement. 'With all due
respect to the Encyclical *Pascendi*, Modernists wear no uniform
nor are they sworn to the defence of any system; still less
of that which His Holiness has fabricated for them.'[1] This
objection to the papal representation of the movement was
raised by nearly all the other leading modernists, *e.g.* by von
Hügel, Miss Petre, Fogazzaro, Buonaiuti, Schnitzer and Le
Roy,[2] and also its justice has been acknowledged by many
who have studied the movement with sympathy from without or in retrospect. Thus, for instance, the Anglican A. L.
Lilley wrote in 1907:

> This supposed Modernist *system* is but a perverse figment of the
> imagination of the clever and inveterately scholastic theologian to
> whom Pius X entrusted the drafting of the Encyclical.... No one
> who knows anything of the various movements co-ordinated by
> this writer... under the name of Modernism can fail to detect the
> unfairness or wilful blindness of that lust of system-mongering
> which has impelled him to his task.[3]

Moreover, an orthodox Roman Catholic may now admit
the abstract and artificial character of the modernist system as

[1] *Medievalism*, p. 106. Cp. *Christianity at the cross roads*, p. 3, *Hibbert
Journal* (January, 1908), pp. 247ff., and a letter from Tyrrell, which is
quoted by E. Buonaiuti, *Le modernisme catholique*, p. 145.

[2] See von Hügel's letters to Loisy in the latter's *Mémoires*, ii, 569f., cp.
ii, 559; M. D. Petre, *Modernism*, pp. 114f.; T. Gallarati-Scotti, *The life of
Antonio Fogazzaro*, pp. 277ff.; Buonaiuti, *Le modernisme catholique*, pp.
47ff.; J. Schnitzer, *Der katholische Modernismus*, p. 4; E. Le Roy, *Dogme et
critique*, pp. 108f. Cp. *The programme of modernism*, p. 16.

[3] *Modernism*, pp. 258f. Cp. G. C. Rawlinson, *Recent French tendencies*
(1917), pp. 37f.; G. la Piana, 'A review of Italian modernism' in *Harvard
Theological Review* (October, 1916), pp. 371, 373; Ch. Guignebert,
Modernisme et tradition catholique en France (1908), p. 154, *Le christianisme
mediéval et moderne* (1922), p. 303, and *Revue historique*, clxix, 104f.;
R. Gout, *L'affaire Tyrrell* (1910), pp. 201f.; F. Heiler, *Der Katholizismus*
(1923), p. xxxi; J. F. Bethune-Baker, *The way of modernism* (1927), p. 3;
M. Goguel, *Revue d'histoire et de philosophie religieuses*, xii, 90.

constructed in the encyclical. Perhaps at the time of its promulgation, when to applaud the encyclical was a condition of orthodoxy, and when its infallibility was being freely canvassed,[1] this admission could hardly be made by those who wished to avoid the suspicion of heresy. M. J. Rivière, however, in his *Le modernisme dans l'Église* (1929), bound as he is to defend the papal condemnation of modernism, at the same time allows that it would be a mistake to look in the encyclical for the reproduction of a doctrine which in the form stated had already existed in the Church. It was not the intention of the pope to summarize the conceptions of any particular author, but rather to disengage by abstraction a general idea from a multiplicity of individual cases. Everyone should agree, he says, with the opponents of the encyclical in recognizing the individual originality of the principal modernists. The pope wanted to present only *un modernisme schématique*, which is useful in discovering the significance and extent of its concrete manifestations.[2]

The modernist system of the encyclical may then be regarded as a convenient fiction, which has been repudiated by those whose conceptions it purports to synthetize. The modernists had not formulated a new system with which they proposed to replace the received system. On the contrary, if we admit their own testimony, their writings represented no more than a number of individual and, for the most part, independent attempts to adapt the received system to the exigencies of modern knowledge and culture. But it may still be asked whether these attempts did in fact have a common philosophical origin in that they proceeded from the acceptance of certain specific abstract principles

[1] Tyrrell showed himself a bad prophet when he wrote in *The Times* (October 1st, 1907): 'Not even the extreme theologians will pretend that an encyclical of this kind has the slightest claim to be considered an ecumenical and so far "infallible" document'. See *Catholic Encyclopaedia*, art. 'Modernism', and J. Rivière, *Le modernisme dans l'Église* (1929), p. 365.   [2] *Op. cit.* pp. 366f.

which, since they constituted a denial of the fundamental
postulates of Catholic orthodoxy, vitiated in advance all
their conclusions.[1] Here, again, the modernists themselves
declare that their proposed reforms of Catholic teaching did
not have their point of origin in the adoption of any philosophical presuppositions, but in a determination to face and
accept the general development of modern scientific knowledge, and, in particular, the results of biblical and historical
criticism.[2] It was this determination that forced them to
realize that much of the commonly accepted system of
traditional orthodoxy, as taught in the theological schools,
required modification and restatement. And it was from this
approach that they proceeded, in so far as they proceeded at
all, to broach wider philosophical and theological questions.
The statement of the encyclical that 'their historico-critical
conclusions were the natural outcome of their philosophical
principles' was therefore an inversion of the facts. The extent
to which, and the manner in which, they proposed philosophical or theological restatements of the orthodox position
depended for the most part on the particular nature of their
respective individual intellectual interests. But, even in the
case of those whose interests were predominantly philosophical, their attitude to history and criticism was the factor
by which their heterodoxy was measured.[3]

---

[1] See, for instance, van Loo, *Kantisme et modernisme* (1917), pp. 148 f.:
'Parti du double principe kantien de l'agnosticisme (subjectivisme
théorique) et de l'autonomie (subjectivisme méthodique), bâtissant son
système doctrinal sur le sable mouvant de la spéculation personnelle, il
était nécessaire que le moderniste, pour défendre et protéger ses élucu-
brations, s'appuyât sur l'*a priorisme* le plus exclusif. Or tout *a priori* étant
d'ordre émotionnel ne peut que troubler profondément l'évolution de la
pensée scientifique et la conduire à l'abîme des erreurs les plus absurdes'.
Cp. *ibid.* p. 170.

[2] The orthodox L. de Grandmaison agreed that modernism originated
in this way, see *Études* (September 20th, 1923), pp. 647 f.

[3] *E.g.* see pp. 187 f. below.

Alfred Fawkes was repeating what Loisy, Tyrrell and others had asserted from the beginning, when in 1927 he said:

In the encyclical *Pascendi*...an attempt...is made to transfer the question with which it deals—that of Modernism—from the ground of fact to that of speculation. It represents the issues as philosophical.... The question between Modernism and the Church is primarily historical; one of knowing, or not knowing, certain facts. These facts are concerned with various subject matter—with Christian origins, with Scripture, with comparative religion, with the science of the mind. If we have a turn for speculation, our knowledge will no doubt arrange itself under certain categories and dispose us to certain generalizations. But to account for Modernism in this way, or to associate it with any particular generalizations or speculative principles, is to put the cart before the horse. It is the premises which lead to the conclusion, not the conclusion to the premises.[1]

Our object is to apprehend the modernist movement as it actually was in its concrete reality; we must refuse to be dominated by any abstract theory about it or to admit the presuppositions of those who have an interest in looking at it from only one angle and in taking only a partial view of it. If we may believe the modernists themselves, their movement was not comparable with, for example, the Tractarian movement in the Church of England; they were not a body of men in close fellowship with one another who set themselves to

[1] *The Modern Churchman*, XVII, 330. Cp. A. Loisy, *Simples réflexions*, pp. 30 f., *Mémoires*, II, 390, III, 215; G. Tyrrell, *Medievalism*, pp. 93, 108 f., 127, *The Church and the future*, p. 15; *The programme of modernism*, pp. 15 ff.; Miss Petre, in the *Hibbert Journal* (October, 1925), writes: 'Catholic Modernism was an effort to combine the latest claims of science and history and democracy with the spiritual teaching of the Church, and to obtain right of citizenship for the scholar, whose sole aim *qua* scholar was scientific and historic truth, in the Church to which he submitted his religious life and conduct' (p. 83). For a recognition of this by an outside observer see H. R. Mackintosh in the *London Quarterly Review* (April, 1915), p. 232: 'The Modernist point of departure is not found, as might be supposed, in the realm of theology proper, but in that of history and Biblical criticism'.

propagate certain clearly defined principles. They did not form a school like the Ritschlians, where a number of disciples extended and developed the thought of an acknowledged master. Nor were they organized like the present-day Anglican Modern Churchmen; they had no society corresponding to the 'Churchmen's Union', they held no annual conferences, they published no official periodical. They were a number of individual Roman Catholics, who in one way or another came to realize that the received teaching of their Church was out of harmony with contemporary thought, and who decided to do what they could to promote a reform of the Church's teaching.[1] Broadly speaking, they opined that it had remained stationary, or at least static, since the middle ages, and that it failed to take account of the immense advance in human knowledge which had taken place since then. But they were never agreed on any one program of reform, and their proposed restatements of Catholic teaching differed substantially from one another. Whether, if the movement had been tolerated by the ecclesiastical authorities, it would have grown into a 'school', an organization, a party, it is impossible to say, and it is idle to speculate. It was in fact condemned and ruthlessly suppressed before it had even approximated to such a stage of growth. The fugitive attempts to organize groups of modernists, which were made after 1907, all proved abortive.

Its lack of cohesion, its incongruous and almost spasmodic character, make every generalization about Catholic modernism hazardous. The very term 'modernism' in itself invites misapprehension; it implies a classification of what can be classified only with severe qualifications. *Il y a autant de*

---

[1] 'L'objet essentiel du mouvement...était, tout en restant sur le terrain catholique et sans porter atteinte à l'unité de l'Église, de rompre l'absolutisme de la croyance théologique, de refondre surtout le régime intellectuel de l'Église et son enseignement' (Loisy, *L'Église et la France* (1925), p. 101).

modernismes que de modernistes is a saying that occurs more than once in French writings on the subject;[1] it is a saying which ought to be constantly borne in mind.

Our method of inquiry into the origins and outcome of the movement will be different from what it would have been if we were able to regard the apparent implications of the encyclical *Pascendi* as justified. The movement cannot be rightly understood unless it is seen as a result of the discord between modern knowledge and traditional Roman Catholic orthodoxy. It consisted of various efforts to remove this discord on the part of convinced Roman Catholics who wanted to combine the culture of their time with the profession of their religion. It has been truly observed[2] that the distinction between a modernist and an innovator, pure and simple, is that the former wanted to maintain a continuity, at least apparent and verbal, an institutional continuity, between the new and the traditional positions. The clash between modern culture and traditional orthodoxy[3] became increasingly evident during the course of the nineteenth century, and several attempts were made to remove it by those who were designated 'liberal Catholics'. The modernist movement was, from this point of view, the last and most thoroughgoing of a series of similar movements,[4] and a survey of those that preceded it will both disclose the historical situation out of which it arose and also serve as a

[1] See A. Houtin, *Le Père Hyacinthe* (1924), III, 117; Loisy, *Mémoires*, III, 212; S. Leblanc, *Un clerc qui n'a pas trahi* (1931), p. 83.

[2] By L. de Grandmaison, *Études* (September 20th, 1923), pp. 644f.

[3] Dr H. L. Stewart, in his *Modernism, past and present* (1932), studies this subject in a much wider context than we need to do here. His book is only incidentally concerned with modernism in the sense in which we are using the term; its real subject is the relation between conservative and progressive tendencies throughout the history of Christianity.

[4] Thus G. Weill, in his *Histoire du catholicisme libéral en France 1828–1908* (1909), treats the modernist movement as the third phase of liberal Catholicism.

background against which its own distinctive characteristics can be more clearly seen. The modernists were the successors of the nineteenth-century liberal Catholics, but they were more than that.

Part I of this essay is therefore intended to portray those aspects of the history of the Roman Church in the nineteenth century which are specially relevant to the origins of the modernist movement. We must, however, be on our guard against supposing that any apparent anticipations of modernism which we may meet contributed directly to the origins of the movement. In 1913 a Protestant professor published a book[1] in which he affected to demonstrate that modernism was a continuation of the work of the Catholic school of Tübingen of which Möhler was the outstanding figure. As a matter of fact, neither Loisy, nor Tyrrell, nor even the Germanic von Hügel, was influenced by Möhler and his school, however similar may be some of the ideas they put forward. In his review of the book, to which reference has just been made, M. Loisy wrote:

> The modernism which we knew was not the following up of another movement; it did not continue a school; it was born chiefly of a situation; and if the solutions which it proposed resemble more or less those of Möhler and the other members of the Tübingen school, that is because the present situation of Catholicism resembles still in many respects that of 1815–40.[2]

Part I purports to convey an accurate impression of what this situation was.

Parts II and III are devoted to a comprehensive study of the careers of the two chief modernists, Loisy and Tyrrell, whose personal history, intellectual interests, and religious temperament were anything but identical. Part IV contains a slighter

---

[1] E. Vermeil, *Jean-Adam Möhler et l'école catholique de Tubingue (1815–1840), étude sur la théologie romantique en Wurtemberg et les origines germaniques du modernisme.*

[2] See *Mémoires*, III, 268 f.

sketch of the other more important manifestations of modernism. Since the movement consisted of a number of individual attempts to set forward a revision of traditional orthodoxy, a complete investigation of its origins would necessitate a study of the life and work of each individual modernist. That is obviously beyond the scope of the present essay; but the procedure which we have adopted, while it avoids the dangers of excessive abstraction and classification, yet ensures that no significant characteristic of the movement will be left out of account. How far the modernists were indebted (*a*) to earlier writers, whether Catholic or non-Catholic, and (*b*) to contemporary influences and experiences, and also how far their own work was strictly speaking original, will become evident in the course of our inquiry.

Part v is a study of the outcome of the movement, first of its effects within the Roman Church, and then of the influence which it has exercised elsewhere.

PART I

THE ROMAN CHURCH IN THE NINETEENTH CENTURY

Chapter I

THE BEGINNING OF THE CATHOLIC REVIVAL

'The French Revolution is the most important event in the life of modern Europe....It brought on the stage of human affairs forces which have moulded the thoughts and actions of men ever since, and have taken a permanent place among the formative influences of civilisation.'[1] These forces were, in the first instance, political—the ideals of liberty, fraternity and equality, the principles of the sovereignty of the people and of personal freedom. But the Revolution was associated in its happening, and still more has been associated in retrospect, with those widespread movements in philosophy and literature, in art and religion, which distinguish the passing of the eighteenth century into the nineteenth. The periods into which history is commonly divided are not of course so 'hard and fast' as our manner of describing them suggests. The characteristic features of a reign or of a century are necessarily generalizations to which there may have been many particular exceptions. Nor do these characteristic features fall down suddenly from heaven; they are moulded by the past as much as by the present. Thus, if we say that the French Revolution, which represents the political birthday of modern Europe, may also be taken to represent the emergence of nineteenth-century culture in general, we do not suppose that the Age of the Enlightenment ended and the Romantic revival began precisely in the year 1789.

The Age of the Enlightenment was not a glorious period in the history of any of the Churches. Its depreciation of religious enthusiasm is notorious, and it cannot be pretended

[1] *The Cambridge Modern History* (1907), VIII, 754.

that the absence of fanaticism was accorded the recompense of solid and profound virtue. It was a time when 'it was easy to talk of the loftiest virtues without practising even the lowliest'.[1] It was an age of rationalism in the sense that the capacity of the self-enlightened human intellect to settle all the problems that were presented to it was hardly doubted. The temper of philosophy was cold and static; the vast enrichment of the field of empirical knowledge, which was to come to fruition in the next century, was almost unsuspected. Its intellectual constructions were at once artificial and superficial. In literature classicism reigned supreme; all novelty and freshness were severely discountenanced. The Churches retained their established positions, and they were content to live on their past. The practice of religion, such as it was, was conventional. The traditional theology, whether in its Catholic or Protestant form, was moribund, and the writers and thinkers of the time, even if for the sake of propriety they treated it with a patronizing tolerance, in effect ignored its claims upon their allegiance. The Roman Church, in particular, produced no giants to compare with those of the *Grand Siècle*, no bishops of the stature of Bossuet and Fénelon, no scholar-mystics like Pascal. The controversies of the period, such as that between the Jesuits and the Jansenists, were barren survivals.

In 1789 a complacent Europe was rudely awakened by the outbreak of the French Revolution. What the ultimate effects of this awakening might be could hardly be foreseen, but at least the whole political and social fabric of the *ancien régime* was shaken to its foundations, and established institutions, not only in France, but everywhere, were sensitive to the upheaval. The Roman Church had been securely bound up with the old order; was it capable of surviving the transition to the new? Events in France, during the last ten years of the century, did not appear to offer many

[1] J. Oman, *The problem of faith and freedom* (1906), p. 142.

grounds for hope. The Revolution had not at first attempted to abolish the Church, or to make a complete and abrupt break with the Catholic religion; but, provoked by the 'essentially reactionary attitude of the Holy See', its hostility grew in intensity until its policy was one of unmitigated persecution. In 1799, when the pope, who had been transported into captivity in France in the previous year, died, 'the triumph of the Republic over the Church seemed complete'.[1]

If the times were politically disastrous for the Church, intellectually they were scarcely less so. It is enough to recall that the whole structure of scholasticism, which, in spite of the inroads of Cartesianism and of the decadence into which it had fallen, had since the Council of Trent maintained its position as the immutable form of orthodoxy, had been lately undermined by the work of Immanuel Kant (1724–1804). 'Kant had done in the sphere of thought what the French Revolution had done in the sphere of politics. He had brought down the long tottering edifice of the established order, and had made a new start possible by clearing the ground once for all of an inveterate growth of old pretensions to transcend the common lot of man.'[2]

However, those who in 1799 may have supposed that the Church of Rome was politically and intellectually bankrupt were soon to be disillusioned. In the very first years of the new century there occurred two events which were an earnest of the revival of Catholicism. In 1801 Napoleon made with the papacy the *Concordat* which, if it did not restore to the Church all the rights that it claimed and had formerly possessed, at least entitled him to boast with some truth that he was rebuilding the altars that had been overthrown in the Revolution. The terms of the *Concordat*, and still more Napoleon's subsequent treatment of the Church,

---

[1] C. S. Phillips, *The Church in France 1789–1848* (1929), pp. 19, 36.
[2] C. C. J. Webb, *A history of philosophy* (1915), p. 210; cp. Wilfrid Ward, *W. G. Ward and the Catholic revival* (1912), p. 424 n.

could not of course be regarded with satisfaction by loyal or discerning Catholics, for it was only too evident that he was interested in religion just in so far as it could be turned to the service of his own ambitions. Nevertheless, the *Concordat* made it clear that the Catholic religion was still a power which had to be reckoned with, even if the reckoning consisted chiefly in its exploitation.

The *Concordat* promised rather than secured to the Church political restoration; the publication in 1802 of Chateaubriand's *Le Génie du Christianisme* was the first important sign of the spiritual and intellectual revival of Catholicism, which indeed it did much to initiate and to promote. This revival is one of the most striking characteristics of the nineteenth century. Chateaubriand's work betokened that the rising stream of romanticism was going to flow into, and revivify, Catholicism. The romantic revival in life and letters stretches far back into the eighteenth century; Rousseau, if not its first, was its most remarkable and influential herald.[1] But it was due to Chateaubriand, and other writers in other countries who followed him, that the romantic movement directly stimulated a revival of Catholicism. For, however this movement be defined, it undoubtedly involved a return from the cold and artificial abstractions of the intellect to romance and emotion, to mystery and adventure, to a sense of the supernatural and the superhuman. It was just on these grounds that Chateaubriand based his new apologetic.

Le christianisme sera-t-il moins vrai quand il paraîtra plus beau?...Sublime par l'antiquité de ses souvenirs, qui remontent au berceau du monde, ineffable dans ses mystères, adorable dans ses sacrements, intéressant dans son histoire, céleste dans sa morale, riche et charmant dans ses pompes, il réclame toutes les sortes de tableaux.[2]

---

[1] For Rousseau's influence on the Catholic revival, see P. M. Masson, *Rousseau et la restauration religieuse* (1916).

[2] *Op. cit.* pt. I, ch. I.

The appeal of an apologetic of this kind was immense to a generation which valued sentiment above reason. It is in effect an appeal to believe in Catholicism, not because it is true, but because it is beautiful, mysterious and charming.

The Catholic revival thus derived its impulse, as it continued to derive its strength, from an appeal that was essentially romantic as contrasted with rationalist. The tendency of the line of its distinguished apologists, of whom Chateaubriand was the first, was to disregard or to despise the contemporaneous movement in the direction of scientific research and historical criticism. This, they supposed, was a legacy of eighteenth-century rationalism, which they could afford to ignore, or blindly to attack. Their appeal was to the glamour of the past; they were not aware of what science and criticism were doing, or were about to do, to render this appeal in its traditional form ineffective.

Le Génie du Christianisme, whatever its defects, had in the circumstances of the time the effect of making Catholicism intellectually respectable and emotionally attractive. Moreover, the persecutions of both the Revolutionary and Napoleonic periods had done much to purify and strengthen the life of the Church. Thus, when at length the yoke of the oppressor was removed and the Church was restored with the Bourbon monarchy, the conditions favoured a genuine revival of religion. But what course would the revival take? Would Catholics adopt a purely reactionary policy? Or would they recognize that, whatever else might be possible, a return to the pre-Revolutionary *status quo* was not? We shall first notice the course of the Catholic revival in France, for it was there that the two movements which it produced—the new ultramontanism and liberal Catholicism—first became conspicuous, and we shall then turn to its corresponding manifestations elsewhere.

Chapter II

THE NEW ULTRAMONTANISM AND LIBERAL CATHOLICISM IN FRANCE, 1814–1848

During the period of the Restoration (1814–30) the official Church, *i.e.* the bishops and clergy, was predominantly reactionary and increasingly determined to 'close up the last wounds of the Revolution'. And in France reaction meant a return to Gallicanism. The royal prerogatives were exalted and the fortunes of the Church were regarded as, by divine providence, inextricably bound up with those of the Bourbons. The propping of the altar against the worm-eaten throne was a suicidal policy, and the re-establishment of Catholicism might have been as short-lived as that of the legitimist monarchy, were it not that meanwhile fresh and gathering forces of life and thought had appeared within the Church.

First, there was the new ultramontanism of which Joseph de Maistre (1754–1821) was the original exponent. Why *new*? Ultramontanism—the assertion of the papal claims, especially the claim to infallibility—was no new doctrine. It had for instance been espoused by Fénelon in opposition to the Gallicanism of Bossuet. But hitherto it had been a matter for theological discussion, which did not necessarily involve anything more than the extent of the papal and royal prerogatives. In any case, the French Church had remained stedfastly Gallican; the prevailing emphasis was on the national, and not on the papal, prerogatives. Now, however, ultramontanism in its most absolute form was advocated as the sovereign cure for all the ills of Europe, as the fundamental principle on which both the order of society and the structure of religion ought in future to be based.

De Maistre had lived through the period of the Revolution and the chaotic years that followed; he had been driven to the conclusion that its principles, and most of all the idea of liberty, were utterly subversive and inevitably resulted in chaos. He did not make the mistake of supposing that a reversion to the conditions existing before was either possible or desirable. A new order of society had to be built, and the first and essential need was a strong and absolute centre of authority to serve as its basis. He argued that the papacy was the only institution that was capable of serving this purpose, and that it was divinely intended to do so. With an extreme assertion of papal absolutism de Maistre himself combined a system of regal absolutism; indeed at every point he exalted the claims of authority and denied those of freedom. But it is his doctrine of papal absolutism that has influenced in one way or another the whole subsequent history of the Roman Church.[1] His most important book, *Du pape*,[2] was published in 1817. Similar doctrines were at the time being advocated by other writers, notably by the philosopher de Bonald; but it was de Maistre who gave them their greatest vogue.

The other new movement, which originated during the period of the Restoration, and which in 1830 was ready to burst into a generous vitality, was that which came to be known as 'liberal Catholicism'. This—the point needs to be stressed in view of later history—was in its origin an offshoot of the new ultramontanism. Félicité de Lamennais (1782–1854), its founder, was in the first phase of his career as completely ultramontane and as completely royalist as de Maistre himself. When he ceased to be a royalist, he remained an ultramontane; in fact he ceased to be a royalist precisely

[1] Cp. Wilfrid Ward, *op. cit.* p. 85.
[2] Eng. trans. by Aeneas McD. Dawson, *The Pope* (1850).

because the monarchy seemed irretrievably committed to Gallicanism.

In 1829 Lamennais published his *Des progrès de la Révolution et de la guerre contre l'Église*, and this may be said to mark the birth of liberal Catholicism, since in it, abandoning his faith in the monarchy, he shows for the first time definite sympathy with liberalism and the principles of the Revolution. The second Revolution (July, 1830) found him and his disciples, of whom the most intimate and the most important were Lacordaire (1802–61) and Montalembert (1810–70), ready to initiate a great crusade. The Revolution was to be baptized; the Church was to unite itself with the aspirations of the people. Thus in the following October began the dramatic story of *L'Avenir*. The newspaper's motto was: 'God and liberty'. The prospectus enunciated the liberties which were claimed for Catholics and for all citizens:

(1) Liberty of conscience. This involves separation between the Church and the state and the suppression of the *budget des cultes*. (2) Liberty of education. The state university, which had been founded by Napoleon and had dominated the whole educational system, would not provide for Catholics the education to which they were entitled; they must therefore be free to have their own schools. (3) Liberty of the press. (4) Liberty of association. (5) Extension of the franchise. (6) The abolition of centralization and the granting of liberty to communes.

It is not difficult to imagine the sensation that was caused when with passionate eloquence a program of this kind was put forward by Catholics. If it enlisted enthusiastic support, it was not slow to encounter fierce opposition. The *juste-milieu* government of the Citizen King was by no means prepared for a thoroughgoing application of liberal principles —least of all in the interests of an extreme ultramontanism. The French bishops naturally viewed with disfavour a movement which they were powerless to control, and which was entirely contrary to their traditional policy. To the older clergy the very idea of reconciling liberalism with Catholicism was absurd. The circulation of the paper decreased rapidly when the episcopate began to prohibit it, and this circumstance together with the interference of the government determined Lamennais and his friends to appeal to Rome. In November, 1831, after a short but glorious life of only thirteen months' duration, *L'Avenir* was suspended.

Gregory XVI was not at all disposed to play the part which these liberal ultramontanes had designed for him. He had not the least sympathy with the principles of the Revolution nor the least ambition to become the patron of democracy. His encyclical *Mirari vos* (1832) condemned unequivocally the policy of *L'Avenir*, and it marks the end of the first stage of the liberal Catholic movement—and its first defeat.

To Lamennais himself, although with Lacordaire and Montalembert he signed a declaration of submission, the condemnation was a crushing blow. His faith in Catholicism was based on his faith in the power of the papacy to regenerate society. The *Mirari vos* undermined the latter; the collapse of the former was only a matter of time. It is easy to say that the policy of *L'Avenir* was too extreme to be practicable; it remains that if the pope had shown the slightest sense of his opportunity and vocation in relation to the modern world, Lamennais might have been saved for the Church.

The liberal Catholics, although abandoned by the founder and leader of their movement, and condemned by the pope, to whom, as ardent ultramontanes, they had deliberately appealed, were not suppressed. Lacordaire and Montalembert were indeed convinced that the policy of *L'Avenir* was impracticable, but their devotion to the principle of liberty was undiminished. The years that followed were given to activity that was at once more prudent and more fruitful. It was during the reign of Louis Philippe that Lacordaire both delivered his courses of sermons at Notre Dame and established the Dominican order in France, and that Montalembert and others began to publish those historical works whose object was to offer an apologetic for Catholicism by painting an alluring picture of its past. They continued the work which Chateaubriand had begun. Gallicanism, though it did not yet entirely disappear, now went finally out of fashion. Ultramontanism seemed to be a doctrine of liberation for the Church of France in its relations with a government that was no longer Christian. The factors, which were later to divide the ultramontanes into rival parties, liberal and intransigent, were not yet apparent. Thus Louis Veuillot was Montalembert's chief lieutenant in the campaign for educational liberty which was the main practical objective of the Church at this time. The demand for liberty was encouraged when in 1846 Pius IX succeeded Gregory XVI and began his pontificate in a way which suggested that he himself was going to pursue a liberal policy. When the Church welcomed and blessed the Revolution of February, 1848, and when in turn its popularity was exhibited at the elections which followed, it seemed that liberal Catholicism had a victorious future before it. 'The alliance between religion and Republicanism seemed for a few short months a *fait accompli*.'[1]

[1] Wilfrid Ward, *op. cit.* p. 110.

Chapter III

LIBERALS AND INTRANSIGENTS
IN FRANCE, 1848–1878

The revolutionary excesses of June, 1848, and the threat of socialism led to a speedy reaction. Only a small minority of Catholics was prepared for experiments in economic, as distinguished from political, revolution. The majority was staunchly conservative. But a much more significant and far-reaching division soon arose in the Catholic camp over the perennial education question. *La loi Falloux* (1850), while it did not give Catholics all that they had asked for, gave them a substantial extension of 'free education'.[1] Montalembert realized that this was as much as they could expect, and he accepted the law with thanks. Veuillot, however, treated him as a traitor, and adopted the attitude of 'all or nothing'. This controversy, typical of many others, occasioned the separation of French Catholics into those two groups—the liberals and the intransigents—which carried on a bitter and continuous feud during the ensuing years. The intransigents grew more and more aggressive and abusive, narrow and irreconcilable; their organ, the *Univers*, was as venomous towards liberals within the Church as towards non-Catholics without. The liberals, on the other hand, attempted under constant provocation to pursue a policy of reconciliation.

We need not follow in detail this feud. Both groups, it must be remembered, were ultramontane and both hoped to

[1] By 'free education' is meant liberty for Catholics to have their own educational system apart from the state system. *La loi Falloux* gave them the right to have their own secondary, as well as primary, schools. Cp. *The Cambridge Modern History*, XI, 130.

carry the papacy with them.[1] Until 1864, and even afterwards, there seemed to be some justification for these contradictory hopes, for the pope by blaming the excesses of its opponents encouraged first one party and then the other. It was not so evident then, as it is now, that from 1848 onwards his own sympathies were entirely conservative. In 1864 his opposition to liberalism, to every policy which savoured of reconciliation with modern society, reached its climax—and remained there. The encyclical *Quanta cura* and the notorious syllabus, with its condemnation of the proposition that the Roman pontiff can and should reconcile himself with progress, liberalism and modern civilization, were the sequel to the *Mirari vos* of 1832, and they represent the second defeat of the liberal Catholic movement. Nevertheless, the liberals made a valiant attempt to deprive the papal condemnation of its force, and to some extent they succeeded in doing so. Dupanloup's ingenious contention, which Montalembert is said to have described as a masterpiece of eloquent subterfuge,[2] that the pope had intended to condemn only what was bad in modern civilization, met with considerable support from the episcopate, and Rome itself went so far as to give it a modified approval. Thus, the liberals, although they were obviously labouring under fresh difficulties, were by no means routed. Needless to say, the intransigents hailed the encyclical and the syllabus with delight, and gave them their most extreme interpretation.

When it became known that Pius IX was going to summon an ecumenical council, the liberal Catholics professed to welcome the prospect. The pope wished no doubt to correct

[1] Cp. A. Sabatier, *The religions of authority and the religion of the Spirit*, p. 134: 'Even the liberal Catholics, strangely blind, taking sides with the papacy against Gallican liberties and the civil power, laboured no less efficaciously for the triumph of the Vatican dogma than the writers of the pure theocratic school'. See also A. Leroy-Beaulieu, *Les catholiques libéraux* (1885), pp. 214 ff.

[2] Lord Acton, *History of freedom and other essays*, p. 424.

and remedy the bad impression that had been made by the syllabus! They scouted the idea that the council would venture upon a definition of papal infallibility. They were not of course opposed to this doctrine; although they avoided the exaggerations of Veuillot and the *Univers*, they were sound ultramontanes. But they regarded the definition as inopportune both on account of the effect which it would have on opinion outside the Church and because of the use that would be made of it by the intransigent party within. The council and its consequences were about as humiliating as they could be for the liberals. The definition was voted on July 18th, 1870; in the mind of the victorious majority it meant the triumph of papal absolutism. 'The decrees of the Council of the Vatican were the decisive effort of the Roman supremacy and of ultramontane doctrines against the liberty of modern societies, against the assertions of reason and science, and the claims and traditions of national Churches.'[1]

Pius IX lived for eight years after his infallibility had been defined. The Church was now a paradise for the intransigents; the liberal Catholics were under a cloud. Any hopes of the Church's reconciliation with modern society that they still cherished had to be deferred. But they were not inactive; some of them played a leading part in political affairs. Their most notable achievement at this time was the securing of a further extension of educational liberty. A law of 1875 made possible the foundation of Catholic universities,[2] and this, as we shall see, had important consequences. The Institut Catholique at Paris became a nursery of modernism.

Before we proceed to observe the manifestations of liberal Catholicism, prior to the accession of Leo XIII, in Germany, Italy and England, we may estimate the character of the

[1] *The Cambridge Modern History*, XII, 92.
[2] See A. Baudrillart, *Vie de Mgr d'Hulst*, vol. I, chs. x and xi.

movement whose course in France we have briefly traced. The chief fact to notice is that the French liberal Catholics were concerned to advocate political, and not theological, liberalism. A. Leroy-Beaulieu went so far as to say, '"Le catholicisme libéral"...est toujours...resté purement politique, étranger à la sphère religieuse ou théologique, à la discipline aussi bien qu'au dogme'.[1] As a general statement this is undoubtedly true, but at the same time it needs qualification. For it is by no means true that the differences between the liberals and intransigents were restricted to political issues. For instance, the liberalism of Mgr Maret, the last of the Gallicans, was not purely political. An indication of its scope can be gathered from the memoir which he addressed to the bishops in 1862, and in the course of which he wrote: 'Nos sciences apologétiques, l'exégèse, la critique sacrée, la critique historique, la philosophie de nos saints dogmes, offrent de grandes lacunes, de grandes imperfections, qui appellent, qui exigent un grand mouvement de rénovation et de perfectionnement'.[2]

Nor, again, was the teaching of Louis Bautain, which was condemned as *fidéisme*, or of Alphonse Gratry, purely political. Some of Bautain's leading ideas, *e.g.* with regard to the psychology of belief, like those of the Tübingen school (see pp. 33 ff. below), reappear in the modernists, and Dr W. M. Horton has for this reason maintained that Bautain was a 'progenitor' or 'grandparent' of modernism, that he 'was to the French philosophical Modernists what Newman was to Tyrrell'.[3] But, in the judgment of the present writer, he fails to make out his case, and indeed he has to admit that Laberthonnière himself stated that he 'had hardly read Bautain at all'.[4] Incidentally, it may be noticed that, on the

[1] *Les catholiques libéraux* (1885), p. 181.
[2] G. Bazin, *Vie de Mgr Maret* (1891), II, 248.
[3] *The philosophy of the abbé Bautain* (New York, 1926), p. 297.
[4] *Ibid.* p. 293 n.

authority of E. Vermeil, Dr Horton makes the entirely un-
justified statement that 'it was largely from the Tübingen
theologians that the Catholic "Modernists" got their
notion of the "evolution of dogma" and of the Church as a
developing organism'.[1] There is no more substance in his own
claim that they were indebted to Bautain.

Whatever isolated cases there were of a comparatively
liberal intellectual attitude, it remains that both parties in
France, liberals and intransigents, were certainly united in
accepting whole-heartedly the traditional dogmatic teaching
of the Church. They differed only in their manner of presenting it. The intransigents stressed violently the opposition
between Catholic and contemporary thought; they exaggerated the supernatural, miraculous and legendary
elements in the ecclesiastical tradition; they encouraged those
cruder forms of popular piety (*e.g.* miraculous apparitions,
cultus of relics, etc.) which came to enjoy much favour
during the nineteenth century. The liberals, too, strongly
attacked the errors of *la philosophie séparée*, but they did so in a
courteous and conciliatory manner. For this and for their
refusal to encourage superstition they were naturally denounced as heterodox by the intransigents. As a matter of
fact neither party was really alive to the intellectual requirements of the time.

Perhaps Lamennais had seen more clearly than those who
succeeded him the need of a general renovation of the
Church's teaching in relation to modern currents of thought,
although his argument from 'common consent' did little to
supply the need. There is a striking passage in his *Des progrès
de la révolution et de la guerre contre l'Église*, which might have
come almost word for word from the pen of a modernist at
the beginning of the twentieth century.[2] Lacordaire had felt

[1] *Ibid.* p. 55; see p. 10 above and p. 37 below.
[2] The passage to which reference is made is reproduced below; see
Appendix II, pp. 272 f. In his earlier *Essai sur l'indifférence* Lamennais had

the same need,[1] and his famous sermons were an attempt
to meet it. But the very success with which they met among
intelligent unbelievers is in itself evidence that the challenge
to traditional orthodoxy from the side of historical and
biblical criticism had not yet become effective. This is shown
also by the success of Montalembert's historical writings;
Döllinger, we are told, 'deplored the uncritical credulity of
the author of *The Monks of the West*'.[2]

It was Renan who was destined eventually to bring the
challenge of criticism home to the mind of Frenchmen, and
neither liberals nor intransigents were in the least ready either
to face it or to understand its seriousness. 'Pour graves
qu'elles fussent (writes M. J. Rivière), les publications de
Renan elles-mêmes ne paraissent pas avoir troublé les
esprits: elles furent réfutées superficiellement ou le plus
souvent dédaignées, sans que personne éprouvât encore, à leur
propos, la tentation de rien changer aux méthodes et positions
classiques de l'exégèse ou de la théologie.'[3] In 1858 Pie, the
intransigent bishop of Poitiers, was rash enough to prophesy
that in twenty years' time Renan as well as Taine would be
unknown.[4]

It is a well-known fact, however curious it may seem, that
those who hold political opinions that are progressive, and
even radical or revolutionary, are often content with a purely
conservative theology. This is partly due to the facility with

clearly recognized that Catholic tradition needed the support of a new
apologetic. Cp. the Hon. W. Gibson, *The abbé de Lamennais and the
liberal Catholic movement in France* (1896), pp. 58 f., 61, 77; A. Houtin,
La question biblique au XIXᵉ siècle, p. 16; *Dictionnaire de théologie catholique*,
IX, 544, 620 f.

[1] H. L. S. Lear, *Henri Dominique Lacordaire* (1887), p. 58.

[2] Acton, *History of freedom and other essays*, p. 385; cp. F. A. Gasquet,
Lord Acton and his circle, pp. 198 f.

[3] *Le modernisme dans l'Église* (1929), p. 66.

[4] G. Weill, *Histoire du catholicisme libéral en France 1828-1908* (1909),
p. 153.

which men keep their thought in watertight compartments. But in the present instance the theological conservatism of the French liberal Catholics can be accounted for more easily. The gulf between the Catholic faith on the one hand and rationalist philosophy and criticism on the other seemed so immense that the possibility of trying to bridge it was not even considered. Renan and Taine belonged to a different world; that there could be any question of meeting them on their own ground did not occur. Politically, on the other hand, Catholics and non-Catholics had to live together, and, however much the 'thesis' of ecclesiastical absolutism might be glorified, in practice the 'hypothesis' which permitted a working arrangement with the state was by circumstances forced upon the Church.

Chapter IV

LIBERAL CATHOLICISM IN GERMANY

Catholicism in Germany during the nineteenth century followed a course both like and unlike that in France. There, too, there was a Catholic revival which derived its impulse from the romantic movement and from the tendency to react against the unsettlement and chaos that resulted from the French Revolution and from the Napoleonic wars.[1] The conversion to the Roman Church of Friedrich Leopold Stolberg (1750–1819) and of Friedrich von Schlegel (1772–1829) had an influence which was the counterpart of Chateaubriand's in France. Stolberg, Schlegel and their followers were also definitely ultramontane, although not to the same extent as de Maistre and de Bonald. At the same time, while there was in Germany a Catholic movement analogous to liberal Catholicism in France, it was both less organized and more complex. Above all, it was an intellectual far more than a political movement.

Nor is this surprising. In Germany there was no need for Catholics to concentrate their efforts on acquiring educational liberty, for this was secured to them already. It was for them to take advantage of it, and indeed they needed to do so. The proximity of a powerful Protestant Church and the constant challenge of its propaganda had a stimulating and comparatively liberalizing effect on the Roman Church in Germany, as contrasted with the Church in France which had no serious competitor. Moreover, it was impossible for Catholic teachers in Germany to disregard or to disdain, like their brethren in France, the development of modern

[1] Cp. *The Cambridge Modern History*, VIII, 776.

philosophy and of historical and biblical criticism.[1] Catholic apologetic, if it was to meet with any success, was compelled to take account of Kant and Hegel, of Lessing and Schleiermacher, of Strauss and Baur.

Liberal Catholicism in Germany had two chief centres, and each of these was dominated by the person of a great theologian. The first was the Catholic school of Tübingen, which flourished from approximately 1815 to 1840, and of which J. A. Möhler (1796–1838) was the outstanding figure. The other was the group which gathered round Döllinger (1799–1890) at Munich at a rather later period in the century.

The Catholic school of Tübingen must, of course, be distinguished from the better known Protestant school of advanced critics of which F. C. Baur was the chief light and which took its name from the same place. Tübingen is one of those German universities, where there are both Catholic and Protestant faculties of theology side by side. The Catholic faculty was founded in 1817. The work of Möhler and the members of this school has been admirably described and analysed by Professor Edmond Vermeil in his *Jean-Adam Möhler et l'école catholique de Tubingue* (1913), to which, in spite of its exaggerated estimate of the subsequent influence of the school, every student of the subject must now be greatly indebted. It is not an exaggeration to claim that the Tübingen school did for Catholic theology what Schleiermacher did, more or less contemporaneously, for Protestant theology. But, whereas the achievement of Schleiermacher has had an epoch-making influence on Protestant thought since, the influence of the Tübingen school was so restricted that it had been almost forgotten until Professor Vermeil's book recalled attention to it.

Schleiermacher, it has been justly said, 'must be regarded as the classical representative of modern effort to reconcile science and philosophy with religion and theology, and the

[1] Cp. *The Home and Foreign Review*, IV, 675.

modern world with the Christian church'.[1] The Tübingen
school made the same effort, but for them 'religion and
theology' meant the whole tradition of Catholicism and
'the Christian church' the Church of Rome. A brief comparison and contrast of their effort with Schleiermacher's will
enable us to judge the nature of their achievement.

The Tübingen theologians agreed with Schleiermacher,
for whom they did not conceal their admiration, in their
criticism of previous theological systems. Thus they both
regarded the separation between natural and revealed
religion, in its commonly accepted form, as erroneous. It had
led to error in two directions: on the one hand, to a false
supernaturalism which denied the capacity of human reason,
in consequence of man's fallen condition, to arrive at
spiritual truth and which therefore treated revelation as an
imposition upon faith entirely from outside the natural
order; and, on the other hand, to a false rationalism which
exaggerated the capacity of human reason and denied the
existence of any revelation which proceeded from the supernatural order. Of the latter error eighteenth-century deism
had been the outcome. If the contrast between reason and
revelation is pressed, one necessarily has to be sacrificed to the
other.

Again, Schleiermacher and the Tübingen theologians both
protested against the custom of regarding Christian dogma as
'un ensemble inorganique de *credenda*'.[2] Their aim was to
substitute a living and organic, for a fixed and static, conception of dogma. 'Organism' was a favourite word of the
Tübingen school, and it is significant that Lessing is the only
theologian of the eighteenth century of whom they expressed
approval. To him was due the idea of revelation as a continuous evolving process, comparable with the process of

[1] *Ency. Brit.*[11] xxiv, 334; cp. L. de Grandmaison, *Jesus Christ* (1932),
ii, 289.
[2] Vermeil, *op. cit.* p. 102.

education. This idea, again, they shared with Schleiermacher, and also the correlative appeal to religious experience, both individual and corporate. Not least, they agreed in emphasizing the element of feeling that there is in all genuine religion, and the priority of experience to intellectual construction, *i.e.* to dogmatic formulation.

On the other hand, the Tübingen theologians objected that Schleiermacher went too far in his reaction from the intellectualist conception of dogma. His theory of revelation as the progressive development of religious experience left no room for the idea of an unique historical revelation of the supernatural order in the incarnation of Christ. For him revelation was only 'relatively supernatural', and in the last resort natural and supernatural dissolved into one another. This is equivalent to the criticism that Schleiermacher's theology is more pantheist than theist, and, although he himself rebutted it, it has generally been held to be a legitimate criticism. The Tübingen theologians also criticized his definition of religion as a feeling of absolute dependence on a power outside ourselves as an over-simplification. The exclusive emphasis on feeling was, they allowed, salutary, and even excusable, after the intellectualism of the preceding century; but an integral definition of religion would have to express the organic union of cognition and morality with feeling.

These instances suffice to show how the Tübingen theologians met contemporary thought on its own ground, acknowledged where possible their agreement with it, and criticized it where it seemed to fail to do justice to the rich volume of spiritual truth which was embodied in the Catholic tradition. Not only the work of Schleiermacher, but the contemporary philosophical systems of Kant, Schelling, Hegel, etc., and likewise the theological systems of other Catholics, especially scholasticism, were submitted to this combination of appreciation and criticism. But this is only the negative side of the Tübingen theology; on the positive side, it was an attempt to elaborate a new and comprehensive presentation of Catholicism adapted to the intellectual conditions of the time.

In particular, it may be noted that Möhler and his school were not afraid of biblical criticism, although at this early stage in its development its conclusions, at least so far as the New Testament was concerned, were largely determined by rationalist or Hegelian presuppositions and were hardly to be reconciled with any form of Christian orthodoxy. The Tübingen theologians eulogized Richard Simon,[1] and maintained that the Catholic has nothing to fear from biblical criticism and certainly less than the Protestant, for his faith is founded not on the letter of Scripture texts but on a dynamic and living tradition. The Catholic critic is undoubtedly committed to the belief that the Bible substantiates the traditional teaching of the Church in regard to faith and morals, but apart from this he is free to recognize in it human imperfections and errors.[2]

The Tübingen theologians, although they were denounced at Rome, and although they anticipated ideas that were later and independently put forward by the modernists, have never been specifically condemned. They never became the cause of any great controversy in the Church—perhaps their methods were too tranquil and pacific—and their work

[1] Richard Simon, the 'father' of modern biblical criticism, was naturally held in high esteem by liberal Catholic theologians and by modernists; e.g. see *Letters to His Holiness Pope Pius X*, by a Modernist (1910), pp. 159–62 and Tyrrell's letter to *The Times* on October 1st, 1907. But they were not influenced by Simon's writings which the progress of the critical movement had rendered obsolete, and the fact that he had been condemned (several of his books are still on the Index) invalidated any appeal to his example as that of one who had combined criticism with Catholicism.

[2] Vermeil, *op. cit.* pp. 30 f., 147 f.; Möhler, *Symbolism* (Robertson's translation, 1894), pp. 296–305.

never received the attention it deserved. It was in fact so lost to sight at the end of the century that the leading modernists, who would have been able to recognize its value and turn it to their own use, were not even acquainted with it.[1] One reason for this was that Möhler and the Tübingen school were quite overshadowed by Döllinger and his associates; from about 1840 the centre of liberal Catholic activity in Germany shifted to Munich. Döllinger became far more famous than Möhler, not only because of the prestige of his vaster learning, but because his methods were aggressive and polemical, so much so indeed that his career ended in excommunication, and for the orthodox Roman Catholic historian he is one of the great apostates of the nineteenth century.

Döllinger had at first been a strong ultramontane on the ground that the papal authority provided the best safeguard against the oppression of the Church by the state, that is to say, he had been a *liberal* ultramontane. But in proportion as the new ultramontanism developed into such an exaltation of the papal claims as was incompatible with any form of liberalism, so he became its most prominent and most determined opponent. In scholarship he was a great ecclesiastical historian, and he ruthlessly exposed the legendary version of Church history which was exploited in the interests of the papal autocracy. It was a characteristic of the Munich school that they claimed scientific freedom in their work as historians, and they deliberately devoted their learning to removing the mass of fables which disguised and distorted the true story of the Church's growth. Although they claimed the same freedom with regard to biblical criticism, they do not appear in this field to have reached

[1] Loisy, *Mémoires*, III, 268 f.; see p. 10 above. Von Hügel, who had himself read only one chapter of the *Symbolik*, did, it is true, recommend Loisy to read some of Möhler's works, but he never did so (*ibid.* I, 415).

conclusions which involved a modification of traditional dogma, at any rate of the received Christology.

The liberal Catholic movement in Germany came to a head in 1863, when Döllinger organized a congress of Catholic scholars and theologians at Munich.[1] The movement had already been severely compromised in the eyes of Rome by the extravagant liberalism of the philosopher Jakob Frohschammer (1821–93), one of the Munich professors, who had been denounced in the previous year by the pope in an apostolic brief. The intransigent theologians who surrounded Pius IX were on the war-path. Döllinger in his presidential address justified their worst suspicions about the Munich school. The following extract from Wilfrid Ward's summary will suggest the tenor of his remarks:

A programme was set before the Congress for treating dogmatic questions on lines more and more removed from the traditional scholastic theology...The Aristotelian starting-point (of the scholastics) imposed limitations. 'Their analytical processes could not construct a system corresponding to the harmony and wealth of revealed truth; and without the elements of Biblical criticism and dogmatic history they possessed only one of the eyes of theology.' ...Scholastic theology was to be regarded as a thing of the past. Catholic doctrine must be presented in its organic completeness, and in its connection with the religious life, 'rigidly separating that which is permanent and essential from whatever is accidental, transitory, and foreign'.... The genuine theologian must reason boldly and thoroughly, and 'not take to flight if the process of his reasoning threatens to demolish some truth which he had deemed unassailable'.[2]

The congress aroused intense enthusiasm among liberal Catholics, not only in Germany, but elsewhere and specially, as we shall see, in England. The enthusiasm was, however, short-lived. A few months later the pope in a brief to

[1] For a full account of the congress, see *The Home and Foreign Review*, IV, 209–44.
[2] *Life of Cardinal Newman* (1913), I, 562 f.

the archbishop of Munich declared emphatically that the scholastic theology and the doctrinal decisions of the Roman congregations must be regarded as authoritatively binding by men of science and could not be opposed without incurring censure.[1] Within a year this was followed by the encyclical *Quanta cura* and the syllabus, the heaviest blow so far received by liberal Catholicism whether in its political or intellectual aspects.

The campaign in favour of papal infallibility and the centralization of all authority in the holy see was now in full swing. Döllinger and his associates were fully alive to the seriousness of the situation. They considered that the Church was being rapidly and irretrievably committed to a condition of papal absolutism and of intellectual obscurantism, and they determined that the liberal case should not go by default so far as it lay in their power. Döllinger was the outstanding leader of the opposition to the Vatican decrees, and when the case was lost he was the most eminent of those who refused to submit. He was consequently excommunicated, but, although the firmness of his opposition to the papacy was largely responsible for the starting of the Old Catholic schism, he himself declined to join it. In any case liberal Catholicism as a movement within the Church in Germany was routed.

[1] See Newman's analysis of the brief, *ibid.* I, 641 f.; full Latin text in *The Home and Foreign Review*, IV, 691–6.

Chapter V

LIBERAL CATHOLICISM IN ITALY

In Italy the liberal Catholic movement never attained the proportions that it did in France or Germany, but it had its representatives, and it enjoyed one brief spell of sunshine. The two leading Italian liberal Catholics were Vincenzo Gioberti (1801–52) and Antonio Rosmini-Serbati (1797–1855). Both were priests who constructed independent and elaborate philosophical systems which, because of their departure from the conventional principles and methods of scholasticism, aroused the hostility of the Jesuits. After a prolonged campaign of denunciation, which in the case of Rosmini was not finally successful until over thirty years after his death, they secured the papal condemnation of both systems. Gioberti was also a politician and one of the prophets of the Risorgimento; it was he who conceived the idea of a free Italian confederacy of which the pope was to be the head. Because of his radical views he was compelled to spend most of his life in exile. Rosmini too was a liberal in politics and also an ultramontane; he had considerable sympathy with Lamennais in the days of *L'Avenir*. But his liberalism was shown most of all in his advocacy of the internal reform of the Church; his best known work in this connexion was *Of the five wounds of the Holy Church*.[1]

This was written in 1832, but was not published till 1846, when 'the pontificate of Pius IX seemed to promise an era of blessings for the Church and for Italy. The liberal reforms granted by the Sovereign Pontiff aroused the greatest enthusiasm amongst the people, who looked on him as an

[1] Eng. trans. by H. P. Liddon (1883).

angel sent from heaven'.[1] What Rosmini described as the five wounds of the Church were the following: (1) the division between the people and the clergy in public worship, (2) the insufficient education of the clergy, (3) the disunion of the bishops, (4) the nomination of bishops by the lay power, and (5) the enforced infringement of the full rights of ecclesiastical property.

Under (2) he made a vigorous attack on the current scholastic theology as taught in the ecclesiastical seminaries. 'Those marvellous text-books now used in our seminaries... I believe, will, in the more hopeful future days of the imperishable Church, be considered to be the most meagre and the feeblest that have been written during the eighteen centuries of her history. They are books without life, without principles, without eloquence, and without system...they require only masters able to read mechanically, and pupils who can listen as mechanically.'[2] For a moment the dreams of Rosmini and Gioberti of a pope, 'who seems destined to renew our failing life and to give to the Church a fresh impulse which will lead her in a new and glorious course',[3] seemed capable of fulfilment. But the revolutionary excesses of 1848 and the humiliations to which he was himself subjected killed all Pius IX's ardour for liberty and progress; from this time onwards he was an unwavering reactionary. *Of the five wounds* was put on the Index in 1849. The intran-

---

[1] G. B. Pagani, *The life of Antonio Rosmini-Serbati* (1906), p. 259. An illuminating account of the opening years of Pius IX's pontificate is given by Wilfrid Ward in *The life and times of Cardinal Wiseman* (1897), vol. I, ch. XVI.

[2] *Op. cit.* pp. 66f. His biographer gives an interesting illustration of Rosmini's own intellectual liberalism; in 1824, when he was living at Rovereto, he brought out a work on geological research by Bellenghi, 'who could not publish it in Rome because the Master of the Sacred Palace was averse to geological opinions not based on Aristotelian theories' (Pagani, *op. cit.* p. 67).

[3] *Of the five wounds*, p. 349.

sigents, who now dominated the Church in Italy,[1] perse-
cuted Rosmini untiringly. Liberalism, whether political or
theological, could hardly expect to thrive, or even to live,
in the atmosphere which now pervaded the papal court.

[1] The Italian Jesuits, who edited the *Civiltà cattolica*, did for Italy what
Louis Veuillot and the *Univers* did for France. Cp. Acton, *History of
freedom and other essays*, pp. 497 f.

Chapter VI

LIBERAL CATHOLICISM IN ENGLAND

In England at the beginning of the nineteenth century Roman Catholicism was the religion of only a tiny minority of the population,[1] which by its inherited circumstances was prevented from exercising any appreciable influence on the life of the nation. But the Catholic revival, whose effects on the continent we have already noticed, was not less conspicuous in its effects on the religious life of England. Here, too, it is generally acknowledged that the revival owed much to romanticism. The writings of Coleridge and Sir Walter Scott were, for instance, one of the factors which prepared the way for the Oxford movement in the Church of England;[2] although they were not themselves Catholics, their place in English literature corresponds to some extent to that of Chateaubriand in France, of Stolberg and Schlegel in Germany, and of Manzoni in Italy. The revival in the Roman Church was mainly a by-product of the Oxford movement in the established Church, and became fully evident only after the secessions of 1845.

The hereditary Catholics had too long been intellectually and politically isolated for them to be capable, by themselves,

[1] Burke put the number at 30,000 or 36,000; see Purcell, *Life of Cardinal Manning*[1], II, 773.

[2] See *e.g.* Newman's *Apologia* (Everyman's ed.), pp. 104f. But the indebtedness of the Oxford movement to romanticism was only partial; the influence of Coleridge at least (note how Newman's remarks, *loc. cit.*, are qualified) was more extensive and constructive in the case of non-Tractarian theologians such as F. D. Maurice, and affected the Anglican Catholic revival more fully at a later period in the century, *i.e.* at the time of *Lux Mundi*. Cp. p. 243 below, and V. F. Storr, *The development of English theology in the nineteenth century* (1913), ch. XIV.

of responding to the fresh currents in European life and thought. The new ultramontanism, whether in its liberal form or not, was entirely alien to their traditional ethos. The infusion of the Oxford converts, with their intellectual vitality and their missionary enthusiasm, was a pouring of new wine into old bottles; the establishment of the new hierarchy in 1850 registered a transformation of the character and prospects of Roman Catholicism in England. Its prospects at first seemed far brighter than they proved to be in the event; for the prayers for 'the conversion of England', which were then offered with intense confidence and hope, have not in fact been answered. The movement in the Anglican Church recovered from the staggering blow of 1845, and the fruits of the Catholic revival in England have thus been shared by Rome and Canterbury. Moreover, Rome has had to be content with the smaller share.

The revival of the Roman Church in England was successfully controlled in the interests of that intransigent ultramontanism which everywhere asserted its power over all other tendencies that were opposed to it. Uniformity of mind and manners was not, however, secured without difficulty. At first there was the division between the hereditary Catholics and the converts, who were like oil and water to one another. It was not the least of Cardinal Wiseman's achievements that he succeeded in making them mix. But what threatened to be a more serious division then became manifest, that between the liberal Catholics and the conservative ultramontanes or intransigents. The latter were in a numerical majority and they were not inferior in enthusiasm, but the liberals composed a group whose intellectual brilliance was of so high an order as to bear comparison with that of any other group of writers of their time, and it was commonly supposed that they had the support of Newman, the most illustrious of his co-religionists. This was not the case, for his sympathies were divided between the two schools, and his subtle mind tried to follow a tortuous *via media* between them.

Sir John Acton, afterwards Lord Acton (1834–1902), himself an hereditary Catholic, was the chief of the liberals in spite of his comparative youth, and round him gathered several of the most able of the Oxford converts, Richard Simpson, J. M. Capes, T. F. Wetherell, H. N. Oxenham, and others. The period of their greatest activity was from 1858 to 1864, when Acton and Simpson were editing first *The Rambler* and then *The Home and Foreign Review*.[1] *The Rambler* had been started by J. M. Capes in 1848; from the first it had stood for a liberal presentation of Catholicism and had consequently aroused criticism. But its liberalism was much more marked from the time when Acton became associated with it. Acton, who on religious grounds had been refused admission to three colleges at Cambridge, had just finished his education at Munich at the feet of Döllinger, and he had freely imbibed his master's spirit. In his hands *The Rambler* became a pronounced organ of liberal Catholicism both in its political and in its intellectual aspects, but chiefly in the latter.

The central truth which the 'Rambler' writers urged (says Wilfrid Ward) was the necessity of absolute freedom and candour in scientific, historical, and critical investigation, irrespective of results. Whether the truth told for or against Catholic polemics, it must not be withheld.... To accept historical conclusions, only so far as they helped Catholic evidences, and to reject them so far as they supplied arguments against the Church, was to depart altogether from an intellectual method which would command respect. Science, physical, historical and critical, must proceed on its own principles and methods.[2]

[1] For details see Gasquet, *Lord Acton and his circle*. In 1859 an attempt was made by the ecclesiastical authorities to place *The Rambler* under the safer control of Newman; but the attempt was unsuccessful. Newman edited only two numbers.

[2] *The life and times of Cardinal Wiseman* (1897), II, 227.

In theory Newman, whose co-operation they naturally desired and to some extent succeeded in obtaining, agreed with this attitude, but its practical application by such writers as Acton and Simpson filled him with misgivings. For Newman throughout his career as a Roman Catholic,[1] however much he regretted the conduct or policy of his ecclesiastical superiors, treated them always with a studied deference. It seemed to him that the 'Rambler' writers put forward their views too aggressively and with too much self-confidence, that they treated the episcopate with insufficient respect, and that they were not careful to avoid shocking those of their fellow-churchmen whose faith was old-fashioned. Thus, for instance, in 1861 we find Acton writing to Simpson:

I have all the pains in the world to keep Newman in good humour. He is so much riled at what he pleasantly calls your habit of pea-shooting at any dignitary who looks out of the window as you pass along the road, that I am afraid he will not stand by us if we are censured. But he will be very indignant with the authorities, and declares that he agrees with us in principle entirely.[2]

In 1862 *The Rambler*, which had been a bi-monthly publication, was transformed into a quarterly, and given the title of *The Home and Foreign Review*. This, like its predecessor, was liable at any moment to be officially condemned. The faction in England, which corresponded to the continental intransigents, and of which W. G. Ward, Manning and Faber were outstanding and typical representatives, was rapidly tightening its hold on the hierarchy, and it was relentlessly hostile to Acton and his friends. On the other hand, if we wish to judge of the real worth of *The Home and Foreign Review* and of the services which it might have

[1] And during his career as Anglican too, when he regarded his own bishop as his pope; see *Apologia* (Everyman's ed.), p. 69.
[2] Gasquet, *Lord Acton and his circle*, p. 192.

rendered to the cause of Catholicism in England if it had been free to continue, it is enough to recall the opinion of it that was expressed by no less competent and unbiased a judge than Matthew Arnold: 'Perhaps in no organ of criticism in this country was there so much knowledge, so much play of mind'.[1]

The *Review* published an enthusiastic account of the congress which was held at Munich in 1863, and to which reference has already been made; and when afterwards the pope condemned precisely those principles of historical criticism and scientific freedom for which the *Review* had been contending, the English liberal Catholics realized that, for the time being at any rate, their enterprise was hopeless, and they appealed to the future to justify them against the policy of the Vatican. The last number was published in April, 1864, and in an article, entitled 'Conflicts with Rome,' Acton explained the reasons for the *Review's* suspension.

Its object (he wrote) has been to elucidate the harmony that exists between religion and the established conclusions of secular knowledge, and to exhibit the real amity and sympathy between the methods of science and the methods employed by the Church. That amity and sympathy the enemies of the Church refuse to admit, and her friends have not learned to understand. Long disowned by a large part of our Episcopate, they are now rejected by the Holy See; and the issue is vital to a *Review* which, in ceasing to uphold them, would surrender the whole reason of its existence....

If the spirit of the *Home and Foreign Review* really animates those whose sympathy it enjoyed, neither their principles, nor their confidence, nor their hopes will be shaken by its extinction. It was but a partial and temporary embodiment of an imperishable idea—the faint reflection of a light which still lives and burns in the hearts of the silent thinkers of the Church.[2]

[1] *Ibid.* p. lxxvii. In 1863 Max Müller spoke of the *Review* as 'one of the best-edited of our Quarterlies'; see W. Ward, *W. G. Ward and the Catholic revival*, p. 144.

[2] See *History of freedom and other essays*, pp. 489, 491.

The principles of the liberal Catholics no doubt remained firm, but it can hardly be denied that their confidence and hopes were shaken, specially when their defeat was emphasized by the encyclical and syllabus, which were published later in the same year. Acton, however, continued to take part in ecclesiastical politics until after the Vatican council, when, like his master, Döllinger, he vigorously championed the cause of the minority. After that, although to the end of his life he remained in private a stedfast, and even somewhat bigoted,[1] opponent of 'Vaticanism', being a layman he escaped excommunication, and he never broke with the Church.

How far in effect did the theological liberalism of Acton and his friends go? How far did they anticipate modernism? Their assertion of the independent rights of scientific research and of historical criticism was in the abstract unequivocal, but when they claimed that this assertion was perfectly compatible with acceptance of the defined dogmas of the Church it cannot be supposed that they realized all that this claim involved. They pressed the distinction between the defined dogmas, which were infallible and binding, and the rest of the Church's teaching, which was open to continual modification. The security of their position depended on the presumption that there was a body of revealed truth, however restricted it might be, which could not come into conflict with the results of free scientific and historical research. They attempted to overcome the clash between the data of revelation and 'the established conclusions of secular knowledge' by denying its existence.

No truce (wrote Simpson) in the contest of science and faith is possible till both parties in this dispute lay aside their exaggerated claims, and own, on one side, that the province of faith is not the

---

[1] Von Hügel observed that anti-ultramontanism became for Acton an *idée fixe*, which seemed to warp his judgment in the latter part of his life; see *Selected letters*, pp. 126 f. Cp. Petre, *Life of Tyrrell*, II, 359.

world of phenomena, but the world of spirit; and that the articles
of faith are not conversant with subjects on which mathematical
proof is forthcoming, but with subjects about which human
reason can give no apodictically certain response, and which it
cannot therefore prove or refute with demonstrative evidence;
and that on the other hand all phenomena, with all particulars of
their place, their magnitude, their time, their succession, and their
number, belong exclusively to the scientific reason, and are
properly out of the province of faith, which is exclusively conversant with invisible things.[1]

A detailed review of the contents of the creeds and definitions
would show that their subject matter is all outside the sphere of
phenomena, which is the realm of science. The Trinity, the
Incarnation, the Fall and the Redemption, Grace, the Sacraments,
the authority of the Church, the inspiration of Scripture, the
immortality of the soul, the resurrection of the body, heaven and
hell, offer no hold for scientific experiments. The philosopher may
theorise upon them in a way that offends faith; but it will be only
theory, not science. He will have once more proved the venerable
truism, that without revelation we have no demonstration of any
Christian doctrine, that each dogma becomes a mere guess, and
therefore as susceptible of denial as of affirmation.[2]

The difficult problem of the relation between reason and
revelation was not to be solved as easily as that. The 'Rambler'
writers were unduly optimistic as to the ease with which
scientific and historical freedom could be harmonized with
dogmatic orthodoxy. But it must be remembered that they
wrote at the time when the opening chapters of Genesis were
the chief battle-ground in theological controversy. Here
they were definitely in the vanguard of theological liberalism.
They were willing to allow freedom to science and biblical
criticism, they rejected theories of scriptural infallibility,
'whether syllabic or of all statements whether of fact or
doctrine', and they pressed the point that the Catholic, whose

[1] *The Rambler* (July, 1861), p. 169; cp. p. 184.
[2] *Ibid.* (September, 1861), p. 327.

faith rested on tradition and the living teaching of the Church, was not disconcerted by new views of the Bible, whereas the Protestant, whose faith rested on its supposed infallibility, was in an insuperable dilemma.[1] If the 'Rambler' writers had flourished when later on the theological battle-ground shifted to the New Testament, to Christian origins, and to Christology, it is impossible to say what their attitude would have been. It was not until towards the end of the century that any serious attempt was made to reconcile the assured results of New Testament criticism with traditional Catholic dogma, and it was this which was to constitute the distinctive crux of modernism. *The Rambler* and *The Home and Foreign Review* contain many suggestive ideas which might have been taken up and developed by the modernists, but as a matter of fact there is no evidence of any direct relation between the two movements.[2]

The reasons why the modernist movement was not a direct continuation or revival of nineteenth-century liberal Catholicism, nor in any particular ways influenced thereby, are not really far to seek. On the one hand, the modernists did not need to go back to the liberal Catholics of an earlier generation in order to discover that there was a conflict between Catholicism and contemporary culture. This was obvious enough to anyone who had eyes to see. The modernists were men of their own time; it was because they were acquainted with the state of culture and science, as it was in their own time—and not as it had been thirty or forty or fifty years earlier—that the problem of dogmatic restate-

[1] Cp. *The Home and Foreign Review*, II, 561–67, III, 214–27, IV, 623–66.

[2] Von Hügel, who was more likely than any to have been influenced by the 'Rambler' school, wrote about 1893 that he knew very little about the events of that time. 'To this hour I have not had a number of that terrible *Home and Foreign Review* in my hands.' See W. Ward, *W. G. Ward and the Catholic revival*, p. 365. In 1908, *i.e.* after the condemnation of modernism, Tyrrell contributed an article on 'The Home and Foreign Review' to the *Rinnovamento*, see his *Life*, II, 359.

ment assumed in their minds the form which it did. And, on the other hand, there was little to induce them to search the works of the liberal Catholics for hints as to the solution of their problem. Their time would be more profitably spent in studying contemporary literature. Liberal Catholicism had been condemned by the holy see; the modernists might, it is true, have discovered precedents for some of their own ideas in the writings of Lamennais or Döllinger or Rosmini or in *The Rambler*,[1] but such precedents, if they had tried to make use of them, so far from assisting their attempt to win toleration for a revision of orthodoxy, would have compromised them in advance.

The modernist movement was not a direct or conscious continuation of the liberal Catholicism which preceded it. But ought we to make an exception to this statement in regard to Newman? Newman is often described as a precursor, even as the only precursor, of modernism.[2] The amount of truth in this description is strictly limited. No doubt he was the only nineteenth-century theologian whom the modernists found useful. But they found him useful, not because he was by any means the most liberal, or progressive, or distinctively modern, theologian that the Roman Church produced in the nineteenth century, but because he had been more liberal than any other theologian whose name was held in honour in official circles. This was not so, of course, during the pontificate of Pius IX, although even then the fact that Newman was the greatest asset that the Roman Church in England possessed kept the official hostility to him respectful. It was the conferring on him by Leo XIII of a cardinal's hat

---

[1] As has been noticed above, the Tübingen school, which they *might* have used with profit, had sunk into obscurity.

[2] *E.g.* 'Dans tous les pays d'Europe où le modernisme s'était implanté et propagé, l'Angleterre était le seul où le mouvement, dans son contenu essentiel: apologétique et histoire du dogme, pût compter un précurseur, véritable et caractéristique' (E. Buonaiuti, *Le modernisme catholique* (1927), p. 130).

(in 1879) that gave to his name a singular prestige both within and without the Church and to his writings an implied authoritative approval which they would not otherwise have had. In communicating to his friend, Dean Church, the news of the honour which had been conferred on him, he wrote: 'All the stories which have gone about of my being a half Catholic, a Liberal Catholic, under a cloud, not to be trusted, are now at an end'.[1]

So indeed it seemed, and so it may have been—for the time being. But by a curious irony it was chiefly because Newman had been made a cardinal that during the modernist movement he was signalled out as the most advanced liberal Catholic theologian of his generation, while the genuine liberals, such as the 'Rambler' writers, who approached far more nearly to an anticipation of modernism than Newman ever did, were overlooked. For the modernists to have recalled *their* work would have been to invite trouble, and they had trouble enough as it was; on the other hand, to invoke the authority of the illustrious cardinal was not only safe, but—in a Church where great store is set on precedents —invaluable.

[1] W. Ward, *Life of Cardinal Newman* (1913 ed.), II, 451 f.

Chapter VII

NEWMAN

Newman would have been horrified by the writings of Loisy and Tyrrell if he had lived to read them, and he would have been as astonished to hear that he was the 'father' of modernism as he was by the suggestion that he 'agreed with Acton and Simpson'[1]—far more astonished. Only by a judicious selection of passages from Newman's works and by isolating these from the rest of his thought would it be possible to argue that modernism was a legitimate child of his. It is perfectly true that some of the lines of thought which the modernists pursued were tentatively explored by Newman, but his explorations never in his own mind involved a calling in question of traditional orthodoxy as an infallible revelation of absolute truth.

Newman was not a systematic theologian; he never tried to set out his religious teaching in the form of a logically coherent system. Indeed his distrust of every such system, of every kind of 'rationalism' (whether infidel or scholastic), was such that he has been freely accused of intellectual scepticism. The accusation is unfair, but it illustrates the futility of looking for rigid consistency in his writings.[2] Obviously no attempt can be made here to describe his thought as a whole. It must suffice to notice the following points which may serve to indicate how far he was, and how far he was not, a precursor of the modernist movement.

(1) Newman accepted *ex animo* and without any apparent

[1] W. Ward, *Life of Cardinal Newman*, II, 496.
[2] Cp. A. Fawkes's remark that 'a primer of scepticism and of Ultramontanism might be compiled from (Newman's) works' (*The Modern Churchman*, XVI, 546). See also *Lord Acton's correspondence* (1917), I, 227.

difficulty the defined dogmatic teaching of the Church. It is antecedently unlikely that one who was credulous enough to believe in the Holy House of Loreto would stumble at the teaching of the creeds or general councils or at the divinely inspired narratives in the Bible. Although he was on opportunist grounds opposed to the definition of papal infallibility in 1870, he accepted the dogma, when it was defined, without hesitation, since he had previously believed in it. He had no desire whatever for a revision of the Church's traditional teaching, nor for a reinterpretation of the sense in which it was to be accepted.

(2) Newman was then perfectly satisfied with what the Church proposed for his belief; but he was not satisfied with the reasons on which, according to the theological schools, belief was supposed to be grounded. From Butler he had learned that the truth of the Christian faith cannot be demonstrated with logical and compelling conclusiveness, and that intellectually the believer must be content with a convergence of probabilities. On the other hand, he realized that certitude in believing is a fact of experience, and his *Essay in aid of a grammar of assent* was an attempt to account for the paradox. Certitude is based not on inference, but on assent; the solution lies in recognizing the function of the will and of other factors beside logical demonstration in the psychology of belief. This was not the normal teaching of the Roman Church, which is that a doctrine such as the existence of God can be demonstrated conclusively by human reason. Newman here was investigating a problem which came to the forefront of philosophical discussion towards the end of the century. It is one of the chief problems that engaged Tyrrell's thought, and Newman at least helped him to realize its importance.[1] It was central to the French 'philosophy of action'.[2] Léon Ollé-Laprune, Maurice

[1] Cp. Petre, *Li e of Tyrrell*, II, 56f.
[2] See pp. 186 ff. below.

Blondel's master, owed much to the influence of Newman.[1]
It will be true to say that Newman's example encouraged
those who read him to put forward opinions about the
psychology of belief that were contrary to the received
teaching of the theological schools. The modernists, however, were condemned not so much because they did this as
because they called in question the content of the traditional
faith. Their heresy concerned not so much *why* one *does*
believe as *what* one *must* believe.

(3) Newman's *Essay on the development of Christian doctrine*
(1845) is commonly held to be the most signal point of his
connexion with the modernist movement. The essay served
a double purpose. (*a*) It was intended to justify his rejection
of the Tractarian appeal to the primitive Church against
subsequent corruptions and his acceptance of Roman
Catholicism in its existing form as the authentic version of
Christianity. To this end he devised the series of tests by
which true developments were to be distinguished from false
(see *op. cit.* pp. 64ff.). (*b*) At the same time, Newman discerned a problem in regard to which the comparative claims
of Anglicanism and Romanism were of secondary importance. It is plain from history that the form of Christian
doctrine and worship has not been identical throughout the
ages; how is it possible to decide what is its true and authoritative form? And how are we to account for the changes and
variations that history discloses? Three common hypotheses
must be deemed unsatisfactory.

(i) The Vincentian canon is an inadequate test, since, for
example, the doctrine of the Trinity was not clearly taught
by the ante-Nicene fathers.

(ii) The second hypothesis is that 'of an early corruption of
Christianity from external sources... (but) it has no claims on
our attention till it is drawn out scientifically;—till we are

[1] Cp. W. Ward, *W. G. Ward and the Catholic revival*, p. 443; M. Blondel, *Léon Ollé-Laprune*, p. 44.

distinctly informed what the real Christian doctrine or evangelical message is, or if there be any; from what sources it is drawn; how these sources are ascertained to us; and what is a corruption'.[1]

(iii) The third hypothesis is that of the *Disciplina Arcani*; but 'it is no key to the whole difficulty...the variations continue beyond the time when it is conceivable that the discipline was in force'.

What then is the hypothesis that Newman himself proposes for acceptance? He summarizes his 'theory of developments' as follows: 'that the increase and expansion of the Christian Creed and Ritual, and the variations which have attended the process in the case of individual writers and Churches, are the necessary attendants on any philosophy or polity which takes possession of the intellect and heart and has had any wide or extended dominion; that, from the nature of the human mind, time is necessary for the full comprehension and perfection of great ideas; and that the highest and most wonderful truths, though communicated to the world once for all by inspired teachers, could not be comprehended all at once by the recipients, but, as received and transmitted by minds not inspired and through media which were human, have required only the longer time and deeper thought for their full elucidation'.[2]

Newman was aware that his *Essay* opened up a dangerous theme. Thus, in 1849, he wrote to the bishop of La Rochelle: 'The book...is but a mere essay; it does but enter upon a subject scarcely mooted up to our days, and of such extreme delicacy, that one hardly dare handle it'.[3] Nevertheless, he

[1] May it not be said that Harnack and the liberal Protestants did draw out this hypothesis 'scientifically', and that Loisy recognized that it did then claim the attention of Catholics? In order to attend to it he had to carry Newman's theory of development to lengths which the latter never contemplated. See Part II, chs. V and VI, of the present essay.

[2] *Op. cit.* p. 27.
[3] *The Rambler*, V, 202.

was not the first Roman Catholic writer to propose a theory of development. He said himself that the view on which his essay was written 'has at all times, perhaps, been implicitly adopted by theologians, and, I believe, has recently been illustrated by several distinguished writers of the continent, such as de Maistre and Moehler' (*op. cit.* p. 27). It is uncertain from what source Newman derived the idea of development;[1] certainly his method of working it out, or of manipulating it, was original.

We shall find that the modernists, while the fact that Newman had opened up the theme was invaluable to them, regarded his theory as deficient because he took for granted the idea of the apostolic *depositum fidei*, *i.e.* of revelation as a body of truths which were 'communicated to the world once for all' in apostolic times. For him, the development of doctrine consisted simply in deducing the consequences and implications of the original, closed revelation. 'The holy apostles would know without words all the truths concerning the high doctrines of theology, which controversialists after them have piously and charitably reduced to formulae, and developed through argument.'[2] The modernists by their acceptance of biblical criticism were driven, and by their sympathy with an evolutionary philosophy were encouraged, to reinterpret, in one way or another, the conception of a final and infallible *depositum fidei*. Newman's theory of

---

[1] A sermon of Wiseman's, preached in 1839, is a close anticipation of the main argument of Newman's essay; see W. Ward, *The life and times of Cardinal Wiseman* (1897), I, 314–19. Dr F. L. Cross, in his *John Henry Newman* (1933), pp. 107 ff., gives reasons for supposing that Newman may have indirectly derived the idea of development from the French Jesuit Petavius (1583–1652); see also his article on this subject in the *Church Quarterly Review* (January, 1933), pp. 245–57. Dr C. C. J. Webb says that it 'had by his own (*i.e.* Newman's) account been suggested to him by the writings of' de Maistre and Möhler; see *Christianity in the light of modern knowledge* (1929), p. 723. But this goes beyond, if it does not contradict, Newman's actual statement quoted above.

[2] *Op. cit.* p. 83; cp. p. 120: 'As all allow, the Apostles were infallible'.

deductive development which began where the New Testament left off gave way to a theory of the evolution of dogma which was based on a reading of the New Testament the necessity of which he is not to be blamed for failing to foresee.

While, however, his essay suffered from these limitations, it still contained a number of statements that could be understood by the modernists to imply more than their author had intended. Consider for instance how they must have relished such passages as the following:

In a higher world it is otherwise; but here below to live is to change, and to be perfect is to have changed often (p. 39).

One cause of corruption in religion is the refusal to follow the course of doctrine as it moves on, and an obstinacy in the notions of the past (p. 61).

A power of development is a proof of life, not only in its essay, but in its success; for a mere formula either does not expand or is shattered in expanding. A living idea becomes many, yet remains one (p. 74).

If Christianity be an universal religion, suited not to one locality or period, but to all times and places, it cannot but vary in its relations and dealings towards the world around it, that is, it will develope. Principles require a very various application according to persons and circumstances, and must be thrown into new shapes according to the form of society which they are to influence.... The refutation and remedy of errors cannot precede their rise; and thus the fact of false developments or corruptions involves the correspondent manifestations of true ones (p. 96).

Sometimes an attempt has been made to ascertain the 'leading idea', as it has been called, of Christianity; a remarkable essay as directed towards a divine religion, when, even in the existence of the works of man, the task is beyond us. Thus, the one idea has been decided by some to be the restoration of our fallen race, by others philanthropy, by others the spirituality of true religious service, by others the salvation of the elect, by others the union of the soul with God. All these representations are truths, as being aspects of Christianity, but none of them is the whole truth (pp. 34 f.).

No wonder that M. Loisy was led to exclaim that Newman must have been the most open-minded theologian that had existed in the Church since Origen.[1] But it would be a gross exaggeration to say that Newman's theory of development gave rise to the modernist movement. All that ought to be said is that, in their attempts to restate Catholic dogma in such a way as to make it compatible with biblical criticism, some of the modernists, and notably Loisy, found Newman suggestive and useful.

If Newman had died before Pius IX, the modernists might still have found his writings suggestive, but they would hardly have found them useful. As a theologian, he would have died under a cloud, and an appeal to him would have been liable to compromise whoever made it.

[1] See p. 94 below.

Chapter VIII

THE ACCESSION OF LEO XIII AND THE EFFECTS OF HIS POLICY

We must now recall the condition of the Church at the end of Pius IX's pontificate in order that we may appreciate the change which resulted from the accession of Leo XIII. When Pius died in 1878, liberal Catholicism, whether in its political or intellectual form, seemed a lost cause. We have seen how—in France, in Germany, in Italy, in England—the liberals were defeated and the intransigents were triumphant. In particular, those who had advocated the independent rights of historical criticism and of scientific research had been either excommunicated like Döllinger or reduced to silence like Acton. Pius IX and the party that had supported him had succeeded in showing that the Church was irreconcilable with modern civilization and with modern knowledge. If the policy of Pius IX had been continued by his successor, it is unlikely that there would have been any modernist movement, not because there would have been no Roman Catholics who recognized the need of a revision of traditional orthodoxy in the light of new knowledge, but because they would have recognized simultaneously the futility of working for any such revision under the conditions that prevailed in the Church. Leo XIII, by modifying the intransigent policy of Pius IX, fostered the illusion that the modernist enterprise was worth attempting.

Leo XIII acquired the reputation of being a liberal pope; if the reputation still survives, it is due chiefly to the comparative difference between his policy and pontificate and those of his predecessor and of his successor. He was not by conviction a liberal in any accepted sense of the term. He did not regard freedom as a political or intellectual ideal or end. It is true that, before he became pope, he had avoided the excesses of the intransigents, but he had not been associated in any way with the professedly liberal Catholics. Moreover, after he assumed control of the Vatican—and few recent popes have controlled the Vatican with a firmer hand—'he withdrew no pronouncement, he disavowed no action, of the previous pontificate.... His ends were those of his predecessor, but he sought them by other means.'[1] As much as Pius IX he desired political privilege rather than political freedom for the Church, and he had as little real sympathy with the intellectual movements of the age. If he maintained that the Church had nothing to fear from the full truth of history, he maintained also that history 'covers an aggregate of dogmatic facts which claim the assent of faith and may not be called in question'.[2]

The difference between Leo and Pius was not that one was a liberal and the other a conservative, but that one was a diplomatist and the other was not. In 1878 Leo saw clearly that the fortunes of the papacy were at a very low ebb, and he determined to restore them. Under Pius IX the papacy had certainly become powerful *among Catholics* as it had never been before. The Vatican decrees had been the culminating point of the ultramontane movement towards papal absolutism, and the misfortunes of the holy see, arising from the loss of the temporal power, had given Pius IX the prestige of a martyr and had won for him the sympathy of those who cared but little for his policy. His character, too, had inspired personal affection or, as some would say, sentimental adulation. Leo was made of different stuff. He wanted to be not a suffering martyr, but a successful statesman. His aims were at once more ambitious and more worldly, and his

[1] A. Fawkes, *Studies in modernism*, p. 87.
[2] Encyclical to the bishops and clergy of France (1899), see *ibid.* p. 107.

character was more virile. The papacy should certainly retain and extend its power among Catholics[1]; but also it should cease to be 'an object of hostility and contempt to the outside world'.[2]

All his great gifts as a diplomatist he used to this end. He wisely realized that in the situation with which he was faced the only policy that could succeed was one of conciliation and compromise. This is the key to his political strategy. In France, for instance, where in truth it proved far less successful than elsewhere, he directed Catholics to rally to the republic and to abandon their legitimist dreams not because he himself cared for republicanism, but because it was only by accepting the existing constitution that the Church could hope to regain its powers and privileges. Wilfrid Ward summed up Leo's attitude in a telling phrase: 'We must use the modern liberties—our ultimate ideal being largely to get rid of them'.[3]

Leo wanted to be not only a successful statesman, but also a patron of letters. It must be allowed that his conception of learning was more medieval than modern and more literary than scientific. Its true method, he supposed, was deduction, its best instrument the syllogism. He had little, if any, personal understanding of the inductive method of modern science and criticism, or of the importance of observation and experiment. Nevertheless, he was sincerely anxious to restore the intellectual, no less than the political, prestige of Catholicism, and here too he was prepared to adopt what he regarded as a policy of conciliation. Thus he opened the Vatican library to students, showed a keen interest in educa-

[1] The movement of centralization, which has been an essential feature of modern ultramontane policy, was continued under Leo XIII. Thus, for instance, his encyclicals and briefs were as frequent as those of Pius IX and not, as formerly, exceptional events. Cp. W. Ward, *Ten personal studies* (1908), pp. 178 f.

[2] *Ibid.* p. 187.

[3] *Ibid.* p. 192; cp. R. Gout, *L'affaire Tyrrell*, pp. 65 ff.

tional reform, and encouraged the foundation and strengthening of universities. But his best known attempt to forward an intellectual revival in the Church was his glorification of St Thomas Aquinas and the Thomist philosophy. This was not, or need not have been, so purely a reactionary a policy as it may seem. For by recalling students from the conventional, cut and dried text-books, that were then in use, to the broader, more creative and elastic teaching of Aquinas himself, the pope could be taken to desire the introduction of a new and more liberal spirit into Catholic theology.[1] Leo's policy was in fact interpreted in two different ways: (1) as being intended to identify Catholic thought with Thomism—the interpretation which eventually conquered under Leo's successor, or (2) as inviting Catholic thinkers to a fundamental reconstruction of Christian philosophy. It was the latter interpretation, as acted upon by Ollé-Laprune and his followers for example, which issued in what came to be known as philosophical modernism and was condemned by Pius X.

The importance of Leo XIII's accession in preparing the ground for the modernist movement will now be evident. His whole policy, specially after the extravagant conservatism of Pius IX, was calculated to create a psychological atmosphere which conveyed the impression that after all Catholicism was capable of a fresh orientation, of coming to terms with political democracy and with modern knowledge. It is not then surprising that a new generation of liberal Catholics should have arisen who were attracted by this possibility and in their enthusiasm failed to recognize how heavily the balances were loaded against it. Far more than the opportunist diplomacy and the pseudo-liberalism of Leo XIII would have been necessary in order to give adequate grounds for the expectation that an orthodoxy, which those

[1] Lecanuet, *La vie de l'Église sous Léon XIII* (1930), pp. 466 ff.; cp. A. Houtin, *Un prêtre symboliste, Marcel Hébert* (1925), pp. 75, 78.

who control it regard as unchanging, and an authority, whose professed infallibility binds it securely to the letter of the past, were likely to come suddenly to terms with forces that they had hitherto opposed with blind obstinacy and the utmost resolution.

There can hardly be a more significant illustration of the hopes which came to be entertained as a result of Leo XIII's policy than the epilogue which Wilfrid Ward added to his *William George Ward and the Catholic revival*.[1] This was published in 1893, *i.e.* during the initial or preliminary phase of the modernist movement, before Loisy's dismissal from his professorship at the Institut Catholique and before the issue of the encyclical *Providentissimus Deus*. Wilfrid Ward's ecclesiastical standpoint was similar to Newman's. His liberalism was of an exceedingly moderate type; his watchwords were caution and patience. His attitude to the modernists was a faithful reflexion of Newman's attitude to the 'Rambler' writers. The hopefulness which he showed in 1893 is therefore all the more remarkable.

Most thinking men, he says, admit that the Catholic Church in communion with Rome is the natural home of the Catholic ideal of spirituality, but there are those who, while accepting this ideal of life and character, resist the claim of the Roman Church to their allegiance because they regard it as plainly incompatible with enlightened thought. 'To this incompatibility the Vatican Council is supposed by many to have set the final seal.' Ward freely admits that 'Döllinger's protest at the Munich Congress of 1863[2] against the unhistorical and uncritical spirit of certain Catholic divines had, in many quarters, considerable justification....

---

[1] References are to the reissue of 1912. Ward says (p. xii) that the epilogue owed so much to von Hügel, that it might almost be regarded as a joint production. The fact that at this time Ward was thus closely in agreement with von Hügel illustrates also the significance of the epilogue.   [2] See p. 38 above.

The prominence in the sixties of what was stigmatised as Ultramontane narrowness' cannot be denied.

But, he continues, 'the real question is, Have the men who were responsible for such a line gained by the Vatican Council, and have its decrees in any sense endorsed their views? Is the Roman Church since the Council committed to the general line of a school which was unhistorical and uncritical, and are its members, therefore, unfit, from an intellectual point of view, to cope with the crucial questions of contemporary thought?' He then suggests 'certain broad facts' which belie the affirmative answer to this question. 'The present Pope (*i.e.* Leo XIII)...has notoriously encouraged historical studies and encouraged their pursuit *in the most absolutely candid and critical spirit*' (italics ours). The pope's actions, *e.g.* his opening of the Vatican archives to Protestant as well as Catholic students, show 'that he has meant what he said—that history is to be pursued by its own methods and independently of its giving such results as are most acceptable to the Catholic controversialist'.

And again, 'while the historical spirit is receiving direct encouragement in the Vatican itself', we have the important fact of 'the growth since the Vatican Council of a school of Ultramontane critics, Biblical and historical, whose accuracy and eminence are beyond dispute'. Among the members of this school are mentioned Professor Bickell, of Innsbruck,[1] Abbé Loisy, 'Professor of Exegesis at the Institut Catholique in Paris...known in Germany and England, as well as in France, as a critic of the first rank', the Bollandist Fathers, and Abbé Duchesne...'known to his friends as the most loyal of Ultramontanes'. It is quite untrue that 'the men whom impartial judges rank as our best critics' are anti-ultramontane. On the contrary, as unbiased critics and historians, they compare most favourably with those who

[1] It was by Professor Bickell that von Hügel had been initiated into the study of biblical criticism.

had opposed the Vatican decrees, *e.g.* Döllinger and the Old Catholics, whose opposition to Rome had borne the marks of fanaticism.

'The consistency of the Ultramontane position itself, both with the historical spirit and with a large-minded and moderate temper of mind, is a matter more readily tested practically than theoretically. *Solvitur ambulando*... (The) effect (of the Vatican decision) on directly intellectual problems has not in fact proved to be in a direction opposed to freedom and thoroughness.... That a phase of the new Ultramontanism was in fact so injurious to the interests of intellectual life in the Church, may make the work of dissociating that phase from the Vatican definition itself in the imagination of rough-and-ready exponents of English public opinion a slow one; but no careful student of the period can identify the two.' The belief that 'the great organised society of the Catholic Church raises no barrier against those minds which now feel that they must in honesty face the problems of the times with perfect frankness' may therefore be regarded as justified.

Such was the situation in which the modernist movement originated. The modernists were those who, in diverse ways, submitted this belief to a practical test. *Solvitur ambulando*. The outcome of the movement was to show that the 'rough-and-ready exponents of English public opinion', who had imagined that the Vatican decrees were the charter of obscurantism, were not so grossly mistaken as Wilfrid Ward ventured to hope.

PART II

LOISY

France was not only the centre of the modernist movement geographically; it was also the country where the movement first came to the surface, and the scene of its most significant crises. In France, too, the movement gained most force, if not by the number of its adherents, certainly by the prestige of its chief representatives. Of these, no less certainly, M. Loisy was the most important, and he has remained the most famous. He was indeed the leading figure in the whole movement, at least until about 1904 when he lost faith in its future, and began to retire from participation in it. It is therefore to be expected that an account of his career, from its beginning until that time, will throw much light on the genesis and character of the movement. Moreover, since the publication in 1930–1 of his Mémoires pour servir à l'histoire religieuse de notre temps, fuller and more direct evidence is available for the investigation of his career than there is, or is ever likely to be, in the case of any other modernist. What follows here is based, in the first instance, upon a study of the Mémoires.[1] To select from the vast mass of material, which they contain, only what bears most closely on the subject of this essay is not an easy undertaking. The reliability of M. Loisy's memory and the accuracy of the facts which he records do not appear to have been seriously challenged.[2] At the same time care has been taken to compare and to supplement his reminiscences with evidence, derived from other sources, and contributed from different points of view, where such exists.

[1] Where specific references are not given, or where there are no references to other authorities, it may be assumed that statements of fact are due to information that is provided in the Mémoires. Specific references to the Mémoires are inserted when actual quotations are made therefrom, or when there is some other special reason for doing so, e.g. when the reference is to a different part of the Mémoires from that which corresponds to the chronological order of events.

Here, as elsewhere in the essay, some of the shorter quotations from French books are left untranslated.

[2] Thus, for instance, Père Lagrange, in his M. Loisy et le modernisme (1932), finds nothing to question in Loisy's account of the facts (apart from one or two unimportant details). His book is an attempt to show that the facts ought to be interpreted differently. It is Loisy's opinions, not the accuracy of his records, that he criticizes.

Chapter IX

VOCATION, 1857–1892

Alfred Loisy was born in 1857. His father was a farmer, and he would have been one too, had not his delicate constitution and the aptitude for learning, which he showed as soon as he went to school, indicated for him some career that would not be one of strenuous physical exertion. It was not, however, through any suggestion or pressure on the part of his parents that he entered upon training for the priesthood. It was he himself who decided that he had a vocation and who took the initiative in regard to its fulfilment. In 1874 he entered the grand seminary at Châlons and donned the ecclesiastical habit which he was destined to wear for the next thirty-four years.

Before he entered the seminary nothing had happened to unsettle his simple faith that the Church was 'a great school of holiness and truth, in which the officers, being in possession of clear and certain teaching, laboured with one accord to keep their charges in the way of salvation'.[1] But he had not been there long before he began to realize that the Church was not precisely what in his innocence he had supposed it to be. Even after the Vatican council there was still liberalism as well as ultramontanism in the ecclesiastical world, and the difference between them was reflected in both the professors and the students of the seminary. Long before he had any clear appreciation of the questions at issue, Loisy was instinctively drawn to associate himself with the liberals. It was as evident at the seminary as it had been in his school days that he had rare intellectual gifts, and he was given an opportunity of beginning the study of Hebrew, nor did he delay to become interested in such biblical criticism as the literature at his disposal made possible.

[1] *Mémoires*, I. 44; cp. II, 373.

It must not, however, be assumed that Loisy was only intellectually precocious, or that he was simply a very clever young man who by force of circumstances found himself committed to an ecclesiastical career which made no spiritual appeal to him. On the contrary, he was genuinely pious and devout; he was inspired by motives that were at once altruistic and mystical. Certainly during his seminary days and during the early years of his priesthood there was real fervour in his faith and devotion, and always (until the final break in 1908) the discipline and dignity of his priestly life were unexceptionable.[1] Nevertheless, almost from the outset (from 1875 onwards) there was a constantly growing tension between his devotional and his intellectual life. His devotional life was naturally based upon the traditional system of doctrinal orthodoxy. As his intellectual powers developed and his opportunities of free research increased, he became acutely conscious of the difficulty of reconciling this system of doctrine in its accepted form with the conclusions to which his studies led him.

In 1878 he was sent from Châlons to complete his training at the newly constituted theological faculty of the Catholic university at Paris. Here he came into contact with Duchesne, who was professor of Church history. Louis Duchesne[2] (1843–1922) was the son of a Breton fisherman; after teaching for two or three years at the seminary of Saint Brieuc,[3] where he had himself been trained for ordination, he went in

[1] Cp. *The Modern Churchman*, VIII, 116.

[2] See E. Dupont, *Mgr Duchesne chez lui en Bretagne* (1923); C. d'Habloville, *Grandes figures de l'Église contemporaine* (1925); *L'histoire et l'œuvre de l'École française de Rome* (1931), pp. 57–64; and a long letter from F. von Hügel in *The Times Literary Supplement* (May 25th, 1922), p. 342.

[3] At the time of the Vatican council he was an ardent ultramontane, and collected signatures for a petition in favour of the definition of papal infallibility, although his bishop was opposed thereto. He was about thirty before he came under liberal influences. See E. Barbier, *Histoire du catholicisme libéral* (1924), III, 202, and Loisy, *Mémoires*, III, 427.

1871 to study at the École des Hautes Études in Paris. Here his talent was noticed, and in 1873 he was invited to join the École Française de Rome, which was founded in that year. At Rome Duchesne became a devoted disciple of J. B. de Rossi (1822–94), the famous Italian archaeologist and epigraphist—'cet illustre savant, la plus belle gloire de la science catholique en ce siècle'.[1] Archaeological expeditions to Greece and Asia Minor served also to determine his future as a scientific historian. When in 1877 he returned to Paris to take up a professorship at the Catholic university, he had already acquired a considerable reputation, and he came as an enthusiastic adherent and apostle of modern critical methods. His appointment met indeed with some opposition, as he had been denounced as 'un prêtre plus que libéral et "d'esprit peu ecclésiastique"'.[2] He was not slow to justify these suspicions. But if the traditionalists were shocked and alarmed, younger men of scholarly bent and progressive temper tended naturally to rally round one whose learning was as unrivalled in its quality as his wit was brilliant and his personality attractive.

Loisy's contact with Duchesne was of great consequence; but its effects were not immediate, as for reasons of health he was prevented from returning to Paris after his first term. Instead he went back to the seminary at Châlons, and was ordained priest on June 29th, 1879. He was at once appointed curé of a tiny village, from which after about six months he was transferred to a slightly larger parish. The full performance of his pastoral duties left him ample time for the prosecution of his studies. He had already thought of embarking upon an exposition of Catholic doctrine 'en rapport avec les nécessités des temps nouveaux'.[3] Towards the end of

---

[1] L. Duchesne, *Les origines chrétiennes*, p. xi; cp. *Bulletin critique*, xv, 374: 'C'est à de Rossi que je dois ma vocation scientifique; ses écrits m'ont sauvé' (quoted by d'Habloville, *op. cit.* p. 19).

[2] Baudrillart, *Vie de Mgr d'Hulst*, I, 361.   [3] *Mémoires*, I, 80.

1880 he entered into communication with Duchesne, who was eager that he should return to Paris. Duchesne had no doubt detected Loisy's ability and planned to enrol him in the group of young students, who were collecting round him, and who, he hoped, would take part in a progressive theological movement. At this time Duchesne still thought that Rome would be favourable to such an enterprise or would at least tolerate it; he himself intended to go bravely forward with his own subject, Church history. It was chiefly owing to Duchesne's influence that Loisy returned to the Institut Catholique[1] in May, 1881. Biblical criticism was the subject to which he was naturally drawn, and Duchesne encouraged him in this direction.

It seems certain that Duchesne himself had not yet realized what would be the effect upon the traditional theology of the full acceptance of the results of biblical criticism. He had hitherto been mainly occupied by his researches in Church history and archaeology, and it was not until August, 1881, and then at the instigation of Loisy, that he gave serious attention to the criticism of the gospels. The following letter, which he wrote to Loisy on August 18th, shows that he recognized at once the need of a new apologetic of some such kind as the modernists eventually put forward.

As our fathers had to modulate the external form of their preaching to suit the capacity of Frank, Saxon, Celtic, etc., intellects, in the same way perhaps we shall have to remove certain obstacles which separate us from the too scientific intellects of our contemporaries. Theology, in its existing form, is finished; the old exegesis is played out. In reading over again during these last few days with the eyes of a critic the first three Gospels, I see that there are in fact many disagreements in detail. One can leave the scholastics ingeniously to combine the genealogies and to show that they harmonize. But two things remain: first, the general impression produced by Jesus Christ on those who approached

[1] A law, passed in 1880, had prohibited the use of the title 'university'; see Baudrillart, *op. cit.* 1, 386.

Him...; secondly, there are these divine discourses set in one way or another in divergent narratives. This is enough. I see that your reading has led you too along this path; do not be afraid to go ahead.[1]

We shall see that before long, after mature consideration of all the issues involved, Duchesne himself drew back, and advised others to do so too.

Loisy had taken his first degree in May, 1881. In the academic year, 1881-2, he read for a further degree, after which he was appointed to a place on the staff of the faculty of theology as lecturer in Hebrew; he also began to specialize in Assyriology. In December, 1882, he began to attend the lectures of Renan at the Collège de France, and was thus initiated into the textual criticism of the Old Testament. Hitherto, he had not read the works, nor otherwise come under the influence, of non-Catholic scholars. It was from Renan, more than from any other single source, that he derived his devotion to, and his proficiency in, the science of biblical criticism.[2] The scientific method of study and the ideal of pursuing it freely and disinterestedly, he had already learned from Duchesne. It was the application of this method and of this ideal to the Bible that he learned from Renan; but from Renan's conclusions and manner of representing the history of religion he widely departed.

Loisy refuses to admit the allegation of his orthodox opponents that his 'apostasy' was due to the subversive influence of rationalist critics.[3] He insists that it was his own

[1] *Mémoires*, I, 98.　　　　　　[2] Cp. *ibid.* III, 99, 437.

[3] This is one of the commonest methods by which the orthodox account for 'the errors of modernism'; see Loisy, *Mémoires*, III, 83 f.; Rivière, *Le modernisme dans l'Église*, p. 96; *Revue historique*, CLXIX, 93 n.; Lagrange, *M. Loisy et le modernisme* (1932), pp. 236f.; D. J. Mercier, *Modernism* (1910), pp. 11, 27f.; L. de Grandmaison, *Jesus Christ* (1932), II, 292; H. Felder, *Christ and the critics* (1924), I, 13: 'All the problems of this modern christology, and the whole opposition of Modernists to the Christ of the Gospels, find their explanation in the preconceived assumptions of rationalist and agnostic philosophy.' Cp. *ibid.* II, 233.

study of the Bible itself, much more than any external influence, which forced him to become a critic and to remain a critic.

The Bible has been the first and principal cause of my intellectual evolution; it is because I read it seriously that I became a critic of it. As the Catholics cannot allow this without denying their absolute dogmas, they are obliged to beat about the bush in order to find other causes; but these secondary causes, when they are not purely fictitious, have significance and point only by reason of the principal cause which they are not willing to allow.[1]

With regard to Renan himself Loisy writes:

I did not seek to enter into relations with him, and I never spoke to him. I still thought that his general position was false and that he had been mistaken in leaving the Church. Thus I instructed myself at his school, in the hope of proving to him that all that was true in his science was compatible with Catholicism sanely understood.[2]

Loisy has preserved the record of an imaginary dialogue between a 'jeune savant' (who is more or less the mouthpiece of Renan) and the Church, which he composed at this period (July, 1883), and which illuminates the way in which his mind was developing. In the course of this dialogue the Church is represented as saying:

I must allow—that my teaching, immutable in its principles and in its end, can and ought to be modified in its form, to be perfected in its exposition, in order that it may better respond to the needs of the generations which it must bring to God. Perhaps my doctors in this century have been inferior to their task and have not understood that it was permissible for them to abandon the old formulas, that they ought almost to forget them, in order to preserve for the world the very substance of the truth which is entrusted to me. God will give me, I hope, men apt for this work, and you will no longer be able to accuse me of ignorance.[3]

[1] *Mémoires*, II, 16.   [2] *Ibid.* I, 118.
[3] *Ibid.* I, 121.

This work Loisy regarded as his vocation; we have here, as early as 1883, the fundamental idea of *L'Évangile et l'Église* and *Autour d'un petit livre*.

During the year 1883-4 he wrote two theses with a view to obtaining the degree of doctor in theology. Before sending them in to be examined he submitted one of them, the subject of which was 'the inspiration of Holy Scripture', to Mgr d'Hulst, rector of the Institut Catholique. The rector considered that the thesis, if published, would be a source of scandal,[1] and the whole project was there and then abandoned. It was not until 1885 that Loisy's teaching began to arouse public suspicions.[2]

The friendly relations that had so far existed between him and Duchesne were brought to an end in June, 1889, by a rather complicated but quite petty quarrel, into which we need not enter. They were not resumed till 1896, when Duchesne had gone back to Rome as director of the École Française, and they never again became so intimate. Already, *i.e.* before 1890, Duchesne had come to the conclusion that 'une évolution scientifique sur le terrain de la Bible dans l'Église romaine'[3] was a moral impossibility, and he played no direct part in the modernist movement. Shortly before this rupture of their friendship he had advised Loisy to confine himself to the study of Semitic philology, and to avoid research and teaching which would inevitably involve a conflict with the theologians. Thus Duchesne, who, as Loisy says, 'did more than anyone to initiate a scientific movement in French Catholicism',[4] withdrew from his position of leadership as soon as he saw that the object of the movement was incapable of realization. His own later work, which was carried out on ground less dangerous than that of

[1] Cp. *Mémoires*, II, 459.
[2] *Ibid.* I, 139; cp. Baudrillart, *Vie de Mgr d'Hulst*, I, 475.
[3] *Mémoires*, I, 164.
[4] *Ibid.* I, 106.

biblical criticism,[1] did indeed cause him trouble with the
Church authorities, but it was free from the distinctive taint
of modernism.

It will be useful at this point to observe more closely the
difference between Duchesne and the authentic modernists.
Those who write in English on the subject of modernism
sometimes give the impression that there was no difference,
or at least that it is not worth taking into account.[2] On the
contrary, the difference is important, and to recognize it is
to go far in the direction of understanding the distinctive
character of modernism. Both Duchesne and the modernists
realized that the science of biblical criticism threatened the
orthodox tradition of theology, and especially the traditional
Christology. Duchesne realized also and from the outset,
i.e. before 1890, that the Roman Church either would not or
could not allow any adequate modification of traditional
orthodoxy, and that therefore the profession of traditional
orthodoxy, or at least the refusal to question it, was the
necessary condition of remaining in the Church. The
modernists, on the other hand, were distinguished by the
hope that it would be possible to secure within the Church
those modifications of traditional orthodoxy which the
science of biblical criticism required, and that pending the
ultimate acceptance of such modifications the Church would
be willing to allow them freedom in their capacity as critics.

[1] Cp. *The Times Literary Supplement* (January 15th, 1904): 'After some
slight indiscretions in his earlier years, (Duchesne) has been resolutely
prudent on Biblical questions.' Also A. Houtin, *La crise du clergé*[2] (1908),
ch. XII, where the first volume of Duchesne's *Histoire ancienne de l'Église* is
submitted to a criticism which shows with what subtlety the author
evaded, or sought to evade, any clash with traditional theology. Cp.
Lecanuet, *La vie de l'Église sous Léon XIII* (1930), p. 330.

[2] See, for instances of failure to distinguish Duchesne from the
modernists, H. D. A. Major, *English modernism* (1927), pp. 19 f., H. L.
Stewart, *Modernism past and present* (1932), pp. 178, 305 f., and W. M.
Horton, *The philosophy of the abbé Bautain* (1926), p. 297.

It is now, of course, obvious that Duchesne was right and the modernists wrong in so far as the anticipation of the future was concerned; whether Duchesne was morally justified in deciding to remain in the Church on the only conditions which he saw to be possible is another question upon which we are not called to pronounce judgment.

Loisy himself has emphasized Duchesne's innocence of modernism more than once. In 1913 he wrote in *Choses passées*:

Duchesne has always had a horror of what is called modernism; he has always taught that the dogmas of the Church are unimpeachable and immutable; he has never written a line for the purpose of attacking or defending them, or to attenuate, correct or modify them by way of interpretation.[1]

And again in his *Mémoires*:

I have already said, and I say it again: in the affair of modernism, from its beginning about 1890 until the end, Duchesne was never anything but a spectator...of our efforts and our tribulations.[2]

Albert Houtin with his accustomed irony described the difference between Duchesne and Loisy as follows:

If Mgr Duchesne and M. l'abbé Loisy, in arriving at the same scientific conclusions, have met with a different fortune, it is because the latter has allowed himself to philosophize upon these conclusions, and to propose a new apologetic of which the Church seems to stand in need.... The theologians cannot let it be supposed that their system is ruined. They have seen to it that those who came to their assistance were condemned. Mgr Duchesne had no such *naïveté*.[3]

But perhaps not the least authoritative description of

[1] *My duel with the Vatican* (American trans. of *Choses passées*), p. 120; cp. *Mémoires*, III, 239, 245, 423–9. C. d'Habloville, *op. cit.* pp. 72 f.

[2] *Op. cit.* II, 278; cp. *Revue historique*, CLXIX, 105.

[3] *La crise du clergé* (1908), p. 165; cp. P. Desjardins, *Catholicisme et critique*, pp. 22 f.; P. Gardner in *The Modern Churchman*, XIII, 537–41.

Duchesne's attitude is contained in a letter which he himself
wrote to Marcel Hébert on January 18th, 1900:

The religious authority rests upon its tradition and the members
of its personnel who are the most devoted—and also the least
intelligent. What is to be done? Are we to hope that this will
change? Are we to try to effect a reform? But this will not
change, and the reform will not be carried through. The only
result of attempts of this kind is to get yourself thrown out of the
window, with no beneficial results either for others or for yourself....It may be that, in spite of all appearances, the old ecclesiastical edifice is going one day to tumble down, that the gates of
Paradise will prevail against it. If it happens so, no one will blame
us for having supported the old establishment as long as possible.[1]

It was the distinction of the modernists that they did hope for
change and that they did try to effect a reform. The story of
Loisy's career from 1890 onwards is a history of this hope, of
the attempt at reform and of its failure.

In 1890 he was appointed professor of Holy Scripture at the
Institut Catholique; at the same time he submitted a new thesis
for the doctorate of theology—on the history of the canon of
the Old Testament. Since the subject of the thesis was 'safe'
and its treatment discreet, it was passed by the examiners.
He was now able to embark upon an ambitious scheme of
teaching. He proposed to work through the whole field of
the scientific study of the Bible. He thought that it was one
of the Church's greatest needs that this should be done on the
basis of a full and frank acceptance of modern critical methods;
the teaching about the Bible which was current in the Church
was obsolete. He realized that he would at almost every
point be breaking new ground and that he was bound to
come into conflict with the official theologians. Neverthe-

---

[1] Houtin, *Un prêtre symboliste, Marcel Hébert* (1925) pp. 114f.; see the
whole letter. Cp. Loisy, *Mémoires*, III, 221, 342. It is not altogether
surprising that Duchesne's literary executor has placed a twenty-five years'
veto on the publication of three volumes of his letters, which are at the
Bibliothèque Nationale; see d'Habloville, *op. cit.* p. 133.

less, since he was entirely convinced of the rightfulness of modern critical and scientific methods, he had brave hopes that his labours would ultimately be acceptable to the Church. Anyhow he felt that it was his vocation to make the attempt, and he expected that many, if not all, his pupils would be disposed to support and assist in the enterprise.

It was in pursuance of this plan of systematic teaching that he followed up his history of the canon of the Old Testament with a history of the canon of the New Testament (1891). Neither of these volumes aroused serious opposition. It was otherwise, however, when in the ensuing year he broached the exegesis of the opening chapters of the book of Genesis. It seemed scandalous to the strictly traditionalist mind of the Superior of Saint-Sulpice (M. Icard) that the historicity of these chapters should be questioned. Students from the seminary of Saint-Sulpice had hitherto formed a considerable part of Loisy's audience; at the beginning of the next academic year (October, 1892) they were forbidden to attend his lectures. A similar prohibition had been applied by M. Icard to the lectures of Duchesne some years earlier (1882).[1]

At this juncture Loisy tried to enlist the sympathy and support of a prince of the Church. He turned naturally to Mgr Meignan, who had ordained him, and who was the most erudite biblical scholar[2] among the French bishops. Mgr Meignan was friendly, but he was not in the least inclined to support or even to encourage Loisy in his projected renovation of ecclesiastical teaching about the Bible. The prudent prelate, who incidentally was on the point of being made a cardinal, was well acquainted with the real question at issue, but he was quite convinced that the Roman Church would allow no substantial modification of its

---

[1] Baudrillart, *Vie de Mgr d'Hulst*, I, 462.

[2] Mgr Meignan plays a considerable, if ignoble, part in A. Houtin's *La Question biblique chez les catholiques de France au XIXᵉ siècle* (1902); cp. Lecanuet, *La vie de l'Église sous Léon XIII* (1930), pp. 318 ff.

traditional teaching about Scripture. He therefore contented himself with benevolently warning Loisy of the danger and futility of the task which he was proposing to undertake. The bishop's attitude was in effect the same as Duchesne's and was the outcome of a longer and wider experience.[1] Events were about to show that his warning was only too thoroughly justified.

Instead of Mgr Meignan's support, which he had solicited in vain, Loisy was now the object of a championship which he had done nothing to solicit and which proved disastrous in its results. The publication by Mgr d'Hulst of his article on *La Question biblique* led to Loisy's dismissal from the Institut Catholique, and it provoked the issue of the papal encyclical *Providentissimus Deus*. We shall examine at some length this series of events, for it is full of significance for the student of the origins of the modernist movement. The crisis of 1893 was in fact an earnest, almost a rehearsal, of the specifically modernist crisis which was to come to a head ten years later.[2]

---

[1] Cp. *Mémoires*, III, 250.
[2] Cp. *ibid*. II, 246.

Chapter x

THE BIBLICAL QUESTION, 1893

Renan had died in October, 1892, and Mgr d'Hulst had contributed to *Le Correspondant*, the established organ of liberal Catholicism, an obituary article which, while written from a perfectly orthodox standpoint, was temperate in its tone. For instance, he went so far as to suggest that Renan's defection from Catholicism might have been prevented if the teaching about history and criticism, which he had received as a seminarist, had been less antiquated. The article was well received, and its author was thus encouraged to go further and to deal with *la Question biblique*. Renan's death had given a general vogue to discussions of this subject. The second article appeared on January 25th, 1893. Loisy received no information about the matter until a few days before, when the rector sent him a finished proof of his article together with a note in which he explained his object in writing it.

Mgr d'Hulst had only a superficial and secondhand knowlege of the questions involved in biblical criticism;[1] nevertheless, he was at this time so infected by Loisy's enthusiasm that he shared the ambition, in so far as he understood what it implied, that the Institut Catholique should be a centre, the centre *par excellence*, from which there should radiate through the Church the new biblical teaching that was necessary if Catholicism was to keep abreast of the times. The realization of this ambition was threatened at the outset by the fact that Loisy's teaching had already become suspect, *e.g.* to the influential Superior of Saint-Sulpice. Mgr d'Hulst judged that the moment was opportune for trying to secure toleration for the progressive movement in biblical study and teaching.

[1] That this was so is allowed by his biographer, Baudrillart, *Vie de Mgr d'Hulst*, I, 399 f.

It was obvious, he said in his article,[1] that *la Question biblique* was a real, and not an imaginary, question. There was a clash between the findings of modern science and the traditional dogma of the inspiration of Holy Scripture. How was this discord to be resolved? He alleged that there were three 'schools' in the Church which advocated three different solutions of the problem—a right and left wing and a centre. All alike agreed in loyally accepting the traditional dogma of inspiration. The right wing urged that, since *ex hypothesi* God was the author of the whole Bible, there was no room in it for error of any kind. In practice this meant that the acquired results of modern knowledge had to be met by a simple *non possumus*, or that, by subterfuge or sophistry, statements in the Bible had to be reinterpreted in such a way as to be made compatible with those results, as for instance when the six 'days' in the first chapter of Genesis were said to mean six 'periods of years'. The left wing, on the other hand, maintained that the inspiration of the Bible covered all statements which involved 'faith or morals', but that it allowed of the recognition of errors in regard to purely scientific or historical matters. The centre, or *école moyenne*, adopted a *via media* between these two extremes; it avoided the rigour of the one and the danger of the other.

The writer denied that in his article he was expressing his own views; he affected to be simply a reporter of opinions which ought to be taken into account. He submitted that all three 'schools' should be tolerated in the Church, while he sought to indicate that his own sympathies were with the *opinion moyenne*. In reality, they were with the *école large* (the left wing), as anyone who read between the lines could see perfectly well. But where was his *école large*? Of whom did it consist? Everyone supposed, and supposed rightly, that it was intended to represent the opinions of Loisy,

[1] The article is analysed and quoted at length by Baudrillart, *Vie de Mgr d'Hulst*, II, 145–57.

although in fact, and evidently by design, Loisy was not mentioned in the article. The object of the article, both in the intention of its author and in the impression which it made on its readers, was to secure toleration for Loisy's teaching.

No instrument could have been more ill-suited to the purpose for which it was intended. So far from securing toleration for Loisy's teaching, it compromised him and his position at the Institut Catholique irretrievably. It was probable, in retrospect it seems almost certain, that sooner or later a crisis was bound to arise in connexion with his professorial teaching, however discreet he and his well-wishers had been. It is ironical that the crisis should have been precipitated by a blatant indiscretion on the part of one who was sincerely friendly to his purpose and who moreover was in a strategic position to forward it. It was a sovereign imprudence that Mgr d'Hulst should have published his manifesto at all; but in any case as soon as the idea entered his head he ought to have consulted Loisy about it. Loisy would probably have succeeded in persuading him to abandon the idea altogether; at least the article in the form in which we know it would never have seen the light. As it was, Mgr d'Hulst, with the best intentions in the world, in effect stabbed Loisy in the back, and at the same time involved himself in a situation from which it was impossible for him to extricate himself with self-respect.

The article on *la Question biblique*, as might easily have been foreseen, immediately provoked a turmoil of controversy. The traditionalists naturally appealed to the Roman Curia to condemn both the author of the article and those whose cause he had espoused. Mgr d'Hulst soon grew alarmed; he was not at all tempted to become an heresiarch. Quite apart from the present controversy, he was not at this time in favour at Rome;[1] and the utmost he could do, or at

---

[1] In politics Mgr d'Hulst was a monarchist, whereas the papacy now stood for the acceptance of the republican régime in France.

least the utmost he tried to do, was to prevent the explicit condemnation of himself and of the persons and writings which his article had compromised.[1] With this proviso—when he saw that the intervention of the holy see was inevitable, he affected to welcome it. The encyclical *Providentissimus*, published in November, 1893, did indeed avoid the explicit condemnation of individual persons and of particular writings, but it gave to the movement for the renewal of biblical science in the Church a setback from which it could hardly recover.

Mgr d'Hulst's indiscretion, as has been already observed, not only provoked the issue of the encyclical; it also resulted in Loisy's dismissal from the Institut Catholique. And here his imprudence is even more conspicuous; it is said that his conscience was troubled about this aspect of the matter until his dying day. We have said that the object of his article was to secure toleration for Loisy's teaching about the Bible; but he had omitted to take the elementary precaution of ascertaining what that teaching really was. As a matter of fact, the rector's *école large* was not a true representation, but a misrepresentation, of Loisy's attitude to the biblical question, and Loisy was not unjustly aggrieved that a misrepresentation of his attitude by one, whom everyone would suppose to be perfectly well informed, had been given wide currency.

To a superficial observer Loisy's quarrel with the *école large* might not seem to have much ground, but, rightly understood, it was far-reaching. Mgr d'Hulst's 'left wing' were united with his 'right wing' and 'centre' in accepting the traditional dogma of inspiration as the starting-point of their thought about the Bible. The 'left wing', instead of interpreting the dogma *au pied de la lettre*, limited absolute inspiration, *i.e.* divine, immutable truth, to those parts of

[1] The rector's predominant motive was to prevent a condemnation which would bring discredit, *i.e.* any imputation of heterodoxy, on the Institut Catholique.

Scripture which were concerned with faith and morals; except in those parts, they held that the dogma permitted them to acknowledge that there were errors in the Bible. Loisy aptly pointed out that this was to make the Bible a mosaic composed of divine truths and human errors—a view which was certainly never contemplated by those who drew up the traditional dogma. The starting-point of his own system, if system it should be called, was not the dogma of inspiration,[1] but a scientific study of the Bible itself. Whatever else it may be, the Bible is in the first instance a collection of human documents; the truth they contain, whether about faith or morals or anything else, is necessarily relative to the time and place and other circumstances of their origin. The primary duty of the Christian scholar is to find out what the Bible has to say for itself, not what an *a priori* dogma has to say about it. The Bible must be studied by the best available methods of literary and historical criticism. The results thus acquired may then be related to the traditional dogma of inspiration, which may have to be revised in the light of them. In an epigram Loisy summarized the difference between his system and that of the *école large*: 'Il ne s'agit plus de savoir si la Bible contient des erreurs, mais bien de savoir ce que la Bible contient de vérité'.[2]

The controversy which followed the publication of Mgr d'Hulst's article made it necessary for him to give fresh guarantees of the orthodoxy of the Institut Catholique. This meant either that he must resign his own position as rector or that he must sacrifice Loisy. But since his own resignation would certainly have involved the sacrifice of Loisy, he

---

[1] He was not concerned to quarrel with the dogma; unlike the *école large*, he did not limit the *extent* of inspiration. What he did do, although he was not at pains to say so in so many words, was to limit its *effects*. Cp. *Mémoires*, II, 15 (the report of his interview with Cardinal Richard in 1900): 'On croit qu'il y a une question biblique, l'inspiration, de laquelle tout dépend. J'ai toujours combattu cette idée. Le dogme de l'inspiration est au-dessus de la critique...'.   [2] *Études bibliques*[3], p. 146.

chose the latter alternative as the less of two evils. Thus at the end of the academic year (June, 1893) the chair of Holy Scripture, which Loisy had filled for three years, was taken from him and handed over to an irreproachable conservative, while Loisy himself was henceforth to confine himself to teaching Hebrew and other oriental languages. The arrangement, which in any case was little more than a temporary compromise, did not last long. It had been agreed that Loisy should continue to publish his review, *L'Enseignement biblique*, in which since 1892 he had reproduced some of his lectures, etc. The final number of this for 1893, which appeared on November 10th, contained a slightly modified version of his last lecture as professor of Holy Scripture, which had been delivered in the previous June. In this lecture[1] Loisy had discussed *la Question biblique* with the object of distinguishing his own position from that of Mgr d'Hulst's *école large*. The lecture contained nothing fresh to those who had followed the course of his teaching, but its publication was regarded as a startling provocation. The council of bishops, who controlled the Institut Catholique, was holding its annual meeting on November 15th. The rector himself brought the matter before them, and without further ado Loisy was dismissed. Thus on the eve of the publication of the encyclical *Providentissimus*, the Institut Catholique was enabled to offer a signal token of its orthodoxy.

The encyclical professed to encourage the serious study of the Bible, and no doubt the pope and his advisers thought that they were serving the best interests of biblical scholarship. But it cannot be said that their view of the nature of those interests was an enlightened one. In effect, the encyclical[2] did little more than reaffirm the dogma of scriptural

---

[1] It was republished in the volume *Études bibliques* (3rd ed. pp. 139–69).

[2] The encyclical is analysed and quoted at length by A. Houtin, *La Question biblique au XIXe siècle*[2] (1902), pp. 165–72.

inspiration as promulgated by the councils of Trent and of the Vatican. Thus it is laid down that 'all the books (of the Bible)...with all their parts have been written under the inspiration of the Holy Ghost. The divine inspiration, far from admitting the co-existence of error, by itself excludes all error....'. In the words of Mgr Barry, the encyclical made 'it impossible for an orthodox defender of Holy Writ to solve its problems by giving up its inerrancy'.[1] The limitation of inspiration to matters of faith and morals is flatly condemned. This part of the encyclical was obviously aimed at Mgr d'Hulst's *école large*.

The rector and the faculty of theology of the Institut Catholique hastened to express their complete submission to the encyclical. Loisy, on his own account, did so too. The practice of expressing submission to papal utterances, which are in reality regarded by those who submit to them as deplorable, savours of insincerity. The practice must not, however, be judged too severely. It was a convention which liberal Catholics, from Lamennais[2] onwards, had found it impracticable to disregard. It is the institution, which applies the principle of authority with such excessive and narrow rigour, that should be blamed, and not those individuals who are doing their best to secure freedom and reform.[3] Clearly a point may come when the demands of authority are absolutely intolerable; then the individual must needs break with the institution. For Loisy the breaking-point came in 1908; it had not come yet.

[1] *The tradition of Scripture* (1906), p. 229.

[2] In 1832 Lamennais, with Lacordaire and Montalembert, submitted to the encyclical of Gregory XVI which condemned *L'Avenir*. It was only later that he broke with the Church. Cp. p. 23 above.

[3] Cp. G. Weill, *Histoire du catholicisme libéral*, p. 289: The opponents of the liberal Catholics 'les ont accusés de mauvaise foi, mais à tort: ces finesses de dialectique sont employées souvent par les sujets d'une monarchie absolue, quand ils veulent concilier l'obéissance vis-à-vis du souverain avec la fidélité à leurs convictions'.

It was not so difficult, as it might at first sight appear to be, for him to justify his submission to the encyclical. In the first place, in reiterating the traditional dogma of scriptural inspiration it maintained the *status quo*; it left matters where they were. The situation, therefore, was no more or less tolerable than it had been before. Secondly, the particular system of Catholic teaching, which the pope condemned, was that of the factitious *école large*, *i.e.* the limitation of inspiration to faith and morals. Not only had Loisy never accepted this system, but he had deliberately and with sincerity dissociated himself from it.[1] On this score at least he could express his cordial agreement with the Holy Father. Thirdly, it required no great ingenuity to find loopholes in the encyclical. Mgr Dupanloup had thus evaded the difficulties which the syllabus of Pius IX had raised for liberal Catholics, and the evasion had been tolerated. A new generation of liberals tried to adopt a similar procedure in regard to Leo XIII's condemnation of biblical criticism. The subsequent history of the modernist movement is the measure both of their success and of their failure.

The events which culminated in Loisy's dismissal from the Institut Catholique and in the issue of the encyclical *Providentissimus* mark a turning-point in the development of the movement and in his own career. It is impossible to say what might have happened if he had been permitted to continue his work at the Institut Catholique for a substantial period, and so perhaps to enlist a large and influential body of disciples. It may be that, if in some such way as this the movement had acquired a larger momentum at the outset, its chances of success would have been greater. It is more likely that Cardinal Meignan and Duchesne were right in supposing that it never had any real chances of success at all.

[1] The difference between these views of inspiration was later recognized in the encyclical *Pascendi*; see Sabatier, *Modernism*, pp. 271 f.

Chapter XI

REVISING DOGMA, 1894–1899

After a delay of several months, Loisy was appointed by the archbishop of Paris, Cardinal Richard, to the chaplaincy of a girls' school at Neuilly. The school was conducted by a community of Dominican nuns. He entered upon his duties there in October, 1894, and during the ensuing five years performed them with a devotion and efficiency that left no room for objection. These duties left him ample leisure for study, and thus he was able to continue his program of work on the Bible. Circumstances also prompted him to widen the range of his studies. At the Institut Catholique his time and interest had naturally been absorbed for the most part by matters of technical scholarship.[1] Now, however, he had an opportunity of investigating the more general questions which arise from the study of religion, and, moreover, his duties of teaching the catechism in school set his mind working along that line of thought[2] which issued in the apologetic of *L'Évangile et l'Église*.

It is well to quote here his own account of what was his attitude to the Church at this time. It must be borne in mind that for him, as for Frenchmen generally,[3] the term

[1] In his *Mémoires*, I. 358, he writes: 'Avec mon installation à Neuilly commence une nouvelle période de mon activité intellectuelle et de mon action morale. Jusque-là, j'avais été à peu près confiné dans l'ordre purement scientifique, étudiant les rapports de la critique avec la théologie sur le terrain de l'exégèse. Maintenant c'étaient l'ensemble du problème religieux et les conditions générales du ministère ecclésiastique qui allaient être l'objet quotidien de mes expériences'.

[2] See *Autour d'un petit livre*, p. 7.

[3] Cp. A. Sabatier, *The religions of authority and the religion of the Spirit*, p. 105: 'The epithet "Roman" has become so firmly attached to Catholicism in speech and opinion as to have become inseparable from it'.

'Catholicism' is synonymous with the 'Roman Church'; that is to say, he has never taken into consideration the possibility of a Catholicism apart from the Roman Church.

I did not accept (he says) any article of the Catholic creed, except that Jesus had been 'crucified under Pontius Pilate';[1] but more and more religion seemed to me to be an immense power, which had dominated, which dominated still, and which promised to dominate always, the history of humanity. All its historic forms had had their limitations, their faults, their abuses; but they represented almost the whole moral life of the human race. The Christian religion, arising out of the religion of Israel, was distinguished among all others by the height of its ideal; the Catholic Church was the mother of the European peoples; a queen, whose power had much declined, yet influential still, she remained the mistress of her future; if she only knew how to speak to the peoples, no adverse power could withstand her. To this Church, in spite of all that she had made me suffer already, I remained sincerely devoted....

My devotion to the Church was certainly more sincere, and I venture to add more disinterested, than that of most of the fanatics and politicians, who were soon to use all their powers to push me outside Catholicism. The service of the Church did not yet seem incompatible for me with that of truth, of humanity. I had been able to see at near enough range the blindness of the hierarchy, the moral shortcomings of its most clear-sighted, and in some cases of its best intentioned, representatives; but it did not seem to me that I had simply to choose between complete adherence to the Catholic beliefs interpreted according to the ignorance of the pope, of Cardinal Richard, of the ordinary theologians, and the immediate repudiation of Catholicism. It appeared to me that the moral action of this religion ought to be supported, and the possibility of a reform which would modify Catholicism without destroying it seemed to me all the more admissible since in all directions many people, on one point or another, more or less

[1] He does not mean that he did not accept the other articles of the creed in any sense whatsoever, but that he did not accept them in the strictly traditional sense, which was the only one that the scholastic theologians and the official Church regarded as legitimate.

timidly or courageously according to their character, seemed to welcome it.[1]

This statement, whose good faith there is no reason to question, may be accepted as a summary justification of the part which its author played in the modernist movement. It is, at least, a sufficient answer to the charges, which were later made against him by critics within and without the Church, that *e.g.* from this time onwards he was playing a double game,[2] or that he was a mere tactician,[3] and that he was not really a Catholic at heart at all. It is true that, if Catholicism is identified with an unbending traditional orthodoxy, Loisy was no longer a Catholic at heart. But was that identification necessary? That was precisely the question at issue.

He was not alone in desiring to work for a transformation of existing Catholicism. From this time onwards he was specially encouraged by the friendship and co-operation of Baron Friedrich von Hügel and Mgr Mignot, two of the most highly cultured Catholics of their generation.[4]

[1] *Op. cit.* I, 363 f.; cp. III, 23 for the date of 'la crise de mes croyances catholiques', and III, 246.

[2] *E.g.* J. Rivière, *Le modernisme dans l'Église*, p. 98.

[3] *E.g.* A. Houtin, *Ma vie laïque*, pp. 155 ff., 260.

[4] On the former, see pp. 204–9 below. Neither the autobiography which Mgr Mignot is said to have left (see L. de Lacger, *loc. cit. infra*) nor any complete biography has been published, although he died in 1918. Presumably, the ecclesiastical authorities do not desire such publication. See, however, in addition to the references in Loisy's *Mémoires*, an article by von Hügel in *The Contemporary Review* (May, 1918), another by A. Fawkes in *The Modern Churchman* (VIII, 111–16), and another by Louis de Lacger in the *Revue d'histoire de l'Église de France* (XIX, 161–205); also Lecanuet, *La vie de l'Église sous Léon XIII* (1930), pp. 331 f., and the fifth appendix in the third volume of A. Houtin's *Le Père Hyacinthe* (1924). The correspondence, etc., contained in the last-named reference enables one to form an adequate idea of the quality and extent of Mgr Mignot's liberalism. The only other French bishop, who actively co-operated with the modernist movement, was Mgr Lacroix of Tarentaise. He resigned his see in October, 1907, nominally on grounds of health, and in 1908 was appointed to a professorship at the Sorbonne. He died in 1922.

A synthesis between Catholicism and modern knowledge seemed to them a cause worth fighting for, and they were as sincerely attached to Catholicism as they were determined to accept the results of scientific and historical research. What modification of traditional doctrine is required by these results is a further question which cannot arise for those who postulate the myth of an unchanging orthodoxy. It would have been reasonable to argue that Loisy's conclusions as a critic went beyond the facts, and that the modification of traditional doctrine which he urged was too great; but was it ever to be expected that he could reach an understanding with those who asserted *a priori* that no such modification was either possible or desirable? It appeared indeed already that the papacy and the hierarchy were committed to this position, but not until 1907 did it become finally evident that the Roman Church as a whole would tolerate and accept it with apparent equanimity.

During the five years which he spent at Neuilly, Loisy contributed numerous articles to reviews,[1] some over his own name, others over pseudonyms. The object of the use of pseudonyms was not so much to conceal his identity as to avoid calling too much attention to his name. The first intimation of the major work, upon which he was engaged at this time, was given to von Hügel in a letter of September 15th, 1896:

Mes catéchismes de persévérance m'ont donné l'idée d'une exposition générale de la doctrine catholique à l'usage de cette fin de siècle, quelque chose de sensé pour tout le monde et de réconciliant pour les gens du dehors. Il m'est venu à l'esprit que peut-être je pourrais trouver un appui et de bons éléments dans

[1] Most important was the *Revue d'histoire et de littérature religieuses*, founded at the beginning of 1896. Loisy was chiefly responsible for its initiation and direction, but it was not under his sole control. It had no official editor, but Paul Lejay acted in that capacity. On the use of pseudonyms, see *Mémoires*, I, 570.

certains écrits de Newman. Je n'en connais aucun. J'ai des extraits d'un livre sur le développement doctrinal, où il y a de bons principes. Qu'en pensez-vous?...Je suis sûr que vous avez tout Newman et que vous pourrez me dire ceux de ses livres qui me seraient utiles....[1]

Such were the conditions in which Loisy set about the work that led to his chief modernist publications. Newman has been described as the parent,[2] and even as the patriarch,[3] of modernism; it is evident that such metaphors are misleading, so far at least as Loisy's modernism is concerned. The idea of development, which he took over from Newman at this time, proved useful in assisting him to express and commend his proposed reconciliation of Catholicism with criticism. But the substance of this proposed reconciliation was already in his mind before he came under the influence of Newman.[4] In any case he extended the application of the idea of development to lengths of which Newman never dreamed.[5]

---

[1] *Ibid.* I, 410; cp. *Autour d'un petit livre*, p. 7.

[2] *E.g.* see A. Fawkes, *Studies in modernism* (1913), p. 380.

[3] A. N. Bertrand, *Revue d'histoire et de philosophie religieuses* (1924), p. 315. C. Sarolea, *Cardinal Newman* (1908), speaks of him as 'the leader of the "Modernists"' (p. 6)!

[4] Cp. P. Desjardins, *Catholicisme et critique*, p. 117; 'Dans le catholicisme de Newman (l'hypothèse du *Développement chrétien*) est une pièce essentielle, qui est seulement adventice dans le catholicisme de M. Loisy. Si je l'entends bien, c'est à ses yeux un échantillon des systèmes apologétiques que la libre critique, une fois admise, permettait aux orthodoxes'. B. Holland justly says that Newman's writings '*fell in with, and accelerated,* the line of thought that Loisy *was already pursuing*' (italics ours); von Hügel's *Selected letters*, p. 16.

[5] For Loisy's exposition of Newman's theory of development see the *Revue du clergé français* (December 1st, 1899), where he urges that Catholics have in Newman's theory one that is far truer and more adequate than those of Harnack and A. Sabatier; at the same time he admits the limitations of Newman's application of his theory. 'La théologie catholique a eu de nos jours le grand docteur dont elle avait besoin....Il lui a manqué peut-être quelques disciples' (p. 20).

In December, 1896, we learn that he was reading Newman 'with enthusiasm'. 'Ce doit être le théologien le plus ouvert qui ait existé dans la sainte Église depuis Origène', he wrote to von Hügel.[1] The unhappy decree of the Holy Office, published in January, 1897, which upheld the authenticity of the *Comma Johanneum*, spurred him on with his apologetic treatise. He says that the works which he had specially in mind, in the construction of this, were Harnack's *History of dogma* (1885–90) and A. Sabatier's *Outlines of a philosophy of religion* (1897). It follows that it was not due to an accident of time or to a mere tactical ruse that his *L'Évangile et l'Église* assumed the form of a refutation of liberal Protestantism. The larger unpublished treatise,[2] which he wrote in 1897, had the same character. This treatise has never been published as a whole; *L'Évangile et l'Église* represents only a part of it.

[1] *Mémoires*, I, 421, 426.
[2] An analysis of it is given in the *Mémoires*, vol. I, ch. XVI.

Chapter XII

PRELIMINARY SKIRMISHES, 1900–1902

The years prior to 1902 were marked by various skirmishes which were preliminary to the real modernist offensive that was launched in that year with the publication of *L'Évangile et l'Église*. One of these skirmishes resulted in a rebuff for Loisy. The *Revue du clergé français*, which began to publish a series of articles on 'the religion of Israel'[1] over the signature of 'Firmin', was forbidden by Cardinal Richard, after the appearance of the first on October 15th, 1900, to publish any more.[2] After this Loisy published no more pseudonymous articles.

In the autumn of 1899, in consequence of a breakdown in health, he had resigned the chaplaincy at Neuilly which he had held since 1894. He now resided at Bellevue, a suburb of Paris. He did not again hold any ministerial appointment in the Church, but he was officially authorized to say mass at home.

Almost immediately after the condemnation of 'Firmin' in November, 1900, he became a lecturer at the École des Hautes Études, a department of the Sorbonne, *i.e.* of the state university. He held this lectureship until 1904. It gave him a certain standing in the world of learning and a certain independence *vis-à-vis* the Church, and it was also a source of

[1] The articles were subsequently published in volume form; the first edition (1901) was for private circulation only. The second edition was translated into English (Crown Theological Library) in 1910.

[2] An attempt to get Loisy condemned at Rome was made at this time without success; von Hügel and Mgr Mignot both intervened on behalf of their *savant protégé*; see *Mémoires*, vol. I, ch. XXI. Tyrrell in his preface to the second English edition of Loisy's *The Gospel and the Church* (p. iv) is mistaken in saying that at this time *La Religion d'Israël* was censured by Rome.

income. During this period he was steadily working at his commentary on the gospels. In a sense, he was already on the frontier of the Church; but it was not yet to him, nor indeed to anyone else, a foregone conclusion that he would have to cross the frontier. On the contrary, at this time both he and his two closest friends, von Hügel and Mgr Mignot, found fresh reasons for hoping that the Church, if it would not yet approve, would at least refrain from any further condemnation of the movement in favour of modern criticism. The fact that Rome had refused to endorse Cardinal Richard's condemnation of *The religion of Israel* was in itself a considerable encouragement, for there was no doubt that he had taken active steps to secure this further condemnation. Then, Leo XIII's appointment of the biblical commission at the beginning of 1902[1] was at first regarded by the modernists as a promising development. The virtual removal of the decision of biblical questions from the juris-diction of the ordinary Roman congregations to this specially appointed commission, whose membership was at the outset comparatively liberal,[2] seemed to imply that there would not now be any immediate and hasty condemnation of the whole critical movement.[3] It seemed reasonable to hope that the attempt to explain away the encyclical *Providentissimus Deus* had been justified,[4] and that the pope had decided to adopt a policy of caution and temporization, which in the circum-stances was the most that could be expected.

Moreover, a further, if more elusive, kind of encourage-

[1] The appointment of the commission became public knowledge in January, 1902. The appointment was actually made on August 31st, 1901, but it was not officially announced by the Vatican until October 30th, 1902. See *Mémoires*, II, 88, 155.

[2] *Ibid*, II, 157; cp. W. Ward, *Ten personal studies* (1908), pp. 195f.

[3] Cp. *Autour d'un petit livre*, pp. xiii, xxi.

[4] Cp. Lecanuet, *La vie de l'Église sous Léon XIII*, pp. 373f. Even the *Civiltà cattolica*, the review of the Italian Jesuits, began to publish liberal articles on biblical questions at this time.

ment was derived from two quite independent invitations which came to Loisy, without any solicitation on his part,[1] to offer himself as a candidate for the episcopate—first, in January, 1902, for the bishopric of Monaco and then, later in the same year, for a French see. It is true that there was never much likelihood that either candidature would prove successful. 'Il est trop probable', he wrote to von Hügel, 'que je resterai, entre mes deux trônes, assis par terre.' But that he should be nominated for a bishopric at all was enough to foster the hope that there might be a future in the Church for one of his convictions.

In the year 1902 the modernist movement may be said to have come to a head, in so far as it ever did this. On March 17th Albert Houtin's *La Question biblique chez les catholiques de France au XIXe siècle* was published. Houtin himself was hardly, in the proper sense of the word, a modernist;[2] but from this time onwards he was the most untiring and capable publicist and historian of the movement. *La Question biblique* is a review of the biblical controversy in France during the nineteenth century. The book is unimpassioned and brilliantly ironical; it reveals the sheer futility of the traditionalist attitude to the Bible. It shows the subterfuges and the sophistries, to which the upholders of tradition had had to resort, and how they had gradually shifted their ground, in regard to such matters as the creation, the deluge, and the Mosaic authorship of the Pentateuch, in order to evade the

[1] Loisy complains with some justice that B. Holland, in his memoir of von Hügel (*Selected letters*, p. 16), gives a false impression of this matter. Cp. *Mémoires*, II, 91. H. P. V. Nunn (*What is modernism?* p. 278) definitely misrepresents Loisy's attitude in this matter as in others.

[2] See the preface to his *Histoire du modernisme catholique* (1913), where he says that from 1903 onwards he had lost faith in the possibility of a synthesis between Catholicism and modernity. Loisy (*Mémoires*, II, 293) points out that in *Une vie de prêtre* (pp. 323–5) Houtin gives a different account of his opinions. For Houtin's attitude to modernism, cp. also Loisy, *Mémoires*, II, 571, III, 71, 158, 251.

plain conclusions of science and criticism. The book naturally caused lively excitement in French ecclesiastical circles.

The excitement was not diminished by the case of Marcel Hébert (1851–1916),[1] which reached its climax at this time. Hébert occupied a place of his own in the early stages of the modernist movement. His influence was due more to the rare personal charm of his character and to the important post which he held—he was director of the École Fénelon in Paris—than to the possession of any special aptitude for intellectual leadership. The bent of his mind was towards philosophy and art rather than towards history or criticism. He had been trained for the priesthood at Saint-Sulpice along strictly scholastic lines, but his director of studies had been the learned and liberal John Hogan.[2] About 1880 his philosophical orthodoxy was undermined, chiefly by the study of Kant, and about the same time he became one of the progressively minded priests who surrounded Duchesne. The knowledge of critical results which he acquired from Duchesne, and later from Loisy, assisted him to the conclusion that the acceptance of the traditional dogmas in a literal sense was no longer possible. He therefore devised a peculiar system by which all the articles of the creed were given a purely symbolical significance.

In 1899 he had printed for private circulation an imaginary dialogue, entitled *Souvenirs d'Assise*, in which he outlined his

[1] See Houtin, *Un prêtre symboliste, Marcel Hébert* (1925); also J. Rivière, *Le modernisme dans l'Église* (1929), pt. II, ch. I.

[2] J. Hogan (1829–1901), after teaching for 32 years at the seminary of Saint-Sulpice where his pupils included d'Hulst and Mignot as well as Hébert, was sent in 1884 to the U.S.A., where he spent the rest of his life. His book, *Clerical studies* (Boston, 1898), is a good, and perhaps the last, example of nineteenth century liberal Catholicism; see *e.g. op. cit.* pp. 116f. His treatment of the biblical question (ch. XII) is much in advance of what was permitted after the condemnation of modernism, see *e.g.* W. Barry's *The tradition of scripture* (2nd ed. 1908); cp. pp. 225f. below.

system. A copy of this dangerous little work fell into the hands of Cardinal Richard in June, 1901, who forthwith gave Hébert the option of retracting or of resigning his post at the École Fénelon. He chose to resign. He wanted to remain in the Church, but after the end of the year he no longer had authority to act as a priest. In July, 1902, seeing no way out of his difficulties, he published in a review an article, entitled *La dernière idole: étude sur la personnalité divine*. Although he signed this article '*l'abbé* Marcel Hébert', its contents, indeed its title, made it evident that he had decided to break with Catholicism. Hébert's favourite doctrines appear to have been the *impersonality* of God and the *possibility* of a future life. His proposed reinterpretation of dogma bore in some respects a real, if somewhat crude, resemblance to Loisy's modernism, but his preoccupation with metaphysical problems and the blatant radicalism of his symbolist system mark him off from the rest of the modernists. A year later (June, 1903) he gave up wearing the soutane, moved from Paris to Brussels, and in so doing passed out of the modernist movement into socialism and journalism.

Meanwhile, for a world already excited and unsettled by Houtin's *La Question biblique* and by *l'affaire Hébert*, Loisy was preparing *L'Évangile et l'Église*. On May 18th (1902) he told von Hügel that the idea of publishing a criticism of Harnack's *Das Wesen des Christenthums*, which had recently been translated into French, had occurred to him. By August 10th the book was finished; it took so short a time to write because the materials for it were already available in the apologetic treatise which he had prepared at Neuilly in 1897. But in August, although the book was finished, he had not decided whether to publish it or not. He submitted the MS. to Mgr Mignot, and it was on the latter's advice that publication was undertaken. 'Sans le conseil de notre bon prélat', Loisy wrote at the time to von Hügel, 'je n'aurais pas osé mettre ce volume au jour.'[1] 'In his reply Mgr Mignot said:

Je viens d'achever...la lecture de votre manuscrit. Vous n'avez encore écrit rien d'aussi complet ni d'aussi objectif: c'est vous dire que j'en suis fort satisfait et que je regretterais vivement que cette étude, qui est tout autre chose qu'une réfutation de Harnack, ne fût publiée.

Je ne pense pas que l'on puisse vous condamner, et, tout au contraire, cette publication vous placera au premier rang des critiques chrétiens.[2]

Loisy describes *L'Évangile et l'Église* as 'un exposé historique du développement chrétien, d'où se dégageraient certaines conclusions favorables au catholicisme, défavorables au protestantisme. Rien de plus, rien de moins'.[3]

It is certain that neither Loisy[4] nor Mgr Mignot anticipated the sensation that the publication of the book was to cause. They realized, of course, that the traditionalist theologians would attack it, but they did not suppose that it would lead ultimately and inevitably to its author's excommunication or that it would go down to history as the *locus classicus* of what the Vatican was to describe as the 'synthesis of all the heresies'. On the contrary, both Mgr Mignot and von Hügel thought that it would strengthen Loisy's position in the Church and even assist his candidature for the episcopate. Thus, Mgr Mignot wrote to him again on November 10th (the book was published early in November):

Ceux qui ne vous ont jamais lu et qui ne vous connaissent que par vos adversaires, qui sont effrayés de vos hardiesses et ne voient en vous qu'un démolisseur, selon l'idée charitable qu'on leur a donnée de vous, seront surpris s'ils vous comprennent, de trouver en vous un défenseur de leur foi.... Je le répète, ce livre, malgré les

---

[1] *Mémoires*, II, 135; cp. III, 216. No one except Mgr Mignot saw the MS. of *L'Évangile et l'Église* before publication.

[2] *Mémoires*, II, 133. [3] *Ibid.*

[4] *Ibid.* II, 149; cp. preface (p. 1) to the 5th ed. of *L'Évangile et l'Église*.

inévitables oppositions qu'il va rencontrer, vous fera le plus grand bien en ce moment.... [1]

At the same time von Hügel wrote with rapturous enthusiasm:

J'ai maintenant lu votre Anti-Harnack jusqu'à la page 140. C'est tout simplement superbe. Jamais vous n'avez rien fait de plus fort, de plus beau, de plus propre à entrer tôt ou tard, plus ou moins, en cette modification de la manière de présenter, de concevoir le catholicisme, *par l'Église officielle elle-même*, qui (la modification) semble si loin de même se soupçonner par elle.

Mais il leur sera fort difficile de condamner cela; car cela se montrera être la seule réponse efficace faite à Harnack; et ces messieurs sont même plus hommes d'affaires qu'ils ne sont étroits.[2]

In retrospect it seems astonishing that Mgr Mignot and von Hügel could have been subject to these illusions as to the effect of Loisy's publication. Duchesne was a better judge of the situation. He wrote from Rome as follows:

Vous êtes tellement en avant de nous que nous serions encore capables de ne pas vous comprendre. Souhaitez-le, car c'est la seule chance que vous ayez d'échapper aux destinées diverses de Giordano Bruno, mon voisin de bronze.[3]

The publication of *L'Évangile et l'Église*, more than any other single event, precipitated the modernist crisis. What then were the origins of this event, whose consequences outran the expectations of the author and his friends? What were the motives which inspired the publication? Before we proceed, let us summarize them as clearly as possible, since they illuminate the origins of the modernist movement as a whole.

(1) For many years, in fact ever since the time of his ordination (see p. 71 above), Loisy had nourished the idea of

---

[1] *Mémoires*, II, 156; cp. p. 144. [2] *Ibid.* II, 157.
[3] *Ibid.*

writing a modernized apology for Catholicism. The idea was
due not to any eccentricity in his own mental constitution,
but simply to the circumstances of the time, *i.e.* to the incompatibility of traditional Catholic theology with modern
knowledge.

(2) But not only had he nourished the idea; he had already
carried it into effect. In the apologetic treatise, that he had
written in 1897, he had all the materials for the task to which
he felt himself called. What was needed was a suitable
opportunity for publication.

(3) The vogue enjoyed in 1902 by the French translation
of Harnack's book provided a suitable opportunity. On the
one hand, quite apart from any apologetic motive, Loisy
regarded the liberal Protestant version of Christianity as
historically untrue and as spiritually unsatisfactory, and he
felt himself qualified to refute it.[1] On the other hand, a
modernized apology for Catholicism would be far more
likely to win the acceptance of Catholics, if it was cast in the
form of a refutation of Protestantism.

(4) There is no doubt that in 1902 there was a movement
of intellectual unrest among the younger French clergy,[2] a
movement which was quickened into excitement by Houtin's
La Question biblique and by *l'affaire Hébert*; nor is there any
doubt that Loisy had a disinterested desire to guide and help
this movement on to what seemed to him the right lines, that
is, in the direction of a Catholicism which was compatible
with the results of modern knowledge. To say, as his orthodox critics would say, that he wanted to exploit the movement of unrest in the interests of a thoroughgoing agnosticism
is entirely unjust. On the contrary, there is clear evidence

---

[1] He was the more disposed to refute it, since certain ill-advised
Catholics, gratified by the moderation of Harnack's criticism of the New
Testament, were openly applauding his work. See *Mémoires*, II, 167;
Autour d'un petit livre, pp. 4 ff.

[2] *Mémoires*, II, 146, 163; cp. Houtin's *La crise du clergé*.

that he wanted to check the tendency of some incipient modernists to react too far from orthodoxy. See his criticism of a passage in Tyrrell's *Oil and wine*, quoted in *Mémoires*, II, 152f., and also his disavowal of Marcel Hébert, *ibid.* II, 49, 130, 136f.

(5) It is true that Loisy knew only too well that he was regarded with keen suspicion by the ordinary theologians and official authorities of the Church, and that his new apology for Catholicism was bound to be attacked and denounced. It might do more harm than good. For this reason he hesitated before publishing. But the encouragements noted above, and more particularly the favourable advice of Mgr Mignot, sufficed to turn the balance.

Chapter XIII

THE CHALLENGE OF LIBERAL PROTESTANTISM

'Protestantism is a form of the Christian religion which desires to go back to the Gospel (the teaching of Christ and of his Apostles) to attach itself to what is most primitive and therefore purest in Christianity; and which, on the other hand, recognises no other authority than the free individual conscience and, consequently, rejects all other authority, especially that of tradition and of the Church.'—Georges Dupont, Liberal Pastor of Montpellier, quoted by Paul Sabatier, *France to-day, its religious orientation* (1913), pp. 198 f.

While *L'Évangile et l'Église* was, as in the event was plainly demonstrated, much more than an attempted refutation of liberal Protestantism, yet its line of argument cannot be properly understood except in relation to that presentation of Christianity of which at the end of the nineteenth century Harnack in Germany and Auguste Sabatier in France were the chief apostles. That *L'Évangile et l'Église* was a perfectly genuine and sincere attack on the liberal Protestant position, an attempted refutation of it, is a point that must be emphasized, for the idea that Catholic modernism was derived from liberal Protestantism and was only a thinly veiled reproduction of it has been sedulously cultivated by those who have an interest in maintaining this misrepresentation.[1] Even Léonce de Grandmaison, who usually avoided tendentious statements, allowed himself to describe A. Sabatier as 'the father of French Modernism'.[2] In England and

[1] *E.g.* see H. Felder, *Christ and the critics* (1924), I, 79, 122, 244.
[2] *Jesus Christ* (1932), II, 295; cp. *Études* (September 20th, 1923), p. 642: 'Auguste Sabatier fut, en effet, le premier, et est resté le meilleur théoricien du modernisme'.

America, where the word 'modernism' is now commonly used to describe liberal Protestantism itself, the essential opposition between the two positions is overlooked, more excusably perhaps, but with no less damage to historical truth.

It was doubtless to be expected that on a superficial view a movement which invited and encountered the hostility of the papacy would be regarded as necessarily Protestant in tendency. For this reason from an early date the modernists saw the need of denying this false supposition.[1] They had indeed no difficulty in declaring that they were incurably Catholic as opposed to Protestant, and the most discerning observers of their movement from without understood this well. Thus, von Hügel, when dealing with this point in a letter which he wrote to *The Times* (March 2nd, 1904) over the *nom de plume* 'Romanus', says: 'Professor H. Holtzmann, the distinguished Protestant scholar, who knows our work well, has described, with frank irritation, how hopelessly Catholic we are'.

As the nineteenth century passed into the twentieth, the liberal Protestant interpretation of Christianity reached the apex of its development and the peak of its popularity. The work of Schleiermacher and Ritschl in particular had marked important stages in the dissolution of traditional Protestant orthodoxy. Doctrines, which had hitherto been an integral part of the religion of the Reformation, such as the infallibility of the Bible, the substitutionary theory of the atonement, and justification by faith alone, were either abandoned

[1] For the opposition between modernism and Protestantism, cp. *What we want* (1907), pp. 6f.; G. Tyrrell, *Christianity at the cross roads* (1910), pp. 44f.; H. L. Stewart, *Modernism past and present* (1932), p. 323; A. Houtin, *Le Père Hyacinthe* (1924), III, 286 (for Mgr Mignot's attitude to Protestantism); Loisy, *Mémoires*, II, 421, 549; Paul Sabatier, *France to-day, its religious orientation* (1913), pp. 207–11; F. Heiler, *Der Katholizismus* (1923), p. xxxii; C. E. Osborne, *Hibbert Journal* (January, 1910), pp. 258f., 263.

or restated in quite a new form. By the end of the century an apologetic for this new type of Protestantism had been developed which seemed peculiarly fitted to appeal to at least the cultured classes in Europe, both because of its compatibility with the supposed results of modern research in science and history and because of its definite abandonment of those characteristics of traditional Christianity, *e.g.* dogmas and institutionalism, which were specially distasteful to the temper of the time. It was possible to claim that Christianity had at last been reduced to its essence, its original essence, and that in this form it would prove impervious to the attacks of secular knowledge and at the same time retain and increase its ancient power as the key to the spiritual and moral progress of mankind.

The classical exposition of liberal Protestantism is Harnack's *Das Wesen des Christenthums* (1900), which was translated into English under the title *What is Christianity?* (1901). Schweitzer, who has done more than anyone except perhaps J. Weiss and Loisy to destroy the historical foundations of Harnack's construction, still describes it as 'the most living presentation' of the 'modernized theory about Jesus'.[1] Harnack professes, be it noted, to examine Christianity simply from the point of view of the historian. 'What is Christianity? It is solely in its historical sense that we shall try to answer this question here; that is to say, we shall employ the methods of historical science, and the experience of life gained by studying the actual course of history' (p. 6).

At the outset he decides that the essence of Christianity is the gospel, and that the essence of the gospel is the kernel of the life and teaching of Jesus, from which the husk must be separated. 'Husk were the whole Jewish limitations attaching to Jesus' message.' While it is true that Jesus proclaimed the coming of the kingdom of God, we must distinguish between that conception of the kingdom which He shared

[1] *My life and thought* (1933), p. 60.

with His contemporaries, and that which was specifically
His own. He did not start the apocalyptic conception, 'but
he grew up in it and he retained it. The other view, however, that the kingdom of God "cometh not with observation", that it is already here, was his own' (p. 54). 'The
kingdom of God comes by coming to the individual, by
entering into his soul and laying hold of it' (p. 56).

It is not at all difficult to say what was the kernel of the
original gospel. 'The whole of Jesus' message may be reduced
to these two heads—God as Father, and the human soul so
ennobled that it can and does unite with him' (p. 63). The
gospel therefore is essentially a message for individuals.
'Individual religious life was what (Jesus) wanted to kindle
and what he did kindle' (p. 11). 'Jesus never had anyone but
the individual in mind, and the abiding disposition of the
heart in love' (p. 111).

The vexed question of Jesus' own place in the gospel is also
quite simple, if we get back behind all the later Christological
development. Jesus was convinced that He was the Son of
God, because He was convinced that He knew God in a way
in which no one ever knew Him before. This fact is established by the saying in Matthew xi. 27: 'No man knoweth
the Son, but the Father; neither knoweth any man the Father,
save the Son, and he to whomsoever the Son will reveal
him'. 'It is "knowledge of God" that makes the sphere of
the Divine Sonship....Rightly understood, the name of Son
means nothing but the knowledge of God' (pp. 127f.). It is
in the light of this consciousness of Divine Sonship that the
Messianic consciousness of Jesus is to be understood. 'Jesus
passed from the assurance that he was the Son of God to the
other assurance that he was the promised Messiah' (p. 138).

The ground is thus prepared for a review of the history of
ecclesiastical Christianity as the covering over, or corruption
of, the original gospel. For instance, the whole edifice of
Christological doctrine is seen at once to be worse than a

distortion. '*The Gospel, as Jesus proclaimed it, has to do with the Father only and not with the Son*' (p. 144; italicized in the original). 'The Gospel is no theoretical system of doctrine or philosophy of the universe; it is doctrine only in so far as it proclaims the reality of God the Father' (p. 146). The stages by which the gospel was transformed into the Catholic Church, and its essence increasingly obscured, are easily traced. 'The religion of strong feeling and of the heart passes into the religion of custom and therefore of form and of law' (p. 197). 'The whole outward and visible institution of a Church claiming divine dignity has no foundation whatever in the Gospel. It is a case, not of distortion, but of total perversion' (p. 262).

In contrast to Catholicism, Protestantism is a return to the original gospel, 'a return to Christianity as it originally was' (p. 272). '(By the Reformation) religion was taken out of the vast and monstrous fabric which had been previously called by its name—a fabric embracing the Gospel and holy water, the priesthood of all believers and the Pope on his throne, Christ the Redeemer and St Anne—and was *reduced* to its essential factors, to the Word of God and to faith' (p. 269; italics in the original). It has, however, to be acknowledged that the Reformation only began this process of reduction; it did not 'make a clean sweep' of what was unessential. The time has now come when those elements of traditional dogma and ecclesiastical exclusiveness which were then retained can be cleared away, and the kernel once and for all separated from the husk.

Auguste Sabatier's religious philosophy closely resembled that of Harnack, and his statement of it was even more patently designed as a challenge to Catholicism. His *Outlines of a philosophy of religion* was published in 1897. It was his intention to fill in these outlines in a series of subsequent volumes, but he died in 1901 when he had just completed only the first of these, viz. *The religions of authority and the religion of the Spirit.* Sabatier makes a rigid distinction 'between the purely moral essence of Christianity and all its historical expressions or realisations' (*Outlines*, p. 164). The former, which consists of a feeling of filial relationship towards God and of fraternal relationship towards man, was the essential element in the consciousness of Jesus, and it is what makes a man a Christian (see pp. 148f.). Compared with this essential principle, all institutions, dogmas and rites are of purely temporary, relative or symbolic worth. It is the vice of Catholicism to have erected these secondary, non-essential things into an absolute system. 'Impotent to arrest the current of ideas and the movement of minds, it can only establish its rule by political measures, by regulations enacted and applied like civil laws—decisions of popes, bishops, or synods, trials for heresy, dogmatic tribunals. Orthodoxy has lost the sense of the symbolical character of Confessions of Faith...Its misfortune and its failing is to be anti-historical' (pp. 338f.).

If, on the other hand, Christianity is identified only with its essential principle, it can freely accept all the results of historical and biblical criticism and of scientific research. There ceases to be any conflict between science and religion, for they are concerned with different things. Science studies what is external and objective; religion is a subjective, inward feeling—'the happy feeling of deliverance, the inward assurance of "salvation"' (p. 312). Sabatier has no use for metaphysics; in effect he abandons the attempt to formulate a Christian philosophy of the universe. The ultimate nature of things is an insoluble enigma; man must be content with the happy feeling of deliverance.

The religions of authority and the religion of the Spirit (Eng. trans. 1904) may also be briefly noticed here, although chronologically it comes a little later. It is a powerful, if one-sided, criticism of the idea of an infallible authority in religion, as developed in the Roman papacy on the one side and in the

It was not due then to a tactical manœuvre or a mere accident of circumstance that what Tyrrell described as 'the classical exposition of Catholic Modernism'[1] took the form of a reply to *Das Wesen des Christenthums*. The genuineness of Loisy's opposition to liberal Protestantism is confirmed, if it needs confirmation, by the fact that he still regards *L'Évangile et l'Église* as a valid refutation of it, although of course he has otherwise abandoned the general position which he took up in 1902. In the preface to the latest edition of *L'Évangile et l'Église* (1930) he writes:

La critique du protestantisme libéral est, de tout le petit livre, ce à quoi l'auteur n'aurait rien à changer, ou si peu que rien. Il lui est toujours impossible, au point de vue historique, de reconnaître en cette forme du christianisme, l'expression exacte du passé chrétien; au point de vue philosophique, une théorie qui soit tout à fait dans le vrai courant de la pensée contemporaine; au point de vue religieux, une foi qui ait de longues promesses d'avenir dans la conscience humaine. Ce n'est pas assez une religion nouvelle, et c'est trop un christianisme réduit.[2]

[1] *Christianity at the cross roads* (1910), p. 92.
[2] P. 6; the new preface was written in 1914, but remained unpublished till 1930. Cp. *Mémoires*, II, 167; *Y a-t-il deux sources de la religion et de la morale?* (1933), pp. 56ff. For Loisy's first published criticism of liberal Protestantism see his article 'La théorie individualiste de la religion' in the *Revue du clergé français* (January 1st, 1899), pp. 202–15, where he anticipated part of the argument of *L'Évangile et l'Église*.

Chapter XIV

'L'ÉVANGILE ET L'ÉGLISE,' 1902

After an introductory reference to Harnack's book, which
has occasioned his own, Loisy says that he at any rate has
attempted to adopt the historical point of view. He claims
that, although Harnack has appealed to the facts of history,
his whole position is in reality based on an unhistorical, *a
priori* assumption, viz. that the essence of the gospel consists
only in filial trust in God the Father. On the basis of this
assumption rest his judgment of the history of the Church
and his condemnation of Catholicism. The reduction of the
whole Christian movement to a single idea is in any case a
proceeding that should be viewed with suspicion, and in the
present instance the single idea that has been selected is
clearly the result of a prejudice. Harnack, like Sabatier,
wants 'to reconcile Christian faith with the claims of science
and of the scientific spirit of our time'. It is for this reason
that they have reduced Christianity to a single sentiment.
'Religion is thus reconciled with science, because it no longer
encounters it. This trust in the goodness of God either
exists in a man or it does not; but it seems impossible for a
sentiment to contradict any conclusion of biblical or philosophical criticism' (p. 6).[1]

From the historical point of view, it is entirely arbitrary for
Protestant theologians at the end of the nineteenth century to
regard as the essence of Christianity only that residuum of
the Christian faith which seems to them still tenable. In
order to discover the essence of Christianity, we must not
extract from the original gospel one idea which happens to

[1] References are to the 2nd ed. of the English translation, *The Gospel
and the Church* (1908).

appeal to us, but rather we must examine the history of Christianity as a whole in order to discern its permanent characteristics. This is the procedure that the historian adopts in regard to Mohammedanism or any other historical religion; it is obviously his duty to adopt the same procedure in regard to Christianity. For the historian, whatever common features have been preserved or developed in the Church from its origin till to-day will constitute the essence of Christianity (p. 9).

The evidence at our disposal does not enable us to draw a rigid line between Jesus and primitive Christianity, for all our knowledge of the person and teaching of Jesus is indissolubly bound up with the development of the movement which He initiated. Whether we approve of tradition or not, it is a fact that 'we know Christ only by the tradition, across the tradition, and in the tradition of the primitive Christians'. It is impossible to define the essence of Christianity apart from tradition, 'for the mere idea of the gospel without tradition is in flagrant contradiction with the facts submitted to criticism' (p. 13). It is useless to regret that this is so, nor is it necessarily a matter for regret; for 'it is in the nature of human affairs that the work, the genius, and the character of the greatest of mankind can only be appreciated at a certain distance, and when the actors themselves have disappeared. Christ, in so far as He belongs to human history, has not escaped this law' (p. 41).

It must be borne in mind that it is the function of the historical critic to trace the development of Christianity, not to decide upon its ultimate truth. He ought to study the evidence neither as an apologist for, nor as an opponent of, dogma. It is for him to elucidate the facts, not to determine their ultimate significance. The ultimate interpretation of history is matter for faith, not for criticism (cp. p. 50). Now, a truly critical, *i.e.* unprejudiced, examination of the evidence reveals that the general theme of the teaching of Jesus was the kingdom of God. 'Repent, for the kingdom of God is at hand' is a just summary of His message. This kingdom was not, as Harnack supposes, conceived of as purely personal and already present, a matter of subjective experience; but on the contrary it was collective, objective, and future (p. 59). The sayings and parables of Jesus are rightly understood in close relation to the eschatological conception of the kingdom. The chief text, on which Harnack depends (Luke xvii. 20f.), is of uncertain authenticity, and its meaning is obscure. 'To sacrifice the rest of the gospel to the doubtful interpretation of a solitary passage would be to go contrary to the most elementary principles of criticism' (p. 72).

The historian needs carefully to resist the temptation to modernize the conception of the kingdom of God. It is perfectly legitimate for the theologian (as distinguished from the historian) to reinterpret the conception to meet the needs of the present day, but he must not read back his reinterpretation into the original gospel texts. This applies equally to the bearing of the gospel on all the different aspects of human life (p. 73). 'The message of Jesus is contained in the announcement of the approaching kingdom, and the exhortation to penitence as a means of sharing therein. All else, though it is the common preoccupation of humanity, is as though non-existent' (p. 86). The gospel was appropriate to the special circumstances in which it saw the light, and for this very reason it had to be detached from its earliest connexions. It did not enter the world 'as an unconditioned absolute doctrine, summed up in a unique and stedfast truth', but as a living faith, at once concrete and complex. It has always and of necessity been conditioned, first by the surroundings in which it originated, and then by those in which it extended and grew.

Harnack's treatment of the Divine Sonship of Jesus lays itself open to criticism quite as much as his treatment of the conception of the kingdom. The idea that Jesus' consciousness of Sonship meant simply His knowledge of God as His Father is founded on a single text (Matt. xi. 27). This text, even if it were authentic, would not really support Harnack's thesis; as a matter of fact the historian must regard it as probably a product of the early Christian tradition and not as an actual saying of Jesus. In any case 'the gospel conception of the Son of God is no more a psychological idea signifying a relation of the soul with God than is the gospel conception of the kingdom' (p. 96). The texts, upon which most reliance can be placed, make it clear that the title, Son of God, was the equivalent of the Messiah. The distinction, drawn by Harnack, is 'absolutely without foundation. The earliest tradition had no suspicion of it; nor would modern criticism have dreamed of it, had there been no theological interests at stake' (p. 104).

The Messiahship of Jesus is an integral part of the original gospel. It is true that He did not openly announce that He was the Messiah during His ministry, but there is no reason to doubt that He was conscious of the Messianic vocation and that His disciples came so to regard Him. This was in fact the ground on which He was condemned to death. For the early Christians it was through the Resurrection that Jesus entered into His Messianic glory. It follows that Harnack's statement that the original gospel had to do with the Father only and not with the Son is grossly misleading. This statement no doubt represents Harnack's own religious belief. 'The historical gospel has none of this mystic and individualistic character' (p. 109). Nor is it historical to divide the original gospel into husk and kernel, relative and absolute. 'The Christ of the gospel did not divide His teaching into two parts, the one comprising all that had an absolute value, the other all that had only a relative value, fitted to the present time' (p. 110). He spoke without the least regard to our categories of absolute and relative. To read back later distinctions of this kind into the New Testa-

ment is just as arbitrary as 'to attribute to Jesus a foreknow-
ledge of the modifications His doctrine must undergo in the
course of centuries after the apostolic age'.

The gospel should be regarded as a concrete whole. The
conception of the kingdom and of the Messiah were not just
accidental or incidental features of the original gospel; since
the faith of humanity has always to be embodied in concrete
symbols, they were the necessary form in which Christianity
had to be born in Judaism before spreading out into the
world (p. 120). The original gospel 'presents itself to the
historian as the greatest manifestation of faith ever displayed
on the earth' (p. 123); but if it was to survive and be preserved, it was equally necessary that it should be embodied in
fresh forms. It is Harnack's unhistorical assumption that the
essence of Christianity is restricted to faith in God the Father
which leads him to place 'the whole development of the
Church, hierarchic, dogmatic, and ritual, outside true
Christianity' and to present it 'as a progressive abasement of
religion'. The development of the Church was a necessary
consequence of the work of Jesus. His disciples were not
'a coalition of fervent and perfect individualists'. Even
during the ministry they formed a society, and 'the Church
can fairly say that, in order to be at all times what Jesus
desired the society of His friends to be, it had to become what
it has become' (pp. 150f.).

Moreover, every genuine society postulates authority as
its preservative element, and the wider the range of the
society the greater is its need of a central government. If the
Church, whose life was indispensable for the preservation of
the gospel, had not developed a form of government, it
must have ceased to exist. A strong central authority was
required by the needs of preserving its unity and of extending
its universality. In the development, which stretches from
the evangelical society that gathered round Jesus to the present
constitution of the papacy, there has been no gap in con-

tinuity and no violent revolution. 'To reproach the Catholic Church for the development of her constitution is to reproach her for having chosen to live' (p. 165). 'Rome claims no new power, or rather, the power is no newer than the situation it is designed to meet' (p. 160).

This must not of course be taken to mean that Jesus consciously and explicitly established the Catholic Church, as it is known to history. 'But a conception far more foreign still to His thoughts and to His authentic teaching is that of an invisible society formed for ever of those who have in their hearts faith in the goodness of God....Jesus foretold the kingdom, and it was the Church that came; she came enlarging the form of the gospel, which it was impossible to preserve as it was, as soon as the Passion closed the ministry of Jesus' (p. 166). The development of the Church is organic, comparable to that of a man. The identity of a man 'is not determined by permanent immobility of external forms, but by continuity of existence and consciousness of life through the perpetual transformations which are life's condition and manifestation'. To be identical with the religion of Jesus, the Church 'has no more need to reproduce exactly the forms of the Galilean gospel, than a man has need to preserve at fifty the proportions, features, and manner of life of the day of his birth, in order to be the same individual' (pp. 170f.).

Nevertheless, it may fairly be claimed that the characteristics of the Church to-day are the primitive characteristics 'grown and fortified, adapted to the ever-increasing functions they have to fulfil'. The essential elements of the original gospel were (*a*) the idea of the heavenly kingdom, (*b*) the idea of the Messiah, the sole Mediator of the kingdom, and (*c*) the idea of the apostolate, or the preaching of the kingdom. It is evident that these ideas continue to live in the Catholic Church, whereas they have more or less disappeared in liberal Protestantism. Thus, for instance, the Church to-day 'for all her apparent want of anxiety as to the imminence of the final judgment...still regards herself as a transitional organization'. The Church on earth is, as it were, 'the vestibule of the Church triumphant, which is the kingdom of heaven realized in eternity....If the dimensions of the evangelical horizon have changed, the point of view remains the same' (p. 168).

Just as in the past the Church has undergone progressive transformation in order to adapt the gospel to the needs of each succeeding age, so it may be well admitted that this process will continue in the future. In particular it may be suggested that the extreme centralization of authority in the hierarchy and the papacy, which was required by past circumstances, may in the future be redressed. 'In any case, it is not true that ecclesiastical authority is, or ever was, a species of external constraint repressing all personal activity of conscience. The Church is an educator, rather than a dominating mistress; she instructs rather than directs, and he who obeys her only does so according to his conscience, and in order to obey God' (p. 175; cp. p. 210).

Again, if the gospel was to be preserved and extended, dogmatic development was no less necessary than institutional development. It is impossible to hold the faith and not to think about it; faith inevitably produces theology. And for the propagation of the gospel, a definite form of teaching is necessary (p. 222). Christian dogma is the outcome of the attempt to give a reasonable account of, and to formulate, the facts of Christian experience; as such it has to be expressed in terms of contemporary thought and knowledge, and is always liable to modification in relation to the progress of thought and knowledge. Dogmas are not truths fallen from heaven and preserved in the precise form in which they first appeared. It may indeed be said that they are divine in origin and substance, but they are human in structure and composition (pp. 210f.). They are a living and not a dead

structure. It must not be supposed that they constitute a
strictly logical and perfectly intelligible system of thought.
For they are not a pure abstraction of the intellect; their
value depends on the extent to which they do justice to, and
hold the balance between, all the data provided by the life of
faith. A dogma may have to hold together truths which seem
to contradict one another, as in the case of the Trinitarian
formula. But the view that ultimate truth may exceed the
measures of our mind and that seeming contradictions may
be 'compatible at the limit of infinity' is a reasonable one.

The problems of theology have had to be resolved 'by
drawing inspiration much more from the Spirit of Jesus than
from His formal declarations', which were not made with a
view to doctrinal development. Hitherto, while the Church
and its dogma have continually developed, the development
has been almost unconscious. Emphasis has been laid only on
the unchanging object of faith, and not on the fact that its
expression is continually changing. (The name of Cardinal
Newman suggests a significant exception to this rule.) Now,
however, since we recognize that 'it is not with the elements
of human thought that an everlasting edifice can be built', the
time may be ripe for the consideration and formulation of a
doctrine of development itself.

Once more, the preservation and extension of the gospel
required not only the development of the Church and of
dogma, but also the development of a ritual, of a cultus.
'History knows no instance of a religion without a ritual'
(p. 226). It is true that 'Jesus no more decided the form of
Christian worship beforehand than He laid down the constitution and dogmas of the Church' (p. 230). As long as the
gospel remained within the bosom of Judaism, the Jewish
cultus met its needs. But as soon as Christianity became an
independent religion, a ritual of its own became 'an intimate
inevitable necessity'. Otherwise, it would have gained no
proselytes, and would have ceased to exist. Various parts of

the Christian cultus may have been derived from pre-existing sources (Jewish or pagan); it is for the historian to inquire what was original and what was derived. Derivation even from pagan sources is not in itself a condemnation, for rites so derived 'ceased to be pagan, when accepted and interpreted by the Church'.

In any case it must be recognized that the Church 'has proscribed all the bloody and magical rites of ancient religions, and thereby has guaranteed, as far as is necessary or possible, the spiritual character of the Christian religion' (p. 237). 'The Christian spirit gave life, and still gives it, to practices apparently trivial, and easily becoming superstitious; but the point at issue is whether those who follow them do not find Christ therein, and whether they would be capable of finding Him more easily elsewhere' (p. 270). In contrast to the Catholic cultus, Harnack's conception of worship is neither rational nor evangelical. 'It would be impossible to unite men in a worship that is purely an affair of the soul.... (Jesus) never recommended to His followers a worship without external forms, and never intended to establish such a worship' (p. 259).

The final paragraph of Loisy's book is so apt a summary of the gist of his argument that we shall quote it in full:

It is true that as a result of the evolution, political, intellectual, economic, of the modern world, as a result of all that may be called the modern spirit, a great religious crisis, affecting Churches, orthodoxies, and forms of worship has arisen to a greater or less extent everywhere. The best means of meeting it does not appear to be the suppression of all ecclesiastical organization, all orthodoxy, and all traditional worship—a process that would thrust Christianity out of life and humanity,—but to take advantage of what is, in view of what should be, to repudiate nothing of the heritage left to our age by former Christian centuries, to recognize how necessary and useful is the immense development accomplished in the Church, to gather the fruits of it and continue it, since the adaptation of the gospel to the changing conditions of humanity is as pressing a need to-day as it ever was and ever will be. It is no part of the present book to say what difficulties—more apparent, perhaps, than real—this work may encounter in the Catholic Church, nor what incomparable resources exist for it, nor in what way the agreement of dogma and science, reason and faith, the Church and society, can be conceived to-day. This little volume is full enough if it has shown how Christianity has lived in the Church and by the Church, and how futile is the desire to save it by a search after its quintessence (pp. 276 f.).

Chapter xv

'AUTOUR D'UN PETIT LIVRE,' 1903

In the event, the 'little volume' proved 'full enough' to show that the difficulties in the way of realizing its ultimate object were not only apparent, but unquestionably real. The Roman Church showed unmistakably that it had no intention of accepting the program which Loisy had sketched for it. But, although the purpose behind *L'Évangile et l'Église* was frustrated, the importance of Loisy's achievement, and the use which the Church might have made of it, ought to be acknowledged. He had done two things. On the negative side, he had submitted the liberal Protestantism of Harnack and Sabatier to a damaging, if not to a fatal, criticism, and he had done this not with abuse but with pure argument. Liberal Protestantism was at the time the most popular and specious line of attack on the Catholic position. On the positive side, he had shown that by accepting the appeal to history a singularly fresh and arresting apologetic for Catholicism could be made out.

He had set out to examine the professedly historical arguments of Harnack and Sabatier; the unbiased student can hardly deny that his refutation of them was successful and even prophetic. In Germany the popularity and vitality of liberal Protestantism of the Harnack type has steadily declined; the recent reaction therefrom, which is chiefly associated with the name of Karl Barth, is receiving much attention in theological circles to-day. In Germany and for German Protestants, it was no doubt J. Weiss and Schweitzer rather than Loisy who most effectively shattered the thesis of *Das Wesen des Christenthums* as to the nature of the original gospel. It is obviously difficult for German Protestants to believe that they have anything to learn from a French

Roman Catholic. In England too, Loisy's part in establishing the eschatological interpretation of the original gospel is sometimes overlooked.[1] In France, however, the importance of Loisy's book, simply as a refutation of Harnack and Sabatier, has been more generally recognized.[2] A noteworthy instance of this is the testimony of Professor Maurice Goguel, the most distinguished of present-day French Protestant scholars:

S'il m'est permis d'invoquer...ma propre expérience, je dirai que *l'Évangile et l'Église* est peut-être le livre qui m'a le plus clairement ouvert les yeux sur la faiblesse de la conception de Jésus et de l'histoire du christianisme primitif à laquelle a abouti la critique libérale du XIXe siècle et qui m'a fait nettement sentir la nécessité de reprendre l'ensemble du problème sur des bases nouvelles.[3]

The worth of *L'Évangile et l'Église* as an apology for Roman Catholicism is of course more disputable. In retrospect it seems clear that it had not the remotest chance of receiving official sanction; but could the Roman Church, it may be asked, have rightly sanctioned so revolutionary an interpretation of its claims? Its novelty is certainly not to be denied;

[1] *E.g.* by Sir E. C. Hoskyns (*Essays Catholic and critical*, p. 155n.), who in this connexion appears to give all the credit to J. Weiss and Schweitzer and to ignore Loisy entirely. The same writer, when referring to Catholic modernism in general and to *L'Évangile et l'Église* in particular, likewise overlooks the importance of Loisy's work as an historical criticism of liberal Protestantism (see *ibid.* pp. 158f.).

[2] This was recognized at the time by an eminent French Protestant, Gabriel Monod; see the extracts from his review of *L'Évangile et l'Église*, which are reproduced in *Autour d'un petit livre*, pp. 287ff. Cp. M.-J. Lagrange, *M. Loisy et le modernisme* (1932), pp. 183 ff., who points out that Loisy realized the importance of the eschatological view of the gospel as early as 1883; and L. Salvatorelli (*Harvard Theological Review*, 1929, XXII, 340), who writes: 'In principle, Loisy's *L'Évangile et l'Église* can be said to mark the disappearance of the "liberal" conception of Jesus'.

[3] *Revue d'histoire et de philosophie religieuses* (1930), p. 199. The writer adds: 'On ne peut manquer de se demander si, au commencement de ce siècle, l'Église catholique n'a pas laissé échapper une admirable occasion qu'elle avait de se redresser dans le domaine intellectuelle' (*ibid.* p. 200).

but a defence of Catholicism which was to meet historical criticism on its own ground could not escape from novelty. Did, however, the novelty of this defence go so far as to involve the abandonment of fundamental truths of the Christian religion, such as the transcendence of God and the historical reality of the Incarnation as an unique revelation of God? That it did do this is commonly alleged by the orthodox opponents of modernism. Much evidently depends on the precise sense in which such doctrines are necessarily to be regarded as fundamental truths of the Christian religion. But in any case it was not Loisy's purpose either to attack or to defend Christian doctrine in the sphere of metaphysics or philosophical theology. He expressly disclaimed the intention of writing a complete defence of the Catholic faith. It was his purpose to show how in the light of modern criticism the history of Christianity could be interpreted as justifying Catholicism.

Because Loisy himself later abandoned Christian theism and belief in the Incarnation, it does not follow that such abandonment was required or implied by the argument of *L'Évangile et l'Église*. It is, on the contrary, to be understood that this was not so, both from the fact that scholars so orthodox on these points as Mgr Mignot, von Hügel and others, regarded it as a valuable defence of Catholicism, and still more decisively from Loisy's own statement:

Ainsi qu'on l'a pu voir (he writes in his *Mémoires*), jusqu'à *Autour d'un petit livre*, inclusivement, mes écrits, même ma pensée réfléchie n'impliquent pas autre chose que la nécessité d'une refonte de tout l'enseignement catholique, la valeur substantielle de la métaphysique chrétienne restant hors de cause.[1]

It must be admitted that Loisy's writings, as indeed much other modernist work, were in harmony with the prevailing tendency towards immanentism in philosophy. In this

[1] *Op. cit.* III, 360f.

respect the modernists were creatures of their own time.[1]
But if this were its only defect, it would not have been
necessary to condemn their work as a whole. It would have
been sufficient for the Church to have directed attention to
the limitations of immanentism and to show how it ought to
be balanced and corrected.[2]

L'Évangile et l'Église was entirely unacceptable to the
ecclesiastical authorities because in it Loisy had insinuated,
discreetly but unmistakably, the need of an essential reform
in the Church's exegesis of the gospels, in its official theology,
and in the methods of ecclesiastical government. But it is an
assumption of Roman Catholic orthodoxy that in these
matters the Church stands in no need of reform, or at least of
essential reform. Thus, although *L'Évangile et l'Église* was on
its first appearance warmly welcomed by discerning judges,[3]
it quickly became the subject of fierce attacks and of official
condemnation.

The book was published, as we have seen, early in
November, 1902. In the January following, serious trouble
began. The *Univers* opened the new year with a series of
articles, which were violently opposed to Loisy, and thus the
matter was carried into the forefront of public ecclesiastical
controversy. Later in the same month, Mgr Batiffol, who
was rector of the Institut Catholique of Toulouse, published
a vigorous attack. On January 17th, Cardinal Richard

---

[1] The prevalence of immanentism during the nineteenth century and at
the beginning of the twentieth is admirably shown in Prof. C. C. J.
Webb's recently published *A study of religious thought in England from* 1850
(1933), where the later reaction towards transcendentalism is also noticed.

[2] Cp. E. Buonaiuti, *Le modernisme catholique*, pp. 50 f.

[3] Among those who were quick to welcome the book we may note the
names of Maurice Blondel, Miss Petre, Rudolf Eucken and Wilfrid
Ward. The last-named wrote to von Hügel that *L'Évangile et l'Église*
'showed a consummate knowledge of what Newman wanted and aimed
at, and that it both extended and wisely limited the sphere of Catholic
evolution'. *Mémoires*, II, 173.

publicly condemned *L'Évangile et l'Église* on the grounds that it had been published without the *imprimatur* and that it was calculated seriously to disturb the faithful. Seven, but only seven, French bishops followed suit. Rome itself was still unwilling to intervene directly.

In consequence of the controversy, of which it had thus become the centre, the first edition of *L'Évangile et l'Église* was practically sold out by the middle of January, and a second edition was in preparation. Loisy's first intention was to meet the Cardinal's condemnation simply by holding up this second edition and to leave it at that. He was, however, advised by Mgr Mignot that, if he remained silent, his silence would be exploited against him, and that some positive act of submission was necessary. He was also advised, not only by Mgr Mignot, but also by Tyrrell,[1] von Hügel and others, to publish a supplement to *L'Évangile et l'Église*, which would serve to clarify those parts of the book that had been misconstructed or adversely criticized. This is to say that it was his friends who urged him to publish *Autour d'un petit livre*. They hardly realized that any further elucidation of *L'Évangile et l'Église* would make more and not less obvious its divergence from orthodoxy and would therefore arouse even more intense opposition.

On February 3rd Loisy complied with the first part of this advice by sending to Cardinal Richard an act of submission to the decree of condemnation. The wording of the submission contained an obvious equivocation, but it was accepted as satisfactory. This was the first of a series of such acts, which Loisy was called upon to make between now and March, 1904. They were the condition of his continuing to play an effective part in the modernist movement. The alternative would have involved abandoning the field of battle as soon

---

[1] Tyrrell first wrote to Loisy after the publication of *L'Évangile et l'Église*, and they occasionally corresponded with each other till Tyrrell's death. They never met. See *Mémoires*, III, 126.

as the first blow was struck. In any case he had much more
than his own inclination to consult. For all who were concerned with the reforming movement in the Church, his was
a test case, indeed the test case; and now that the battle had
definitely begun he had to fight it through to a finish in the
interest of all those who looked to him as in some sense their
representative.

The prospects of victory, *i.e.* the prospects of securing
toleration for a revision or modification of orthodoxy, were
never bright; and at this moment they became appreciably
darker. The character of the biblical commission, which at
first had been comparatively liberal in complexion, was
changed by the appointment of a large number of new
members.[1] It was certain that henceforth it would be a
bulwark of reaction, as has in fact proved to be the case. The
encouragement, which the modernists had derived from the
original appointment of the commission, was thus dissipated.

During the spring and summer of 1903 there were several
influences at work which were leading Loisy to force to a
head the issue that the publication of *L'Évangile et l'Église* had
raised. His submission to Cardinal Richard's condemnation
did not bring to an abrupt end the campaign of criticism and
misrepresentation which had been directed against him. On
the contrary, even theologians of the standing of Batiffol and
Lagrange continued to accuse him of mystification and
equivocation. He was invited to clarify his position with
regard to orthodoxy. Moreover, he was aware that his
opponents were still trying to secure his condemnation at
Rome. All this was provoking, and Loisy never professed to
have the patience of a saint.

Again, his commentary on the fourth gospel had for some

---

[1] For a full list of the members of the commission, see A. Houtin, *La
Question biblique au XXᵉ siècle*[2] (1906), pp. 288 f. On the change in its
constitution, see also P. Desjardins, *Catholicisme et critique*, pp. 95 f., and
What we want, p. 55.

time been ready for the press, and his commentary on the
synoptic gospels was steadily approaching completion. As he
proceeded, he realized increasingly that his conclusions about
the synoptics would be quite as objectionable to his orthodox
opponents as his conclusions about St John. There was no
point therefore in deferring the publication of the latter until
after the publication of the former. Anyhow he was not
willing to postpone the publication of both indefinitely. His
position in the world of scholarship, and consequently to
some extent also in the Church, would be fortified by the
reputation as a *savant* which he felt confident these volumes
would earn for him. The result of all these influences and
considerations was that in October, 1903, he published not
only the second edition of *L'Évangile et l'Église*,[1] but its
sequel, *Autour d'un petit livre*, and also *Le Quatrième Évangile*,
a volume of 950 pages, a work of pure scholarship.

Autour d'un petit livre is in the form of a series of letters.
They were never actually sent to those to whom they are
addressed. We need not examine these letters in detail here;
they are designed to reiterate and amplify the chief con-
tentions of *L'Évangile et l'Église*. But here Harnack has almost
disappeared from the picture; there is little effort to disguise
the fact that a new interpretation of Catholicism is being put
forward. Loisy no longer writes with diplomatic caution,
like a prudent ecclesiastic; he expresses his thought fully and
frankly.[2] It will be enough for our purpose to notice the
main points on which he seeks to insist.

In the forefront we must place his claim that biblical
criticism is an autonomous science. Its conclusions must not
be dictated or determined by dogmatic presuppositions. The

---

[1] In order to 'respect the censure of Cardinal Richard' (!), the second
edition was published *chez l'auteur*, *i.e.* at Bellevue in the diocese of
Versailles, and did not bear the name of the Parisian publisher. *Mémoires*,
II, 248.
[2] Cp. P. Desjardins, *Catholicisme et critique*, p. 26.

Catholic critic must be as free as anyone else to give an
unbiased description of the facts of history. The facts thus
described cannot be in real contradiction with any dogma,
for dogmas are ideas representative of faith, which has for its
object not human knowledge, but the divine order, eternal
and incomprehensible. The description of events, as they
appear to have happened in the natural order, is perfectly
compatible with a supernatural explanation of them. Dogma
is not a description of history but an appreciation of it, or
rather it is an attempt to express in human thought and
language the ultimate truths which are implied by the spiritual
experience of Christians.[1] But human thought and language
are not fixed and absolute things; like all things human they
are living and continually changing. The terms in which
dogma is formulated are necessarily relative and are therefore
liable to require modification in accordance with the general
progress of knowledge.

Thus, for instance, the divinity of Christ is a dogma of the
Church, and this means that Christ is God for faith. But the
divinity of Christ is not a fact of history, nor would it be that
even if Jesus Himself had taught it. It is a judgment of faith,
made by the religious conscience. The historical process by
which the dogma was formulated does not affect its truth,
although it may suggest where its formulation is likely to
need revision. Traditional Christology has attributed to
Christ, omniscience, *i.e.* unlimited knowledge. This attribu-
tion is true for faith in so far as it is, or was, the best available
means of affirming the truth of the Saviour's divinity. But it
is not an authenticated fact of history; indeed as an historical

---

[1] Cp. '*Vidi's*' account of Loisy's thought in a letter to *The Times*
(January 21st, 1904): 'Doctrine and dogma cannot be historically proved,
he (*i.e.* Loisy) argues, though their development can be historically
ascertained; they are matters for faith and must be believed by a free act of
faith'. On the importance of experience, individual and collective, see
also *Mémoires*, II, 428.

hypothesis it is inconceivable. Here we have an instance of the distinction between truths of history and truths of faith, which figured prominently in the modernist controversy.

It is important to notice that, if these two kinds of truth are distinguished, they are not entirely divorced from one another. Loisy does not cut Christian dogma loose from its historical origins, as many of his critics have alleged, or suggest that its origins can be a matter of complete indifference to the believer. 'The fundamental reality of Christianity is the historical apparition of Jesus', *i.e.* His life and death. This is the initial fact and all the rest is the outcome of this. Nor does the proposed interpretation of dogma result in a belittling of the Jesus of history. It is not Loisy who invented, or offered a proper pretext for, such expressions as 'the delusions of a Jewish fanatic'. 'The historic Christ in the humility of His "service" is great enough to justify the Christology, and the Christology need not have been expressly taught by Jesus in order to be true' (p. 136). The distinction between the Jesus of history and the Christ of faith, important and necessary as it is for a right understanding of theology, is not held to involve a separation of the one from the other. There is no reason to suppose that the Christological dogma has reached the term of its development. Modern knowledge has raised fresh problems for theology. No ecclesiastical definition will ever be absolutely true in the sense that it contains the complete and final truth about its object. The faithful adherent of the Church accepts defined dogmas as being the best and surest formulations of the truth that have yet been found possible. He accepts the relative and imperfect formulation, and his intention in doing so is to accept the absolute and full truth.

Chapter XVI

'RES DISSOCIABILES', 1904–1908

Autour d'un petit livre explains how the modernists were able to subscribe conscientiously to the traditional teaching of the Church, while they desired its revision. They were not so stupid as to suppose that the Church ought to reform its creed from day to day according to the requirements of science. What they asked was that the Church should not use its creed in such a way as to shackle science.[1] The development of theology is necessarily a slow process. The legitimate need of preserving unity and discipline in the Church involves the duty of submission to the current phase of theological development. But this submission must not imply the surrender on the part of scientists, critics, and historians of their freedom and sincerity.[2]

When Loisy published *Autour d'un petit livre*, he realized that he was challenging the ecclesiastical authority as to whether it would or would not tolerate this position. There seemed to be only two possible consequences. If *Autour d'un petit livre* and his other books escaped ecclesiastical

[1] See *Mémoires*, II, 255.
[2] Cp. the letter of 'Romanus' (= von Hügel) in *The Times* (March 2nd, 1904, *i.e.* after the condemnation of Loisy's books): 'We can, and do, sincerely accept, as to discipline, the decree of the Index..., even though this possibly inevitable *hic et nunc* protection of the majority may in great part have been rendered necessary by the mental inertia and neglect of many generations of both taught and teachers. We can and do sincerely accept, as to doctrine, the decree of the Holy Office, in so far as it adjourns or checks the Abbé's (*i.e.* Loisy's) apologetics, since the Church authorities are clearly the official spokesmen for one of the two members of the attempted synthesis. But we cannot make our submission to the decree of the Holy Office in so unqualified a form as to let it include historico-critical method and its direct subject-matters, as such, even though these latter be the records of primitive Christianity'.

censure, then he would be free to continue his work as a historical critic without further distraction. On the other hand, it was far more likely that the Church would condemn as heretical the position he had adopted, and in this case the only way out of the difficulty would be excommunication. He did not intend, in order to remain in the Church, to submit to condemnation again and to abandon his work as a historical critic. This at least, he tells us, was his intention in October, 1903, when *Autour d'un petit livre* was published. If afterwards he appeared temporarily to compromise this intention, he says that it was only because he was harassed into doing so by the stress of persecution.

Leo XIII had died on July 20th, 1903; it was not easy to judge from the previous career of the new pope what his attitude would be to doctrinal liberalism. On August 7th Loisy had written to von Hügel: 'Pius X has the bearing of a good *curé*, and perhaps he will be better or less unfavourable to us than a diplomat'.[1] The illusory nature of this hope was soon to be disclosed. In his first encyclical (*E supremi aposto-latus*, October 4th, 1903) Pius X warned the clergy against the 'insidious manœuvres of a certain new science which adorns itself with the mask of truth.... false science, which, by means of fallacious and perfidious arguments, attempts to point the way to the errors of rationalism and semirational-ism'.

The piety of Pius X was not indeed open to question, but it was a piety akin to that of Cardinal Richard, a narrow and intense piety which, since it was completely satisfied by traditional orthodoxy, was quite incapable of realizing the need of theological development.[2] Moreover, the new pope had none of his predecessor's disposition to pose as a liberal

---

[1] *Mémoires*, II, 260.

[2] Cardinal Richard told Duchesne at this time that he persisted in believing that the works of St Dionysius the Areopagite, bishop of Paris, were authentic! See *Mémoires*, II, 277.

or as a benevolent patron of modernity. Thus the modest concessions to the new movement which Leo XIII had made, notably the appointment of the biblical commission, were speedily modified in a reactionary sense. The forces of conservative domination reasserted their normal hold on the Roman Curia.

As we have already seen, Cardinal Richard had for some years been trying to induce the Roman authorities to condemn Loisy, but hitherto without success. Up to the last Leo XIII had temporized.[1] The Cardinal did not hesitate to take advantage of the new opportunity that was provided for him, and this time he met with success. Although Mgr Mignot once more used what influence he could on Loisy's behalf, it was to no purpose. On December 16th, 1903, the Holy Office decided that the following five books by Loisy were to be put on the Index: *La religion d'Israël, Études évangeliques, L'Évangile et l'Église, Autour d'un petit livre,* and *Le Quatrième Évangile.* The decree was sent to Cardinal Richard by the Cardinal Secretary of State (Merry del Val) who in the course of an accompanying letter wrote: 'The very grave errors which abound in these volumes concern principally: the primitive revelation, the authenticity of the evangelical facts and teaching, the divinity and knowledge of the Christ, the resurrection, the divine institution of the Church, the sacraments'.

On January 11th, 1904, Loisy wrote to Cardinal Merry del Val that he 'received with respect the judgment of the Sacred Congregations, and that he himself condemned in his writings whatever they might contain that was reprehensible'.

I must nevertheless add (he continued) that my adhesion to the sentence of the Sacred Congregations is purely disciplinary in character. I reserve the right of my conscience, and I do not

[1] See Rivière, *Le modernisme dans l'Église*, p. 190.

intend, in inclining before the judgment delivered by the Holy Office, to abandon or retract the opinions which I have put forward as a historian and critic....[1]

Obviously this 'submission' would not be accepted as adequate by Rome, and, when officially informed to this effect, Loisy wrote again to Cardinal Merry del Val (January 24th): 'I accept...all the dogmas of the Church, and, if in exposing their history in the books which have just been condemned, I have unintentionally put forward opinions contrary to the faith, I have said and I repeat that I myself condemn, in these books, whatever they may contain that, from the point of view of the faith, is reprehensible'.[2]

In due course Loisy was informed that this was no more satisfactory than his former letter; nothing less than an unqualified submission would be accepted. On February 23rd, in response to renewed pressure from Cardinal Richard, he refused to add anything to his two letters to Cardinal Merry del Val. Everything now pointed to his excommunication and both Loisy and his friends were preparing themselves for it. There is indeed adequate evidence[3] that a decree of excommunication was prepared in Rome and that its promulgation was committed to the discretion of the archbishop of Paris. For reasons, which we are about to notice, the decree was not actually promulgated or made public, and therefore the fact of its existence has never been acknowledged by the Roman authorities. Cardinal Richard's biographer deliberately suppresses all reference to it.[4]

At the last moment, when excommunication was almost a *fait accompli*, the situation was changed in consequence of a fresh line of action pursued by Loisy himself. He tells how, at the end of February, the exhaustion of his physical powers by the nervous tension of the preceding months, assisted at a crucial moment by the persuasions of two friends who

---

[1] *Mémoires*, II, 313.　　[2] *Ibid.* II, 322.　　[3] See *ibid.* II, 314–60, 642.
[4] M. Clément, *Vie du Cardinal Richard*[2] (1924), pp. 402–6.

happened to visit him, culminated in an apparent *volte-face*. On February 28th he wrote a letter to the pope, in which he offered, as evidence of his goodwill, and for the pacification of spirits, to abandon his teaching in Paris, *i.e.* his lectureship at the École des Hautes Études, and to suspend the scientific publications which he had in preparation.

On March 12th he was summoned by Cardinal Richard to hear the pope's answer to his letter. This was to the effect that it was 'absolutely necessary that, confessing his errors, he should submit himself, fully and without restriction, to the judgment pronounced by the Holy Office against his writings'. So far from imposing silence on him, the Church would wish him to conform to the precept: *Succende quod adorasti, et adora quod incendisti.* With lively emotion Loisy has described the effect that this communication had upon him. Inspired by sincere and noble, if irrational, sentiments, he had offered for the Church's sake to sacrifice his lectureship and his publications, his most precious possessions. With what seemed to him incredible heartlessness, the head of the Church rejected his offer and demanded of him intellectual and moral suicide. This event, he says, more than any other killed his affection for the Church. He tried in vain, at the interview which was occasioned by the communication of the pope's letter, to show Cardinal Richard how impossible it was for him to retract *en bloc* the conclusions at which he had arrived as to the facts of history. But what hope could there ever be that two such entirely different mentalities should reach an understanding? Nevertheless, since he was now eager above all things for a measure of peace at any price within the limits of reason, Loisy made one last gesture. Later on the same day (March 12th) he sent to Cardinal Richard the following note:

Je déclare à votre Éminence que, par esprit d'obéissance envers le Saint-Siège, je condamne les erreurs que la Congrégation du Saint-Office a condamnées dans mes écrits.

In itself this note was a pure equivocation, and the ecclesiastical authorities no less than Loisy himself regarded it as such.[1] But it provided a basis on which the final resolution of the conflict could be postponed. It was as a matter of fact postponed for just four years. At the same time, the terms of the note obviously laid Loisy open to the suspicion of grave insincerity by those who were not able or who were not willing to recognize its utility as an instrument of ecclesiastical diplomacy or to appreciate the subtle reasoning which made it possible for him to sign it. We are not therefore surprised to learn that he has never ceased to regret that he made this declaration.

Hitherto, with whatever reservations, Loisy had been sincerely attached to Catholicism. But now this ceased to be true. He no longer believed that a revision of traditional orthodoxy was a practical proposition. He no longer believed that it was possible for him to be at once a critic and a Catholic. On May 12th, 1904, he wrote in his journal: 'Je veux rester prêtre et savant, *res dissociabiles*'. And on June 7th he clearly anticipated what his future would be after he was excommunicated: 'Il est certain, d'ailleurs, que, si je me trouvais hors de l'Église, ce ne serait pas pour tenir le rôle de docteur incompris, attendant que la porte s'ouvre pour rentrer dans le bercail. Je vivrais en savant laïque, intéressé aux choses morales, et je mourrais de même'.

It is not, therefore, far from the truth to say that from 1904 onwards the outcome of the modernist movement, so far as Loisy himself was concerned, was settled. The next four years, during which he lived in retirement in the country and completed his commentary on the synoptic gospels, served only to defer the inevitable conclusion of his life as a

---

[1] It is evident that both Rome and Cardinal Richard appreciated the declaration at its true worth. It was not published by them, as it certainly would have been if they had looked upon it as a genuine submission. See Clément, *Vie du Cardinal Richard*, p. 406; Loisy, *Mémoires*, II, 372.

Catholic.[1] Already, in 1904, it was rumoured that Rome was going to issue a new syllabus of errors[2] and probably the decree *Lamentabili* would have been issued long before 1907, if various circumstances had not adjourned its publication, notably the preoccupation of the Vatican with the controversies relating to the disestablishment of the Church in France. Although this question had no direct bearing on the modernist crisis, yet the intransigent attitude of the papacy in regard to it, and the refusal of Pius X to allow even that modified acceptance of the laws passed by the government, for which the episcopate was prepared, did much, in Loisy's case at any rate, to deepen the despair of a compatibility between any form of liberalism and loyalty to the Church.[3] In any case, the succession of modernist books which were put on the Index during these years, and also the decisions of the biblical commission,[4] left no doubt as to the intentions of the holy see.

Why then, it may be asked, since Loisy had virtually lost his faith in Catholicism, did he not voluntarily leave the Church? The answer to this question is that, in his judgment, the responsibility for his loss of faith rested on the Church itself, that is on the ecclesiastical authorities, and he was not willing, either in his own interest or in the interest of those Catholics who in any way depended on him, to relieve the authorities of their responsibility. He would have been false to the attitude that he had adopted throughout his career in the Church if he had given any final justification for the idea that his rupture with Catholicism was spontaneous.[5]

While living thus in retirement, he continued to say mass

[1] See his letter to Houtin, *Mémoires*, III, 14 ff.
[2] *Mémoires*, II, 411; Rivière, *Le modernisme dans l'Église*, pp. 333 f.
[3] See Loisy, *L'Église et la France* (1925), p. 103; *Mémoires*, II, 440, 454 f., 519.
[4] For details see Rivière, *op. cit.* pp. 333 f.; Loisy, *Mémoires*, II, 411.
[5] Cp. *Mémoires*, II, 323, 456, 459, 509.

at home. The official authorization to do so, technically called an indult, which he had received after his serious illness in 1899, needed to be renewed in November, 1906, as it was valid for only seven years. When Loisy applied for a renewal of the indult, the French ecclesiastical authorities, who were evidently acting upon instructions from Rome, raised difficulties, and he therefore ceased to say mass. 'This act', he says, 'had not lost for me all religious significance; but latterly it had become burdensome to me, as it seemed to imply the profession of official Catholicism.'[1] It was now beyond all doubt that the final rupture could not be indefinitely delayed, and accordingly Loisy sent the MS. of *Les Évangiles Synoptiques* to press. In 1907 Rome at last began the series of acts by which the modernist movement was condemned,[2] and Loisy wrote a number of letters which were designed to clarify his attitude in regard to the issues that were in dispute between official Catholicism and himself. These, together with some earlier letters and relevant documents, were published in book form (*Quelques lettres sur des questions actuelles et sur des événements récents*) shortly after his excommunication, which took place on March 7th, 1908. *Les Évangiles Synoptiques* and *Simples réflexions*, the latter being his commentary on the decree *Lamentabili* and on the encyclical *Pascendi*, were published a month or so before the excommunication. It was not, however, these publications, but his refusal to make an act of submission to the papal acts of 1907, which was the immediate cause of his excommunication.[3] With his excommunication his life as a Catholic and as a modernist ended.

[1] *Ibid.* II, 493.
[2] Papal allocution on April 17th; the decree *Lamentabili* on July 3rd; the encyclical *Pascendi* on September 8th; the 'motu proprio' *Praestantia* on November 18th.
[3] *Mémoires*, II, 635, III, 371. *Simples réflexions* and *Quelques lettres* were not publications whose intention was to forward the modernist movement so much as commentaries on its condemnation.

PART III
TYRRELL

M. Loisy has been described[1] as the chief scientific, and Father Tyrrell as the chief religious, exponent of modernism. The distinction is a just one, although it would be misleading if it were held to imply that the one was interested only in science, and the other only in religion. It was equally the object of them both to unite an unfettered search for truth with the practice of the Catholic religion, with active membership of the Roman Church. But M. Loisy has ever been a savant, so that for him science was the paramount, though not the only, interest. Tyrrell, on the other hand, was a mystic, a prophet, a martyr; his interest in science as such was secondary and almost indirect. Because of this difference between them, if for no other reason, a study of Tyrrell's career brings to light fresh and further aspects of the modernist movement.

And again, Tyrrell's chief contributions to the life and literature of the movement belong to a later period than Loisy's. By the time that Tyrrell came to the forefront, Loisy had already 'shot his bolt' and had recognized that failure was inevitable. From 1906 until his death, says Archdeacon Lilley,[2] Tyrrell was the 'universally acknowledged leader' of the movement. The expression may suggest too much, but it is true that as the story of Loisy's career illuminates its earlier stages, so that of Tyrrell's illuminates its later stages.

The chief and most authoritative sources of information, in addition to Tyrrell's own published works, are his Autobiography and life (1912) and Letters (1920), both of which are edited by his friend and literary executor, Miss M. D. Petre. Of all these full use has been made,[3] nor have other special studies of his life and thought been ignored. Every book about the movement necessarily contains some estimate of the part he played in it. Diverse and conflicting as these estimates may be, according to the viewpoint of their authors, yet each is in its way instructive.

[1] By Professor Karl Holl, see M. D. Petre, Modernism, p. 224.
[2] Article on 'Modernism' in E.R.E., VIII, 765.
[3] With regard to references, what was said on p. 68 above about Loisy's Mémoires applies in this Part to Tyrrell's Autobiography and life.

Chapter XVII

A CONVERT DISILLUSIONED, 1861–1901

George Tyrrell was by birth an Irishman. He was born in Dublin on February 6th, 1861; his father, who was a journalist, had died in the previous December. His mother was left very poorly off, and had a severe struggle to provide for the upbringing of her three children. She belonged to the Church of Ireland, and the character of Tyrrell's early religious training was extremely Low Church. He was taught to regard Roman Catholicism as a religion for vulgar and uneducated persons. As a boy he was clever, but he was idle at school. He achieved no academic success, and, in spite of his great intellectual gifts, he never became a scholar in the stricter sense of the term. As a boy also he went through a period of religious unbelief under the influence of his brother who was older and more brilliant than himself. Then, through seemingly accidental circumstances, he began to come under the spell of Catholicism, and started to attend one of the only two High Churches in Dublin.

As happens to many who have been brought up in a Low Church atmosphere, it was the very different atmosphere of Catholicism, rather than its doctrines, that in the first instance appealed to him. Here was something mysterious, unknown, and forbidden. But the quest for truth was already strong in him, and his reflective powers were quickly developing; he could not for long remain content with any thing that was superficial. He happened now to read Butler's *Analogy*, and, little as he understood it, he woke thereby to 'a dim sense of there being a great and pressing world-problem to be solved for myself and for others, either positively or negatively'.[1]

At this juncture, early in 1878, he became closely attached to Robert Dolling (1851–1902),[2] who was working as a layman in Dublin. Tyrrell was greatly attracted by Dolling's ardent and evangelical Catholicism, and he soon came to share his friend's dissatisfaction with the moderate and austere High Churchmanship which was the most that the Church of Ireland had to offer them. Dolling, however, had no inclination to become a Roman Catholic. His religion was essentially practical; he was not harassed by intellectual difficulties or by the alleged incoherence of the High Anglican position. Nevertheless, his keen insight into character enabled him to recognize the different bent of Tyrrell's mind, his present desire for a faith that was logical and final in its claims. He did not try seriously to dissuade Tyrrell from doing what he had no intention of doing himself. The dominant characteristic of Tyrrell's mind was, in the words of his friend Canon C. E. Osborne, 'his analysing intensity, his truth-chasing capacity'. Given the conditions in which he first became sensitive to the appeal of Catholicism, it was almost inevitable that he should press straight through to the Catholic system in its most complete and consistent form, *i.e.* to the Roman Church. He must needs test its truth there, and not in any half-way house.

Thus, when in March, 1879, at the age of eighteen, he left Ireland for England, his course was practically determined. Dolling had arranged to open a house in London in connexion with a guild for postmen, and Tyrrell was to live with him

---

[1] *Medievalism*, p. 99; cp. a letter from Tyrrell, quoted by R. Gout (*L'affaire Tyrrell*, p. 11): 'A perfectly unintelligent and uncritical reading of Bishop Butler's *Analogy* first made me realise that there was a world-problem to be solved'.

[2] See a letter from Tyrrell in C. E. Osborne's *The life of Father Dolling* (1903), pp. 19–23.

for a time. Dolling thought that there was a remaining possibility that an experience of Anglican Catholicism at work might satisfy Tyrrell; but a brief intercourse with ritualist clergy and laity in London only served to confirm his impression that they were 'playing at' Catholicism. He says in his autobiography that if he had been 'brought in contact with some more thoughtful representatives of Anglicanism, the results might have been different'. As it was, he was predisposed to accept the syllogistic arguments for the Roman position. His emotions were for the time being captivated by 'the old business, being carried on by the old firm, in the old ways'.

In particular, he had formed from reading and hearsay a naïve and highly idealized picture of the Society of Jesus. He conceived of it as 'an Order whose every member was governed, from first to last, by a zeal for the propagation of truth and religion, such as inspired St Ignatius and his first companions'. He was himself now eager to embrace the truth so understood, and eager also to devote his life to its propagation. Thus it came about that he had been in London only a month or two when he got into touch with the Jesuits. After a rather perfunctory preparation he was received into the Roman Church, and the possibility of his becoming a member of the Society was immediately broached.

He did not become a novice at once, but went for a year's probation to teach in Jesuit establishments, first at Cyprus, and then at Malta. From the first his experience of the Society from within led to a certain disenchantment; but the ideal he had formed was not easily to be shattered. It was in September, 1880, that he formally entered the novitiate. His novice-master was a man whose mentality was narrowly and extremely ultramontane, but a man of exalted ideals and of intense devotion. He did not fail to detect in Tyrrell a mental indocility, a pride of intellect, which unfitted him for

membership of the Order. Tyrrell, however, was so determined to learn the Catholic and Jesuit way of life and
thought, that he suppressed his doubts and questionings and
trode the path of dutiful, if reluctant, submission. From this
time onwards too he became bound to the Society by many
ties of friendship with its members.

After the year's novitiate, which was spent at Manresa
house, Roehampton, he was sent to Stonyhurst to begin
seven years' training in philosophy and theology. Here he
became a diligent student of scholasticism and a disciple of
St Thomas Aquinas. The desire for a coherent scheme of
thought and knowledge was strong in him; the claims of
scholasticism were imposing, and there was no other system
available for him. He learned it 'under the direction of men
whose infectious self-assurance was not easy to withstand'.[1]
In his enthusiasm for this system—the enthusiasm, it must be
remembered, of a convert—he went through a phase of
militant orthodoxy, which lasted till about 1897 and is
reflected in some of his earliest writings.[2] Yet within the
Society itself there were influences at work which were
sufficient to preserve in his mind the independence of judgment that, from the point of view of orthodoxy, was
ultimately to lead to his downfall.

The long period of preparation, which included a further
three years spent in teaching, ended at last in 1891, when he
was ordained priest. The next two or three years were spent
chiefly in parish work, and then he was appointed to the
chair of philosophy at St Mary's hall, Stonyhurst, which he
occupied from 1894 to 1896. Here his troubles began and,

[1] *Medievalism*, p. 159.

[2] See *Life*, II, 51 f.; cp. Tyrrell's article in *The Times* of October 1st,
1907; R. Gout, *L'affaire Tyrrell*, p. 32. At least two essays in *The faith of the
millions*, viz. 'The prospects of reunion' and 'An apostle of naturalism'
are trenchantly orthodox. This period of Tyrrell's career seems to be overlooked by those who say (like P. Gardner, *Modernism in the English
Church*, p. 51) that 'he never really absorbed the Roman position'.

strange as this may seem in the light of later developments, they were due in this instance to his excessive devotion to St Thomas Aquinas. The scholasticism, which was in general favour in the Society of Jesus, was not that of St Thomas himself, but scholasticism as interpreted by the Jesuit Suarez (1548–1617). Tyrrell and a small minority in the Society, which was encouraged to some extent by Leo XIII, advocated a revival of non-Suarezian Thomism, that is, of a more elastic system of philosophy than that which the dominant tradition and the vast majority of present members of the Society favoured.

The fact is (Tyrrell wrote later with reference to this time) that Aquinas represents a far less developed theology than that of the later scholastics, and by going back to him one escapes from many of the superstructures of his more narrow-minded successors, and thus gets a liberty to unravel and reconstruct on more sympathetic lines. I would thus use the neo-scholastic movement to defeat the narrow spirit which animates many of its promoters. Aquinas was essentially liberal-minded and sympathetic.... This was what I fought for, for two years.... My feeling is that, under cover of Aquinas, much might have been quietly introduced and assimilated unconsciously, that will be opposed if presented in an alien and hostile garb.[1]

In 1896 he was relieved of his charge at Stonyhurst, and sent to Farm street to join the staff of writers there. Although he had not yet published any book, he had since 1886 contributed a number of articles to *The Month*, the periodical of the English Jesuits. These articles, some of which were published later in his *The faith of the millions* (1st and 2nd series), excited no particular comment at the time, nor are they of much importance for our present purpose. They belong on the whole to the earliest, the orthodox and

[1] Letter to von Hügel (December 6th, 1897), see *Life of Tyrrell*, II, 45. Cp. *The faith of the millions* (1st series), p. 20, and *The Church and the future*, pp. 106f. See also p. 63 above.

dogmatic phase of Tyrrell's development. Such traces of his later ideas as can be detected in them are so slight as to be hardly significant.

His first book was *Nova et vetera* (1897); this was followed by *Hard sayings* (1898) and *External religion: its use and abuse* (1899). These books consisted of meditations, conferences and addresses. They were mainly devotional, and not theologically controversial. Nevertheless, they were distinguished by a spirit that was fresh in such Roman Catholic literature, by a freedom from the traditional and conventional manner of spiritual or pious writings.[1] They therefore attracted attention and met with appreciation in those circles where there was a desire for something of the kind.

Most important of all, *Nova et vetera* attracted the attention of Baron von Hügel, who in September, 1897, wrote to express his gratitude for the book and his desire to make Tyrrell's acquaintance. The friendship thus begun was of great, and for Tyrrell himself of decisive, consequence. Hitherto, he had not been intimately associated with anyone of the Baron's intellectual calibre. 'This was, perhaps,' writes Miss Petre, 'his first intimate acquaintance with a *scholar* in the true sense of the word, a man of finished general education, wide reading and vast knowledge on a considerable number of subjects.'[2] Tyrrell was growing increasingly dissatisfied with scholasticism and was feeling after some fresh approach to truth. Von Hügel brought him into contact with those movements in Catholic thought which were independent of scholasticism and tending towards a more liberal theology and a new apologetic. In this way, for instance, Tyrrell was introduced to the philosophical work of Maurice Blondel and Laberthonnière, as well as to that of the non-Catholic Bergson, and, what influenced him quite as much, he was initiated into the science of modern biblical criticism.

During the first period of their friendship von Hügel's

[1] Cp. Fawkes, *Studies in modernism*, p. 13.　　[2] *Life of Tyrrell*, II, 87.

attitude to the received theology was more radical than Tyrrell's. 'Every time I meet you or hear from you,' Tyrrell wrote to him in 1901, 'I am poked on a little further.'[1] And again in 1902: 'All the vast help you have given me— and surely I have grown from a boy to a man since I knew you—has been in opening up my eyes to an ever fuller and deeper knowledge of the data of the great problem of life'.[2] 'In the early stages of their companionship (writes Miss Petre) the influence of Baron von Hügel tended rather to forward than to retard the advance of his friend's mind; later on the positions were somewhat reversed, and we find him endeavouring to check the rapidity of one to whom quick movement was all too natural.'[3]

Quick as the movement of Tyrrell's mind was, he did not become a modernist in one bound. Approximately from 1897 to 1900, he went through a phase of what he called 'mediatorial liberalism'. During this time he was more or less in sympathy with the position occupied by Wilfrid Ward,[4] a position from which the latter never moved. It was a judicious compromise between liberalism and conservatism. Intellectual liberty in science and criticism is good, but it must be limited and provisional. There must be no rash criticism of ecclesiastical authorities, nor must science intrude upon theology. If the scientist exercises caution, it is reasonable to expect that the ecclesiastical authorities will show moderation. 'Patience' should be the motto of both. Tyrrell with his 'truth-chasing' temperament was not likely to rest for long in a position like this.[5] He was rapidly coming

---

[1] *Life of Tyrrell*, II, 95.

[2] *Ibid.* II, 96. Cp. *Lex orandi* (1907 edition), p. xxxii, and von Hügel's *Selected letters*, p. 12.

[3] *Life of Tyrrell*, II, 94. Cp. von Hügel's *Selected letters*, p. 113.

[4] Cp. Tyrrell's essays on Ward's *Life of Cardinal Wiseman* and on 'Liberal Catholicism' in *The faith of the millions* (1st series), pp. 22–39, 68–84.

[5] See his description of this attitude in *Medievalism*, p. 153.

to recognize the extent to which the received tradition of Catholic theology was behind the advance of modern knowledge, and to realize the difficulties which this involved for those who like himself were in search of religious truth. As a result of his writings and his priestly work he was constantly being called upon to minister to souls who were troubled by these difficulties; more and more keenly he felt the need of some other remedy than patience.

He had joined the Roman Church in search of truth, and not of peace, and he had become a Jesuit because he believed that the Society was in the intention of its founder and by the record of its history the most potent instrument available for the propagation of truth. This belief, or at least that part of it which concerned the history of the Society and its present capacity, was now in ruins. He no longer believed that scholasticism, specially that form of scholasticism which was dominant in the Society, was the only or the most adequate method of arriving at and propagating truth. For a time, after he realized this, he was inclined to hope that the Society might become the agent of a reinterpretation of Catholicism in relation to the modern situation. But the forces of tradition were obviously too strong, and he had to abandon the hope almost before it was formulated.

It was already evident that his membership of the Society of Jesus was full of embarrassment and that a rupture was becoming inevitable. Nevertheless, he did not intend himself deliberately to precipitate a rupture, partly because of the scandal it would cause to those who in various ways depended on him,[1] and also because it did not appear that he would be better able in any alternative position to promote that transformation of Catholic doctrine, which he now felt to be necessary. It was, however, morally certain that sooner or later the Society would have to take action against him.

[1] See *The Church and the future*, pp. 8 f.

The first definite external symptoms of cleavage were occasioned by an article, entitled 'A perverted devotion', which he contributed to the *Weekly Register* (December 16th, 1899).[1] The subject of the article was similar to that in connexion with which Dr St G. Mivart had been condemned a few years before,[2] the difficulties of belief in the traditional doctrine of hell. It does not appear whether or not Tyrrell realized how perilous a theme this was. Here, if anywhere, nineteenth-century orthodoxy, both Catholic and Protestant, would allow no modification of traditional teaching.

The substance of the article was a plea for agnosticism with regard to the Church's teaching about the everlasting punishment of the damned and a criticism of theological rationalism. It should be acknowledged that the Church's teaching on this point, as generally stated, 'seems, and is intended to seem, absurd and impossible; for it causes man to appear more just, more kind, than his Maker'. And what applies to teaching about hell

holds good in reference to other difficulties against our faith in the absolute goodness and wisdom of God, arising from the existence of suffering, the permission of sin, the problem of predestiny. The attempt to rationalise these mysteries, to level them down to our range of vision, to patch them up, to whittle them away, is responsible for the widespread decay of faith which they have occasioned—well-meant ingenuity no doubt, but surely misguided and ill-judged!... Thousands would willingly submit to these mysteries were they allowed to preserve that agnosticism in their regard which is one of the elements of real faith....

The difficulties in question are not solved, nor even eased, by such theological expedients as minimizing the probable number of the damned. Rationalism should 'cease its

[1] Reprinted in *Essays on faith and immortality* (1914), pp. 158–71.
[2] An article, entitled 'Happiness in hell', which Mivart contributed to the *Nineteenth century* (December, 1892), was put on the Index. See W. L. Knox and A. R. Vidler, *The development of modern Catholicism* (1933), pp. 152–5.

elucidations'. The finite mind is essentially incapable of seizing the absolute end, which governs and moves everything towards itself. 'We must purge out of our midst any remnant of the leaven of rationalism that we may have carried with us from earlier and cruder days, when faith needed the rein more than the spur.'

Here we have the authentic voice of Tyrrell the modernist; he has broken with scholasticism, implicitly at least, and in effect with 'mediatorial liberalism' also. He is insinuating the need of a new attitude to dogma as such, and not merely advocating a more careful statement of one particular dogma. The article gave rise to a considerable controversy. The Jesuit authorities in England could find in it 'no proposition worthy of theological censure'. Not so those in Rome. Two censors appointed by the Father-General of the Society found in it ample grounds for objection. Their leading objection (writes Miss Petre) was

to the anti-rationalistic tone of the article, its 'moderate agnosticism'.... They defend the use and cogency of reason in the elucidation of dogma and deny that its 'illustrations and analogies' can ever serve to aggravate, and not to lessen, the difficulties of faith. They object to seeking help for such difficulties in the very mysteriousness of the doctrine.... They maintain that the doctrine (of hell) is sufficiently elucidated by the traditional explanations of theology; that if it cannot be proved by reason, all objections to it can be defeated by reason; that its use and salutariness must not be lessened by appeals to mystery....[1]

After several months' correspondence, Tyrrell published in the *Weekly Register* (June 1st, 1900) a meaningless 'submission'. But his position in the Society was compromised, and he was henceforth under suspicion. His liberty as a writer was curtailed; he was no longer allowed to conduct

---

[1] *Life of Tyrrell*, II, 120 f.; for the full text of the *censurae* see appendices I and II.

retreats; and he went to live in virtual retirement at a small Jesuit mission at Richmond in Yorkshire.

There he continued to write, indeed more than ever before, for he had no other prescribed occupation. His powers of self-expression were now at their height, and he was conscious that he had a message to deliver. If he produced no *magnum opus* (we are told that during these years he was working at the rough draft of one),[1] it was because his pen was always busily occupied with the ecclesiastical events and controversies of the time, and also because of the peculiar conditions under which he had to publish what he wrote. He wanted to publish, and not merely to write, because he felt that what he had to say was of immediate import. Moreover, he wanted to publish what he could with the official *imprimatur*, since in this way he could reach and influence a wider range of Catholic opinion. But during this period (1900–5) he also published pseudonymously or anonymously and circulated privately books and articles, which clearly would not pass ecclesiastical censorship. This proceeding was contrary to the rules of the Society of Jesus, but he justified it to himself on the ground that his position was admittedly anomalous and recognized as such by the Society; in short it was the less of two evils.[2]

In 1901 *The faith of the millions* (two volumes) was published with the *imprimatur* of Cardinal Vaughan. These essays, as we have had occasion to remark, belong for the most part to the middle or transitional phase of Tyrrell's development, and some even to the earliest, purely orthodox phase. In republishing them his main motive was to gain a favourable hearing for the newer ideas about which he intended to write forthwith. Thus he wrote to a friend: 'My chief desire for it (*The faith of the millions*) is that it collects

[1] See *Life*, ii, 192.
[2] Cp. his chapter on 'The ethics of conformity' in *The Church and the future*, pp. 139–46.

into one my "doctrine", and gives proof of how sober and moderate it has been all along, which proof may be useful to me later'.[1]

Even so, it did not pass the censors without difficulty. There is one essay, 'The relation of theology to devotion', which is a definite and explicit anticipation of what was to come. Its significance was not yet fully appreciated either by himself or by others;[2] but on re-reading it in 1907, with a view to publishing it again in *Through Scylla and Charybdis*, Tyrrell wrote: 'I am amazed to see how little I have really advanced since I wrote it; how I have simply eddied round and round the same point. It is all here—all that follows—not in germ but in explicit statement—as it were a brief compendium or analytical index'.[3] The theme of this essay should therefore be carefully observed.

Tyrrell begins by explaining his use of the term 'theology'. It 'may be used in a wider or a more restricted sense. Here we employ the term to signify what is known as scholastic theology, that is, the essay to translate the teachings of Catholic revelation into the terms and forms of Aristotelian philosophy; and thereby to give them a scientific unity'. He proceeds to distinguish between 'the philosophical and the vulgar way of conceiving and speaking about things'. 'The former is abstract, orderly, and artificial; the latter, concrete, disorderly, and natural.' This is true with regard to Nature. The backwoodsman's knowledge of Nature is of a different kind from that of the scientist. The two kinds of knowledge may assist one another, but they are distinct. 'The more abstract, general, and simple our classification is, and the further removed it is from the infinite complexity of con-

[1] *Life*, ii, 48.

[2] We are told, however, that in December, 1901, after *The faith of the millions* had received his *imprimatur*, Cardinal Vaughan had misgivings about this essay; *Life of Tyrrell*, II, 172.

[3] *Through Scylla and Charybdis*, p. 85; see also von Hügel's *Selected letters*, p. 166.

crete reality, the more we need continually to remind ourselves that its truth is merely hypothetical, and holds only in
the abstract.'

And if this is true of the natural world, how much more
true is it of the spiritual and supernatural world! Here 'we
are under a further disadvantage; for we can think and speak
of it only in analogous terms borrowed from this world of
our sensuous experience, and with no more exactitude than
when we would express music in terms of colour, or colour
in terms of music'. A metaphysical theory is an attempt 'to
comprehend the incomprehensible, to equal a sphere to a
plane'. 'In saying this, we do not deny for a moment, that
the infinite can to some extent be expressed in terms of the
finite; but are only insisting on the purely analogous character of such expression....The use of philosophy lies in
its insisting on the inadequacy of the vulgar statement; its
abuse, in forgetting the inadequacy of its own, and thereby
falling into a far more grievous error than that which it
would correct.' Thus, for instance, 'the error called " anthro-
pomorphism" does not lie so much in thinking and speaking
of God humanwise—for that we are constrained to do by the
structure of our minds—as in forgetting that such a mode of
conception is analogous'.

Tyrrell now passes on to apply this to the Christian revelation. 'It is a fact that the Judaeo-Christian revelation has been
communicated in vulgar and not in philosophical terms and
modes of thought.' 'Revelation', this is to say, is not
theology, but rather the data of theology. Theology is an
attempt to 'unify and elucidate' the data provided by concrete Christian experience, and just because it tends, like
all philosophizing, to 'excessive abstraction and vague un-
reality' it needs constantly to be tested and checked. 'It has
to be reminded that, like science, its hypotheses, theories, and
explanations, must square with facts—the facts here being the
Christian religion as lived by its consistent professors.'

Now it can hardly be denied that some of the abstract theories of theology do belie these facts. Thus 'the whole doctrine of Christ's κένωσις or self-emptying can be explained in a minimising way almost fatal to devotion, and calculated to rob the Incarnation of all its helpfulness by leaving the ordinary mind with something perilously near the phantasmal Christ of the Docetans.... When the theologian has finished his treatise: *De scientia Christi*; when he has impressed upon us that Christ was exempt from the two internal sources of all our temptations, *sc.* the darkness of our mind and the rebellion of our body; that in His case, temptations from without met with no more response from within than when we offer food to a corpse; we cannot help feeling that under whatever abstraction this may be true, yet it cannot be the whole truth, unless all who have turned to Christ in their temptations and sorrows have been wofully deluded—unless the *lex orandi* and the *lex credendi* are strangely at strife'.

Tyrrell is content to suggest, rather than to assert, that they are at strife; but the implication is obvious. He illustrates the same point from the theology of the blessed sacrament. His conclusion is as follows: 'Devotion and religion existed before theology, in the way that art existed before art-criticism.... Art-criticism, as far as it formulates and justifies the best work of the best artists, may dictate to and correct inferior workmen; and theology as far as it formulates and justifies the devotion of the best Catholics, and as far as it is true to the life of faith and charity as actually lived, so far is it a law and corrective for all. But where it begins to contradict the facts of that spiritual life, it loses its reality and its authority; and needs itself to be corrected by the *lex orandi*'.

Chapter XVIII

'LEX ORANDI,' 'LEX CREDENDI,' 1901–1906

'The relation of theology to devotion' discloses the essential features of Tyrrell's thought—the distinction between theology and religion or revelation corresponding to the distinction between the abstract and the concrete, the analogical character of all affirmations about the spiritual and supernatural world, the sense that living the Christian life is more important than acceptance of the orthodox creed and that the truth of the creed must be brought to the test of experience, and at the same time an intense appreciation of Catholic, sacramental devotion as mediating the fullest spiritual life. It is also to be noticed that he suggests the need of a revision of the traditional Christological teaching, not here because of its incompatibility with the results of biblical criticism, but because Christian experience postulates a Christ Whose humanity was genuine, *i.e.* subject to real limitations, which traditional theology has in effect obscured.

To what extent, it must be asked, was the substance of Tyrrell's thought, from 'The relation of theology to devotion' onwards, original or derived from others? He said himself, speaking of modernism, that he was 'not conscious of having contributed a single idea of (his) own to that interpretation of Catholicism'; that he let himself 'be taught by abler and more learned men who had won the battle long before (he) appeared on the field'; and that his own work had been one of 'vulgarisation'.[1] But in saying this he did less than justice to himself. It is true that he was not an expert in any branch of science, history or criticism. His first master was St Thomas Aquinas, for whom, even after

---

[1] *Medievalism*, pp. 107f.

the break with scholasticism, he retained a profound respect. The influence of Newman on his mind was secondary and more temporary. His friendship with von Hügel was the most decisive influence. From the time of its beginning he read widely all kinds of literature relevant to theology, both English, French and German, and thus for purposes of his apologetic he utilized ideas derived from a large variety of sources. But it is not easy to trace these sources in detail, for it was not, generally speaking, his habit in writing to give references or to make quotations.[1] It is probable also that what he derived from others he made so much his own as to be hardly conscious of its origin.

Tyrrell was a thinker. 'A thinker (it has been said) is not a person with a bag into which he collects so many ideas from other people and adds so many more of his own. The real interest is to see a man's attitude towards the great elemental truths, to see what interest preponderates for him, and from what point of view he regards the world.'[2] But it is probable that Tyrrell was specially influenced by at least two contemporary writers, William James[3] and Arthur James (later Lord) Balfour.[4] One has only to read *The will to believe*, *The varieties of religious experience* and *The foundations of belief* to realize how much there was in common between Tyrrell's 'attitude towards the great elemental truths' and theirs; and in fact acknowledgments of indebtedness are extant in his correspondence. Nevertheless, it would be hazardous to catalogue

[1] Cp. C. W. Emmet, *The eschatological question in the gospels* (1911), p. 5.

[2] J. Oman, *The problem of faith and freedom* (1906), p. 27.

[3] *The will to believe* (1897); *The varieties of religious experience* (1902). For an avowal that *Lex orandi* was indebted to the former see *George Tyrrell's letters*, p. 22.

[4] *The foundations of belief* (1894); Tyrrell told Buonaiuti that his objection to *pure* pragmatism was drawn from this book, *Le modernisme catholique*, p. 146; *George Tyrrell's letters*, p. 116. He had reviewed it sympathetically in *The Month* (May, 1895), pp. 16–32.

Tyrrell's ideas and to affirm that each must have been derived from one particular source; all that could really be shown is that each might have been so derived. At the same time it is safe to say that the anti-intellectualist tendency of his own thought after his reaction from scholastic rationalism was encouraged and fortified by the writings of James and Balfour, and also of Bergson. Pragmatism, voluntarism, intuitionism, were 'in the air'.

That he was consciously indebted to other Catholic modernists is shown by his statement which was quoted at the beginning of the last paragraph but one. In this connexion a peculiar interest attaches to the judgment expressed by Henri Brémond. Brémond (1862–1933) was an intimate friend of Tyrrell,[1] and he was also well versed in English literature. He wrote in 1913 to Loisy: 'Pour Tyrrell, vous l'avez façonné, ainsi que Laberthonnière; et les grands libéraux anglais ont fait le reste, Mat. Arnold, *Literature and dogma,*—un tiers de Tyrrell est là-dedans,—Jowett, etc.'.[2] The statement about *Literature and dogma* may at first sight appear to be extravagant, and Miss Petre in her *Life of Tyrrell* says nothing to suggest, still less does she emphasize, this affinity. If, however, one reads *Literature and dogma* in close conjunction with Tyrrell's writings, the justice of Brémond's estimate is confirmed.

An antipathy to metaphysics and rationalism and to making theology a matter of abstruse reasoning and philosophical speculation; the sense that religion is primarily concerned with

[1] The full extent of Brémond's friendship with Tyrrell was not brought out in the *Autobiography and life* for prudential reasons; see von Hügel's *Selected letters,* p. 199.

[2] Loisy, *Mémoires,* III, 268. J. Lewis May, who notices M. Arnold's influence on Tyrrell, attributes Brémond's statement about *Literature and dogma* to Loisy himself, but this appears to be an error; *Father Tyrrell and the modernist movement* (1932), p. 272. P. Gardner (*Modernism in the English Church,* p. 50) says: 'Many of Tyrrell's sayings remind one strongly of Matthew Arnold, whether the influence was direct or not'.

life and conduct and experience; the inadequate, analogous and non-scientific character of religious affirmations; the falseness of the common antithesis between natural and revealed religion; the abandonment of the attempt to prove the truth of Christianity by the argument from prophecies or miracles; and an intense personal devotion to Our Lord:[1] all this is in *Literature and dogma*, and all this is in Tyrrell.

A letter written by Tyrrell on September 20th, 1899, suggests by an allusion which it contains that he had read Arnold by then.[2] There are occasionally explicit references to Arnold in his writings.[3] They are, however, critical, and do not express any consciousness of indebtedness on Tyrrell's part. In the absence of more definite evidence we may hesitate to put forward any certain conclusion as to the extent to which he was directly influenced by Arnold and the other 'grands libéraux anglais'. But to whatever extent or in whatever ways he was influenced, it seems a reasonable hypothesis that he was keenly affected by English liberal Protestantism. Affected, we say, rather than influenced, for in any case Tyrrell's differences from *Literature and dogma* are no less significant than his affinities thereto.

His reaction from the excessive abstraction of scholasticism disposed him to meet those of Arnold's way of thinking on their own ground, to accept the appeal to the concrete,

[1] M.-J. Lagrange is probably justified in saying that Loisy in his writings never betrays any such devotion; *M. Loisy et le modernisme* (1932), p. 105. The point is significant of the difference between Loisy and Tyrrell; cp. pp. 180 f. below.

[2] See *Life*, II, 73. 'The relation of theology to devotion' was first published in November, 1899, and it is possible that this was largely inspired by a reading of Arnold, but it may equally well be regarded as an extension of suggestions derived from Newman's *Grammar of assent*.

[3] *The faith of the millions* (1st series), pp. 193 ff., (2nd series), p. 60; *Lex credendi*, pp. 39 f., 78; *A much-abused letter*, p. 71; introduction to Brémond's *The mystery of Newman* (1907), p. xiv. Cp. *Lex orandi*, p. xxxi; *Christianity at the cross roads*, p. 177; *Autobiography and life*, II, 398; *George Tyrrell's letters*, pp. 103, 221, 239.

living experience of humanity. The aim of his writings is to show that the criterion of experience justifies not Arnold's vague liberalism, but a full and rich Catholicism. That is to say, he accepts Arnold's methods, his presuppositions even, and applies them not only to the Bible, but to the whole stream of religious experience in general and Catholic experience in particular, and claims that they issue in a justification not merely of 'morality touched by emotion', but of the whole complex of Catholicism as realized in history, its institutions, its worship, its sacraments, its asceticism, its mysticism, its ethics. He shows too that dogma is necessary because of the need of thinking about religion, of attempting an intellectual formulation of religious experience, and that dogma is useful since it assists or ought to assist the development of religion. While he agrees that the traditional dogmatic systems, whether Catholic or Protestant, are in many ways unsatisfactory, yet he shows that some of the dogmas which Arnold had laughed out of court, *e.g.* the Trinity, the Atonement, the Mass, can be defended, or at least restated, on the basis of the appeal to experience. Moreover, he agrees with the liberals in accepting the scientific criticism of the Bible, but shows that the Christ to whom criticism points is by no means the Christ of Arnold. The Christ of Arnold was in fact practically identical with the Christ of Harnack, just as *Literature and dogma* is an earlier and English version of *Das Wesen des Christenthums*.[1]

Tyrrell's modernism may then, like Loisy's, be reasonably

[1] The two following sentences from *Literature and dogma* may alone suffice to illustrate the resemblance between the two books: '"The kingdom of God is *within* you!" Such an account of the kingdom of God has more right, even if recorded only once, to pass with us for Jesus Christ's own account, than the common materialising (*i.e.* eschatological) accounts, if repeated twenty times' (5th edition, p. 160). 'Jesus never troubled himself with what are called Church matters at all; his attention was fixed solely upon the individual' (*ibid.* p. 293). For *Das Wesen des Christenthums*, see pp. 106 ff. above.

regarded as an attempt to meet liberal Protestantism on its own ground, to show that its premises led to a different conclusion. He was well aware of the attraction which liberal Protestantism had for cultured Englishmen to whom traditional Protestantism no longer made an intellectual or spiritual appeal, but who still wished to believe in some form of Christianity. 'At the present moment (Arnold had written) two things about the Christian religion must surely be clear to anybody with eyes in his head. One is, that men cannot do without it; the other, that they cannot do with it as it is.'[1] It was to persons of this sort that Tyrrell was most anxious to commend Catholicism.

The foregoing points might all be illustrated from *Oil and wine*, which, however, is one of Tyrrell's devotional, rather than apologetic, works. It was printed with a view to publication in 1902, but it was refused the *imprimatur* and could only be circulated privately. It was not actually published until 1906. The Jesuit censors of the book considered that 'the supernatural nature of Faith requires bringing out more; and the excellency of Catholic teaching, in spite of accidental defects in minor details. The impression on many minds at present would be that Catholic doctrine has so much error mixed with it as to be seriously compromised'.[2]

It is all the more surprising that *Lex orandi*,[3] which is one of the most important of Tyrrell's apologetic writings, was duly authorized by the ecclesiastical authorities for publication in 1903. It is true that archbishop Bourne said shortly afterwards that 'had he read Chapter XXIII of "Lex Orandi" he

---

[1] *God and the Bible*, p. xiv.

[2] *Life*, II, 170.

[3] *Religion as a factor of life*, which is more or less a rough draft of *Lex orandi*, was printed for private circulation in 1902 under the pseudonym of Dr Ernest Engels; it may be noticed that Maurice Blondel is here quoted at length (see pp. 39–42), but not in *Lex orandi*.

should have hesitated about the *Imprimatur*'.[1] The argument of the book is that the criterion, by which Christian beliefs must be judged, is their prayer-value; *lex orandi, lex credendi*.

'Beliefs that have been found by continuous and invariable experience to foster and promote the spiritual life of the soul must so far be in accord with the nature and the laws of that will-world with which it is the aim of religion to bring us into harmony; their practical value results from, and is founded in, their representative value. Not indeed that the spirit-world can be properly represented in terms of the natural world.' But we can be sure that a certain analogy does exist between the formulation of religion as embodied in the creed and the eternal realities of the spirit-world because of the creed's universally proved value 'as a practical guide to the eternal life of the soul—a proof which is based on the experience not of this man or that, however wise or holy, but of the whole Christian people and of the Church of the Saints in all ages and nations, on the consensus of the ethical and religious *orbis terrarum*' (pp. 57f.).

'It is...Christian devotion rather than Christian metaphysics, the need of the soul rather than the need of the intellect, that has selected the orthodox faith in preference to heterodox error' (p. 153). The faith therefore does not depend on any metaphysical system; nor again is it necessarily dependent on any particular affirmation about history. 'Certain concrete historical facts enter into our creed as matters of faith. Precisely as historical facts they concern the historian and must be criticised by his methods. But as matters of faith they must be determined by the criterion of faith, *i.e.* by their proved religious values' (p. 169). Here we have the distinction between history and faith which Loisy also stressed; but it is reached by a different approach. Tyrrell is primarily concerned with faith, and his concessions to history are incidental, and also in *Lex orandi* they are not in

[1] *Life*, II, 182.

detail defined. For Loisy, on the other hand, history is the dominant interest, and faith must be conceived in such a way as to be compatible therewith, as to be compatible, that is, with the freedom of the historian.

It must be allowed that Tyrrell's apologetic savours largely of 'pragmatism'. Christian beliefs are held to be true, because they are fruitful in practice, *i.e.* because they work. It is not, however, pure pragmatism. He does not hold that absolute or ultimate truth is unknowable. In prayer, in all forms of genuine religious experience, we have a real knowledge of God and the spiritual world; but we can express this knowledge only in analogous or relative terms. It would be unfair to regard *Lex orandi*, or any other of Tyrrell's writings for that matter, as more than a preliminary essay. Its epistemology may be ill-digested; but in any case its implications are revolutionary with regard to scholastic theology.

The Church and the future, which was printed in 1903 under the pseudonym of 'Hilaire Bourdon' for private circulation only,[1] is a bolder and more outspoken challenge to traditional orthodoxy. It is evident that Tyrrell had read and been much impressed by *L'Évangile et l'Église*.[2] So far from trying to mitigate, he emphasizes the contrast between his restatement of Catholicism and the official theory. 'It may be well...to remember what the official theory is. Christ and His Apostles are held to have delivered the complete "Depositum fidei" (*i.e.* the dogmas, Sacraments and other essential institutions of Catholicism as now existing) to St Linus and the episcopate united with him; who in their turn have transmitted it infallibly to their successors, without

[1] It was published in 1910, after Tyrrell's death, by the Priory Press; reference is here made to this edition.
[2] Cp. his letter of November 20th, 1902, to Loisy (*Life of Tyrrell*, ii, 394); he had also been greatly impressed by J. Weiss's *Der Predigt Jesu*, see the *Hibbert Journal* (January, 1910), pp. 239 f.

substantial increment but only more fully "explicated", illustrated, systematised' (p. 29).

This theory, with its correlative doctrines of the inerrancy of the Bible and of the Church, is now in ruins as a result of biblical and historical criticism. Tyrrell proceeds to outline a restatement of Catholicism which combines the critical views of *L'Évangile et l'Église* with the interpretations of dogma of his own *Lex orandi*. He accepts the eschatological view of the original gospel, and accepts it with enthusiasm. There is always a prophetic and mystical strain in Tyrrell's writings, while Loisy is *par excellence* the critic, the *savant*. At this time Tyrrell, in writing to von Hügel, speaks of his own 'somewhat incurable Christo-centricism, which survives and thrives upon all that should overthrow it'. And, with regard to *The Church and the future*, he adds: 'Of course, neither Blondel nor even Loisy, nor perhaps even you will follow me in my radicalism...I have only one unclearness about Loisy's view remaining, and that is that it is too indiscriminatingly conservative, that it does not give us what Newman tried (vainly I think) to give us, a criterion to distinguish true from false developments'.[1]

With great subtlety Loisy had insinuated that it was possible to reinterpret traditional orthodoxy in a sense compatible with the results of criticism. Tyrrell makes no such pretence. In the epilogue to *The Church and the future* he writes:

The 'liberalism' of this restatement of Catholicism lies not in an attempt to reconcile the data of science and history with dogmas by giving to these latter a sense which their framers would have repudiated, but in a frank abandonment of the 'official' in favour of a broader theory of ecclesiastical inerrancy; in a wider conception of the nature of dogmatic truth; in a modification of our view of the Church's claim to infallibility parallel to, and dependent on, that which we are forced to adopt in regard to the

[1] *Life of Tyrrell,* II, 187.

Sacred Scriptures. As to the heterodoxy of these views from the 'official' standpoint, there can be no manner of question (p. 170).

We may pause here, as Miss Petre does in her *Life of Tyrrell*,[1] to observe how far he has broken with 'Newmanism'. During the period of his 'mediatorial liberalism' (1897–1900) he had been a Newmanite like Wilfrid Ward, although even then, as we have said, Newman had never been his master in the same way as St Thomas had been in the earlier phase. But now, however suggestive he had found Newman's theory of development as expounded in the *Essay*, he no longer could regard it as satisfactory. It was vitiated by its acceptance of the idea 'of the *depositum fidei* as being a divinely communicated "Credo" or theological summary'; between this and evolutionary philosophy no synthesis was possible. Here Tyrrell's modernism was certainly in form more radical than Loisy's, explicitly so in *The Church and the future* and implicitly so in his *Semper eadem* articles[2] which belong to this time. Tyrrell made a direct attack upon the idea of the *depositum fidei*; Loisy simply ignored it, as at an earlier stage he had ignored the dogma of scriptural inspiration, and by formulas, that were more ingenious than ingenuous, affected to save the face of orthodoxy. He did so to such effect that Wilfrid Ward at first regarded *L'Évangile et l'Église* as a legitimate interpretation of Newmanism.[3] The object of both modernists was the same, viz. to substitute for the official theology one which took full account of the facts of history as disclosed by criticism. But they followed a different method just as they used a different terminology.

Tyrrell's method was to advocate a new conception of 'revelation'. From the traditional point of view, revelation

[1] On the extent to which Tyrrell had read, and been consciously influenced by Newman, see *op. cit.* II, 208 f.

[2] Published in *Through Scylla and Charybdis*, pp. 106–54.

[3] See p. 126 n. above.

was an infallible body of doctrine which had been given once for all in apostolic times, its truth being attested by prophecies and miracles, etc.; the Church was charged with the duty of preserving this unchanging deposit of faith and, when necessary, it was authorized to make infallible explications or applications of it in order to preserve it. This was the only kind of development that it could recognize. The whole conception is static and oracular.

Against this, Tyrrell puts forward a conception that is dynamic and evolutionary. Revelation is not a fixed body of doctrine, but the spirit or idea of Christianity which has been, and is still being, continuously realized in the experience of Christians. The ultimate object of this experience, belonging as it does to the eternal order, is unchanging. But its theological formulation or rationalization is continually being modified, enriched and improved. Thus Tyrrell assigns the difference between his conception and the traditional one

to the fact that liberal theology, like natural science, has for its subject-matter a certain ever-present department of human experience which it endeavours progressively to formulate and understand, and which is ever at hand to furnish a criterion of the success of such endeavours; whereas our school-divinity finds its subject-matter in the record or register of certain past experiences that cannot be repeated and are known to us only through such a record.... We do not ask if Copernican be true to Ptolemaic astronomy, but if it be true to experience. Nor does the liberal theologian ask or care that his theology be substantially identical with that of the past, but only that it be truer to experience than that which it supersedes.[1]

We have here gone somewhat beyond the chronological order of Tyrrell's writings. His authorship of *The Church and the future* was a carefully guarded secret; otherwise it

[1] *Through Scylla and Charybdis*, p. 136; cp. *The Church and the future*, pp. 26 f.

would certainly have provoked his rupture with the Society of Jesus. As it was, a slighter, anonymous writing became famous on this account. The 'Letter to a professor' was written about the end of 1903, and printed for private circulation early in 1904. The professor's person was fictitious, although perhaps founded on fact.[1] The letter is an *ad hominem* statement of the attitude to Catholicism, which Tyrrell had put forward in *Lex orandi* and *The Church and the future*. The professor, who is perplexed by the accumulation of scientific and critical objections to the received theology, is invited to distinguish between the official, formulated Catholicism, which does violence to his intelligence and moral sense, and the as 'yet unformulated Catholicism, or rather the living multitudinous reality thus perversely formulated', which draws and holds him 'by ties of affection and of instinctive spiritual sympathy'.[2] In remaining a Catholic it is to the latter, and not the former, that he will be adhering. Tyrrell concludes the letter by asking the question which in his latter years he was increasingly disposed to answer in the affirmative: 'May not Catholicism like Judaism have to die in order that it may live again in a greater and grander form? Has not every organism got its limits of development after which it must decay, and be content to survive in its progeny?'[3]

There remains one book to notice, which belongs to this period, *i.e.* it was written before, although published after, his rupture with the Society of Jesus. *Lex credendi*, published early in 1906, is, as its title suggests, a sequel to *Lex orandi*. It

[1] *Life of Tyrrell*, ii, 193 f. J. Schnitzer (*Der katholische Modernismus*, p. 14) says that Mivart was the professor in question. Mivart died, excommunicated, in 1900; he had been advised to consult Tyrrell about his difficulties (*Life*, ii, 169), and what Tyrrell says in the introduction to *A much-abused letter* (pp. 26 f.) suggests that the Mivart case may have prompted the fiction. See also R. Gout, *L'affaire Tyrrell*, p. 115.

[2] *A much-abused letter*, p. 60.

[3] *Ibid.* p. 89.

purports to elucidate 'points there lightly touched'. In the first part Tyrrell attempts to define what he means by 'the Spirit of Christ', when this is regarded as the content of the Christian revelation, by which creeds and theologies must be judged. The second part is an exposition of the Lord's prayer, clause by clause, which is also designed to show the priority of prayer, in the wide sense of spiritual experience, to formulated belief. The frequency with which he seeks to guard himself against the charge of undue pragmatism shows that he is uneasy on this score. The objection can hardly be met by repeating that 'a belief which constantly and universally fosters spiritual life must so far be true to the realities of the spiritual world, and must therefore possess a representative as well as a practical value' (p. 252). The objection can in fact only be met by relating the argument from experience to a wider theory of knowledge and of the universe; but into the sphere of metaphysics Tyrrell is not prepared to enter. 'We leave aside the metaphysical problem of the relation of the Divine Being to our own, of sameness and otherness, and speak simply of those manifestations of the spirit of which each man's soul is the theatre, though God is also their author in some mysterious way' (p. 68).

In this book he emphasizes more than he has done before the idea that Catholicism has appropriated 'the fruits of the general religious process of humanity', *i.e.* of pagan as well as of Jewish religion. 'We should not then admit it as a reproach when attention is drawn to the likeness between many points of Catholic and ethnic worship.... We see in it a proof that such practices are the spontaneous natural creation of man's religious needs—needs which the Church purifies and to which she ministers' (p. 97). This idea was welcomed by other modernists besides Tyrrell as a way of meeting the difficulties resulting from the comparative study of religion. Good apologetic as it may be, it made them over-ready to accept contemporary theories which held that primitive Catholicism had largely and directly borrowed from the oriental mystery religions, etc., theories which have been modified by subsequent research.

Lex credendi does not, however, deal with the subject in detail and, as Miss Petre says, it 'belongs, in some ways, rather to the devotional than to the scientific class of his works'.[1] Certainly Tyrrell's treatment of the gospels is devotional rather than critical or historical. However effectively he may disguise the fact, he continually reads back his own ideas into the original texts. At times, as for instance when he discusses the petition 'Thy kingdom come', we seem to catch echoes of Harnack.

[1] *Life of Tyrrell*, II, 203.

Chapter XIX

PROPHET OF REVOLUTION, 1906–1909

Meanwhile, before *Lex credendi* was ready for publication, Tyrrell had ceased to be a Jesuit. During the whole time that he had spent at Richmond (1900–5) his relation to the Society had been under consideration, and from time to time he corresponded with his superiors both in England and in Rome with regard to it. Thus in 1904 and again at greater length in 1905, with a view to securing a pacific termination of his membership, he explained to the Father-General how completely he was now out of sympathy with the Society. It was precisely the institution which represented everything in Roman Catholicism to which he was most keenly opposed. In the autumn of 1905 a definite application was made for his secularization, *i.e.* that he might be dispensed from his vows as a Jesuit and become a secular priest. The negotiations were, however, impeded by technical difficulties, and they were still proceeding when on December 31st, 1905, some extracts from the 'Letter to a professor' were quoted, or rather misquoted, in an Italian newspaper and ascribed to an 'English Jesuit'.[1] The General hereupon asked Tyrrell if he were the author of the 'Letter', and, when he acknowledged that he was, and furthermore refused to publish an adequate repudiation of it, he was without more ado dismissed from the Society. He received the form of dismissal on February 19th, 1906; he had said his last mass on February 14th.

His ecclesiastical status was now peculiar, since he had been dismissed and not secularized. He could communicate, but not celebrate. During 1906 some attempts were made to regularize his position as a priest, but they were abortive.

[1] As to how this happened see R. Gout, *L'affaire Tyrrell*, p. 134.

The conditions on which alone a *celebret* would be granted to him included the censorship of his 'epistolary correspondence', and not unnaturally he regarded this as intolerable. For about fifteen months after his dismissal he had no fixed residence, but travelled or stayed with friends, until in May, 1907, he settled at Storrington.

At first it seemed that he might be able to remain on peaceful, and even friendly, terms with the English Jesuits. In May, 1906, for instance, *Lex credendi* was sympathetically reviewed in *The Month*. But henceforth he was destined for perpetual warfare with official Catholicism in all its forms. His temperament was such that, while at times he yearned for peace and tranquillity and keenly realized the mischief caused by religious controversy, yet when provoked or urged on he could not resist the temptation to fight vigorously and even angrily. Nor was provocation lacking. Articles against him soon began to appear in the continental ecclesiastical reviews. Many of his English friends too were alienated as a result of the disclosure of his pseudonymous and anonymous writings. And it was not easy to be patient when Rome wanted to impose intolerable conditions on him if his position as a priest was to be regularized. Moreover, and most of all, he felt that he was called to a prophetic mission[1]—the reformation of Catholicism. Indeed it was revolution more than reformation which he now began to preach—the pouring of new wine into the old bottles until they burst.

But it would be idle to look for rigid consistency, still less for finality, in Tyrrell's conduct or teaching. It was difficult enough for men of steadier temper than he to steer an even

---

[1] Cp. 'I feel my work is to hammer away at the great unwieldy carcase of the Roman Communion and wake it up from its medieval dreams. Not that I shall succeed, but that my failure and many another may pave the way for eventual success' (from a letter of November 28th, 1907; see *Life*, II, 373).

course amid the turmoil of the time; and, more than most men, he was liable to be swayed this way and that by the events of day to day and by personal influences. Thus, almost on the eve of the issue of the encyclical *Pascendi* the negotiations for the *celebret*, which had recently been reopened, were nearer a favourable conclusion than they had been before. After *Pascendi*, however, Tyrrell sealed his fate, so far as Rome was concerned, by his defiant articles in *The Times* (September 30th and October 1st, 1907). On October 22nd he was deprived of the sacraments.

If he now preached revolution, *i.e.* a radical transformation of the Church's theological teaching and method of government, he never preached revolt, *i.e.* the organization of a modernist schism apart from the Church. This is borne out by his remaining publications, to which we may now turn. *A much-abused letter* (see p. 168 above) was published in the autumn of 1906, and need not detain us further.

Through Scylla and Charybdis: or the old theology and the new (1907) is a collection of essays and articles, most of which had been previously published, and several of which we have had occasion already to notice. Tyrrell says that in this volume 'he throws down his cards on the table'; and, having done so, he appears to have thought at the time that he might have nothing more to say by way of apologetic. His object, therefore, is to place beyond all doubt the nature of his apologetic, the keynote of which is the distinction he draws between revelation and theology, between the 'prophetic truth' of the former and the 'fact-truth' of the latter. He entitles his book 'Through Scylla and Charybdis' because he thinks to avoid the errors both of the old theology—with its unchanging dogmatic system—and of the new—with its reduction of Christianity to a mere evolutionary process without any necessarily permanent content. For since he denies that there can be any development in revelation—'God our Father; Christ crucified and risen; the Holy Spirit, etc., are

identical values for all times and capacities' (p. 353)—he can
claim that his thought is in some respects more conservative
or 'old-fashioned' than that of Newman or Loisy (p. 335),
though in other respects he admits it is more radical. It is
unquestionably more radical than Newman's, because in
refusing any final or absolute truth to theological propositions
or formulas it involves a complete break with traditional
views of the nature of dogma.

The strength of the position is that, since the conclusions of
theology are admittedly provisional and analogous, it can
fearlessly profess its willingness to come to terms with
science and historical criticism. None the less Tyrrell still
maintains that the Church's 'belief in herself as an historical
religion implies her assurance that there are parts of her
traditional history against which criticism will, as a fact,
never prevail'. He transmutes the idea of the original
depositum fidei by saying that the apostolic revelation is
'classical and normative'; but it is not clear why it should be
so, except that it has been. This weakness is a consequence of
his failure to recognize or to require that a theology or
theory of religion, which is ultimately to satisfy the mind,
must be coherent with a theory of the universe as a whole.

Medievalism, published in 1908, is a reply to Cardinal
Mercier's Lenten pastoral of that year, in which he had communicated to his diocesans the encyclical *Pascendi's* condemnation of modernism and singled out Tyrrell as its leading
exponent. *Medievalism*, we are told, was written at great
speed; it is not the most profound of Tyrrell's writings. It
savours too much of controversial propaganda, and the style
is sometimes more rhetorical than eloquent. Nevertheless,
it is a vigorous and clear-sighted exposition of the pretensions
of papal absolutism and an incisive criticism of their historical
development. Tyrrell writes with prophetic fire as though the
days of papal absolutism were numbered, and affects an
optimism about the modernist movement which was hardly

justified by its circumstances. He has in fact to admit that it is only by a *tour de force* that he can maintain the authenticity of his own interpretation of Roman Catholicism. Miss Petre informs us that it was at about this time that he was most strongly tempted to return to the Church of England.[1]

Christianity at the cross roads, which was published post-humously, is the last declaration of Tyrrell's faith (he died on July 15th, 1909). We will not say the *final* declaration, for his early and unforeseen death prevented his thought from reaching any final term. But it is a declaration of faith, and not of scepticism, and of faith both Christian and Catholic, however incompatible it may be with existing Roman Catholicism. It is necessary to insist on this since from two different sides a contrary impression has been given currency. Albert Houtin, in *Ma vie laïque* (1928), p. 255,[2] says, 'Tyrrell was a pure sceptic', and quotes a letter to himself which is supposed to confirm this statement. It is certain—his biographer had shown that this was so—that in some moods and to some correspondents Tyrrell did make sceptical, negative and reckless remarks which are quite inconsistent with his published work, but it is by the latter that his real and considered attitude must be determined.[3] Again, on the other side, Bernard Holland, in his memoir of von Hügel,[4] misrepresented Tyrrell's attitude, although from a different motive, when he wrote: 'Virtually (Tyrrell) had reached, on the negative road, the same point as Alfred Loisy or Marcel Hébert'. Loisy himself has shown how crudely misleading such an assertion is.[5]

Christianity at the cross roads is the enunciation, rather than a proffered solution, of a problem (see p. xvi). Tyrrell had

[1] *Life of Tyrrell*, II, 373.   [2] Cp. also *Une vie de prêtre*,[2] p. 434.
[3] Cp. *Life*, II, 399; von Hügel in the *Hibbert Journal* (January, 1910): 'His works...are the fullest expression of his deliberate thought'; and *Selected letters*, p. 165; and A. Fawkes, *Studies in modernism*, p. 11.
[4] *Selected letters*, p. 26.   [5] *Mémoires*, III, 129 ff.

recently read Schweitzer, and this had quickened his realization of the contrast between the Christ of liberal Protestantism (Harnack) and the Christ of eschatology (J. Weiss and
Loisy). He felt, and felt with some truth (cp. p. 170 above),
that hitherto, while accepting the latter, he had tried to retain
much of the former. The problem, as he sees it now, is as
follows: The Christ of eschatology is substantially the same
as the Christ of Catholic tradition and experience, that is, a
supernatural, otherworldly, transcendent, essentially mysterious Christ. But it is exactly these characteristics of the
original gospel and of Catholicism too that are most alien to
the modern outlook. For modernity is distinguished by its
belief in evolution and progress; its idealism is purely
humanitarian, the goal of its aspiration a perfected human
society on earth. With all this liberal Protestantism is quite
harmonious.

But Catholicism, like the historic Christ, cuts right across
modernity, and in doing so represents far more truly than
liberal Protestantism the abiding content of religion as
something more and other than morality touched with
emotion or a sanctified worldliness. With prophetic conviction Tyrrell declares that modern faith in humanity and
progress is doomed to disillusion and that the human spirit
will never find ultimate satisfaction in the reduction of
religion to so impoverished a faith. Yet, while Christ and
Catholicism do justice to the world's need and to the abiding
truth about human life, the official Church, in its present form,
is failing to do this, because of the corruptions and errors
against which modernism exists to protest. The universal
religion of the future will have, for instance, fully to accept
the results of the scientific movement.

Because Roman Catholicism preserves most completely
all the values of the past, it is of existing Christian institutions
the best qualified by radical transformation to become the
body out of which the Church of the future will grow.

Modernists do not believe that 'the Roman bureaucracy, that exploits even the Papacy', will ever resign its ascendancy. 'Their whole hope is in the irresistible tide of truth and knowledge, which must at last surround and overmount the barriers of ignorance, buttressed up by untruthfulness; and, above all, in such inward and living Christianity as may still be left in a rapidly dying Church' (p. 280).

This paragraph ends the book:

It is the spirit of Christ that has again and again saved the Church from the hands of her worldly oppressors within and without; for where that spirit is, there is liberty. Deliverance comes from below, from those who are bound, not from those who bind. It is easy to quench a glimmering light caught by the eyes of a few; but not the light of the noon-day sun—of knowledge that has become objective and valid for all. It is through knowledge of this kind that God has inaugurated a new epoch in man's intellectual life and extended his lordship over Nature. Shall He do less for man's spiritual life when the times are ripening? and are they not ripening? Are we not hastening to an *impasse*—to one of those extremities which are God's opportunities? (p. 282).

It was then a dilemma that Tyrrell bequeathed to any who cared to receive his bequest; but it was a dilemma of faith and not of scepticism. He did not believe, we are told, that his statement of it was 'likely to please any party'.[1] The Roman Church was busily occupied in the suppression within its ranks of every manifestation of modernism. And as for the modernist movement itself, this was virtually defunct. It would not be incorrect to describe *Christianity at the cross roads* as its swan-song. 'Modernism', Loisy justly remarks, 'as a party of open resistance to the Roman absolutism, passed away with Tyrrell.'[2]

[1] See Miss Petre's preface to *op. cit.* p. x.
[2] *Mémoires*, III, 127. Loisy said almost the same thing as early as November, 1909; see Houtin, *Histoire du modernisme catholique*, p. 269. Von Hügel also regarded Tyrrell's death as marking the end of the modernist movement, *Selected letters*, p. 248.

We need not tell here the familiar and moving story of Tyrrell's death and burial; for the attendant circumstances in no way altered his position *vis-à-vis* the Church. That he received the sacraments on his death-bed is irrelevant. He had not 'retracted his errors', and Miss Petre, by immediately making a public statement to this effect, prevented the growth of a contrary legend. The ecclesiastical authorities therefore had no other course open to them but to refuse Catholic burial; their refusal was perfectly consistent with their principles, and is simply one more illustration of the way in which they applied those principles in their treatment of the modernists. That a heretic should retract on his death-bed the convictions for which he has lived is in itself of little consequence, but such a retractation can be handsomely exploited for the edification of the faithful. In the case of an heresiarch the edification is greatly increased. Tyrrell had not intended that his memory should be exploited in this way.

Chapter XX

LOISY AND TYRRELL

The foregoing account of Tyrrell's career will have shown that, however much there was in common between what modernism meant to him and what it meant to Loisy—and there was much—yet there was almost as much that was different between them. Before we pass on, it may be instructive to notice the contrast between Tyrrell and Loisy in their respective reactions to the failure, or at least to the condemnation, of the modernist movement. M. Loisy himself has provided a text for any such comparison in his reviews of *Christianity at the cross roads*, which appeared in two French periodicals in 1911:

The mystical point of view (he wrote) is so predominant in Tyrrell's book that undoubtedly he draws nearer to Protestantism (than to Catholicism). A book, which Tyrrell well understood, and which he even defends in his own against mistaken interpretations, *L'Évangile et l'Église*, while making faith the vital element in religion, insisted far more on the social character of Christianity, on the necessity of a control of faith by reason, and on the function of ecclesiastical authority, of which Tyrrell now speaks only to desire and to predict its ruin. *L'Évangile et l'Église* contained a modest program of perhaps necessary reforms; Tyrrell's work is a prophecy of revolution; both may rest together in the graveyard of heresies.

And again:

Between (Tyrrell's) modernism and that of *L'Évangile et l'Église* there is the distance which separates a very ardent mysticism from the simple examination of a given belief, of a given institution, of a given situation. Of *L'Évangile et l'Église* it has been said that it was quite Catholic, but hardly Christian in the

Protestant sense of the word. Tyrrell's book, on the other hand, is thoroughly Christian, but hardly Catholic.[1]

In France there might be no need to add anything to these words; in England they require some commentary, for we do not use the terms 'Catholic' and 'Protestant' in the same context here as there. As we have observed above (see pp. 89 f.), in France Catholicism means the Roman Church as it at present exists. Belief in God, in Christ, in the Church, each is an integral, not a separable part of the profession of Catholicism. Hence when a Frenchman abandons Catholicism, he does not normally pass over to Protestantism, nor does he remain a Christian nor even a theist, but he becomes an unbeliever. For this reason too attempts to provide a *via media* between Roman Catholicism and Protestantism, as for instance that made by Père Hyacinthe Loyson,[2] have met with no success. In England the position is far more complicated. We are familiar with an almost infinite number of different forms of Christian profession. Individuals and groups and sects, not to mention the established Church as such, combine acceptance of some elements of the Christian tradition with rejection of others in a bewildering variety of ways. In particular, the acknowledgment of devotion to the person of Christ on the part of individuals, who have a very uncertain degree of theistic belief and who more or less deliberately disown all forms of existing institutional Christianity, is a common phenomenon.

Now it is this last kind of faith, this personal devotion to Christ, which we suppose Loisy to have in mind when he speaks of the Protestant sense of the word 'Christian'. It is the faith of an individual, which is determined by his own particular thought or temperament, and which does not, consciously at least, proceed from, or depend on, membership

[1] See Loisy, *Mémoires*, III, 139.
[2] See Houtin, *Le Père Hyacinthe, réformateur catholique*, 1869–1883 (1922).

of a religious society, 'une patrie des âmes', a Church. Loisy's own faith in Catholicism, and in modernism too, had been of the latter kind, and thus from the moment when he ceased through excommunication to be a member of the Church his profession of Catholic or Christian or modernist faith ceased also.[1] It seemed absurd to him to profess to be a Catholic 'malgré le pape'. Because Tyrrell had faith of the individual kind as well, his modernism survived, and even thrived on, his excommunication, and he died professing to defend Catholic principles against the Vatican heresies.[2]

[1] Cp. Petre, *Hibbert Journal* (April, 1922), p. 405.
[2] See Tyrrell's will; *Life*, II, 434.

PART IV

OTHER MODERNISTS:
OTHER MODERNISMS

Since, in our judgment, a right understanding of the modernist movement depends on a recognition of the fact that it consisted mainly of individual attempts to advance a revision of traditional orthodoxy, and since these attempts differed considerably according to the particular motives and the specialized interests of those who made them, it follows that a complete study of our subject would require an investigation of the origins and outcome of the work of each individual modernist. This essay does not pretend to be a complete study of the movement, but it is intended to be a veracious and an objective one. We have refused to base our study on any partial theory about the nature of modernism; we have insisted on the importance of remembering that there were as many modernisms as there were modernists. For this reason, the careers of those who were, by general consent, the two leading modernists have in Parts II and III been traced in some detail. In Part IV we must be content to indicate in more summary fashion the most important of such other attempts to revise traditional orthodoxy as fell under the condemnation of the encyclical Pascendi, or which at least were intended to do so by those who drew it up. In some cases the task will be facilitated by the possibility of referring by way of comparison or contrast to the work of Loisy and Tyrrell.

The references to books, in the text as well as in the footnotes, will show from what sources information has been derived.

Chapter XXI

IN FRANCE

What is called philosophical modernism was a prominent, if secondary, feature of the movement in France. Here it may be supposed that we have to do with a group which has sufficient cohesion to be regarded as a single school of thought. Maurice Blondel (b. 1861),[1] Père Laberthonnière (1860–1932),[2] and Édouard Le Roy (b. 1870)[3] were all exponents of what is known as 'the philosophy of action', but they did not collaborate and a close view reveals that there was a considerable difference between them, specially in the extent to which their writings were ostensibly inconsistent with traditional orthodoxy. Thus Blondel, the originator of the philosophy of action, applied it to Catholic dogma in such a way as to support the traditional views about the history of Christian origins, and probably for this reason, although as early as 1894 his first book, *L'Action* (1893), had been

[1] Blondel was a pupil of Ollé-Laprune (1839–1898), to whom *L'Action* is dedicated, and who was to some extent influenced by Newman; cp. pp. 54 f. above. Blondel has protested against the suggestion that his master was 'among the initiators of modernism'; see his *Léon Ollé-Laprune* (1923), p. 109. In *Le problème de la philosophie catholique* (1932) he recapitulates his earlier work, and he is said to be preparing a complete statement of his whole philosophy.

[2] Laberthonnière directed the *Annales de philosophie chrétienne* from 1905 to 1913, when the review was put on the Index, and he himself prohibited by the holy see from all further publications. See M. D. Petre, *Hibbert Journal* (April, 1933), pp. 417–26. Cp. *Revue de métaphysique et de morale* (Oct.–Dec. 1932), supplement, p. 16: 'Lui, qui débordait de pensées...lui qui prononçait en son fond le mot de saint Anselme: *Potius mori quam tacere*, il souffrit plus que la mort en se taisant près de vingt ans'. His books, *Essais de philosophie religieuse* and *Le réalisme chrétien et l'idéalisme grec*, were put on the Index on April 4th, 1906.

[3] On Le Roy, see pp. 188 ff. below.

threatened with condemnation, and although he has been commonly classified among the modernists,[1] he was never actually condemned.

On the contrary, Pius X is said (after 1910) to have sent him a message through the archbishop of Aix to the effect that he was 'sure of his orthodoxy'.[2] E. Buonaiuti in his *Le modernisme catholique* (1927), p. 92, writes: 'Profoundly attached to the external discipline of the Catholic society, and besides perfectly consistent with himself, Maurice Blondel has stubbornly denied that he had any responsibility for the modernist movement'. J. Rivière too in *Le modernisme dans l'Église* (1929), p. 122, gives him a certificate of good character.[3] Nevertheless, although both friends and foes of modernism are now prepared thus to exonerate Blondel, it cannot be denied that it was an adaptation or interpretation of his philosophy, as well as of Bergson's, Boutroux', etc., that gave rise to the modernism of Laberthonnière and Le Roy.

The philosophy of action is anti-intellectualist in the sense that it denies that ultimate truth can be reached simply through intellectual processes, dialectic, etc., and finally secured by such means in abstract formulas. The attainment of truth involves the activity of the whole of our being— willing and feeling as well as knowing. The word 'action' is used to mean not one particular kind of activity, *e.g.* doing as opposed to thinking, but the whole of our life with all that is given in our experience, that is to say a reality that is always in movement, always incomplete, always becoming. Faith accordingly does not consist in accepting with our

---

[1] *E.g.* P. Sabatier, *Modernism* (1908), p. 163; cp. B. Holland in von Hügel's *Selected letters*, p. 12; F. Woodlock, *Modernism and the Christian Church* (1925), p. 55. Guido de Ruggiero, *Modern philosophy* (1921), refers to Blondel as 'the spiritual father' of the modernist movement (quoted by K. Gilbert, *Maurice Blondel's philosophy of action* (1924), p. 2).

[2] K. Gilbert, *op. cit.* p. 4.

[3] Cp. J. Wehrle, *Revue biblique* (July, 1905), p. 330.

intellect dogmas which are revealed to us from entirely beyond our experience and, as it were, imposed upon us from outside. We approach and realize the supernatural from within. Our thinking, willing, feeling, when closely scrutinized, are found to demand an object beyond the natural, finite order. The method of immanence, as it was called, *i.e.* the analysis of our own inmost life, is thus shown to lead to a doctrine of transcendence: it shows that the natural postulates the supernatural. Faith is not a final or static condition; it is an attitude or orientation of the whole personality.

This is, of course, a very inadequate summary of the general tenor of the line of philosophical thought, which was worked out in various ways by Blondel, Laberthonnière, and Le Roy. It was obviously alien to the traditional teaching of the theological schools, and it inevitably provoked discussion and controversy. Nevertheless, its expediency as a method of apologetic, *i.e.* as a means of commending Catholicism to those who shared the common presuppositions of much contemporary non-Catholic thought, might have been allowed, as indeed it has been in the case of Blondel himself; but, when the philosophy of action was put forward as a substitute for scholasticism, and still more when it was applied in such a way as to call in question the traditional views of dogma in general and of this dogma or that in particular, it was unlikely to meet even with toleration from ecclesiastical authority. It was because Laberthonnière[1] and Le Roy did this that they were condemned, while Blondel escaped. It was in fact precisely in so far as they urged such a revision of the idea of dogma as would make it compatible with the conclusions of modern biblical and historical criticism that they were modernists, and consequently our view is once more confirmed that this was, more than any other, the crucial issue in the modernist movement.

Just as Loisy appropriated the suggestions contained in

[1] *E.g.* see E. Barbier, *Histoire du catholicisme libéral* (1924), IV, 215.

Newman's *Essay on development* and extended and applied
them in ways from which Newman himself would have
shrunk in horror, so in like manner Laberthonnière and Le
Roy (and Tyrrell too) utilized the suggestions contained in
The grammar of assent, notably the idea that the certitude of
faith is not the outcome of a conclusive intellectual demonstration, but that it depends largely on the will. This is not
to say that the philosophy of action (or 'moral dogmatism'
as it is also called) was, any more than *L'Évangile et l'Église*, a
direct consequence of Newman's work;[1] it was inspired and
evoked by influences and circumstances which Newman at
most dimly foresaw. William James, Boutroux, Bergson,[2]
contributed more to it than Newman. But Newman's work
at least provided an impressive precedent for the attempt
to put forward a new philosophy of faith independently
of scholasticism. The scholastic theologians had viewed
Newman with suspicion, not to say with hostility; in the
modernists the dangerous tendencies which they had suspected seemed to be fully realized.

The clearest and most provocative expression of French
philosophical modernism was Le Roy's *Dogme et critique*
(1907). Le Roy was a lay professor of mathematics, and in
philosophy a thoroughgoing Bergsonian.[3] *Dogme et critique*
contains an article entitled 'Qu'est-ce qu'un dogme?' that he
had published in 1905, together with letters and further articles
designed to answer criticisms. He definitely rejects what he
calls the 'intellectualist' conception of dogma. A dogma is

---

[1] It is significant, for instance, that Le Roy's references to Newman in
Dogme et critique are all second-hand; there is no evidence that he had
himself read Newman.

[2] Cp. E. Hermann, *Eucken and Bergson*[2] (1912), pp. 35, 132 f.; P.
Sabatier, *France to-day, its religious orientation* (1913), *passim*. Dr W. M.
Horton says that Laberthonnière 'named Boutroux and Maine de Biran
as the two philosophers who had most deeply influenced him'; *The
philosophy of the abbé Bautain*, p. 293 n.

[3] See his *Une philosophie nouvelle*[2] (1913), p. iv.

not to be regarded as a proposition that must be accepted as absolutely true and binding on the intellect. He admits that this is the ordinary conception. 'God is represented, in the act of revelation, as a very learned professor who must be taken at his word when he communicates to his audience results of which it is not capable of understanding the proofs' (p. 16).

Instead of this conception, which is treated as ridiculous, a dogma is said to have, in the first instance, a negative sense. 'It excludes and condemns certain errors rather than positively determines the truth.' Thus the dogma that 'God is personal' in no way defines the divine personality; it is equivalent to the statement 'God is not impersonal', *i.e.* He is not 'a simple law, a formal category, an ideal principle, an abstract entity'. In so far as they contribute to our speculative knowledge at all, dogmas are the statement, rather than the solution, of problems (cp. p. 277). 'If they formulated absolute truth in adequate terms (if we may suppose such a fiction to have any sense), they would be unintelligible to us. If they provided us only with imperfect, relative, and changing truth, they could not rightly command unconditional acceptance' (p. 23).

But a Catholic can and does accept dogmas unreservedly, and he does so rightly because a dogma is above all *une prescription d'ordre pratique, une règle de conduite pratique* (p. 25). Thus 'God is personal' means 'behave in your relations with God as you do in your relations with a human person'. Or again, 'Jesus is risen' means 'your attitude to Him should be what it would have been before His death; you are to regard Him as a contemporary'.

Le Roy denies that this pragmatic conception of dogmas should be interpreted as involving absolute agnosticism with regard to their theoretical or historical truth. But it is their practical implication which is of first importance and which has to be accepted unconditionally by all the faithful. He tries to maintain that this is what the Church has always been concerned to insist on, and that it is only the intellectualism of the dominant theological schools which upholds the ordinary conception of dogma, a conception which raises insuperable difficulties from the point of view of modern philosophy or of historical criticism.

However this may be, in attempting to answer the attacks of his theological critics, Le Roy made admissions which the official Church was in no temper to allow or to endorse. For instance, with regard to the Resurrection (pp. 155–258), he specifically abandons belief in the miraculous disappearance of the Lord's Body from the sepulchre. *Dogme et critique* was put on the Index on July 26th, 1907.

Chapter XXII

IN ITALY

'No one dreams of denying the existence and the virulence of Italian modernism,' says J. Rivière.[1] But it is not so easy in Italy, as in France, to differentiate between the various forms which the movement assumed. For in Italy the development of theological or doctrinal modernism, the sort of modernism which is the subject of this essay, was closely bound up with, and to some extent consequent upon, the 'Christian democrat' movement,[2] whereas in France they were comparatively distinct. The Christian democrat movement was prior in point of time; in the closing years of the nineteenth century it attracted a considerable following among the younger generation of Catholics. At the death of Leo XIII there was in Italy, writes A. Houtin, 'a large party of young men who had, it is true, neither moustaches nor money, but who loved liberty and who wanted to believe that it was compatible with the religion in which they had been brought up'.[3]

The leader of this party was Don Romolo Murri (b. 1870). Originally, its liberalism was purely political and social, and Murri himself remained a scholastic of the scholastics even

[1] *Le modernisme dans l'Église*, p. 89. On Italian modernism, in addition to the books which will be cited in the text, see the following which contain useful information: L. H. Jordan, *Modernism in Italy* (1909); A. Houtin, *Histoire du modernisme catholique* (1913), pp. 106–12 *et passim*; E. Buonaiuti, *Le modernisme catholique* (1927), chap. v; J. Rivière, *op. cit.* pp. 89–93, 274–87, 402–15; J. Schnitzer, *Der katholische Modernismus* (1912), pp. 114–51; R. Murri, articles in the *Hibbert Journal* (July, 1922, and July, 1926); G. la Piana, 'A review of Italian modernism' (*Harvard Theological Review*, October, 1916).

[2] On the aims of the Christian democrats, see Jordan, *op. cit.* p. 28, and la Piana, *loc. cit.*

[3] *Histoire du modernisme catholique*, p. 110.

during the later stages of the movement.[1] It was chiefly among the Christian democrats that the French modernists, when their teaching began to penetrate into Italy, found disciples. Thus the two movements converged, although they never became identical. Theological modernism in Italy was *un sous-produit*.[2] On its critical side it was derived largely from Loisy, on its philosophical side from the French philosophers of action. This is not to say that Italian modernism had no scholars of its own. On the contrary, priests, such as G. Semeria, Genocchi and Minocchi, who disseminated the results of biblical criticism, etc., through their lectures and reviews, were men of genuine learning and wide culture, if not of marked originality.

A. Houtin suggested[3] that von Hügel sowed the seeds of doctrinal modernism during the visits which he paid to Rome about 1891–3. Von Hügel did no doubt from that time onwards act as the international liaison officer of the movement, but in this particular case Houtin's suggestion appears to be too conjectural, and if true is of too little consequence, to be regarded as of much importance. Buonaiuti, who in this matter is a more reliable authority, considers that January, 1901, ought to be reckoned as the birthday of modernism in Italy, since Minocchi then began the publication of the periodical, *Studi religiosi*, which continued to be the principal organ of the movement during the following years. Biblical and other theological questions were there expounded with prudence, but from a definitely critical standpoint, and new ideas were insinuated largely through book reviews, a favourite device of those who wish to innovate with caution.

[1] Murri was a priest; H. D. A. Major (*English modernism*, p. 20) is mistaken in saying that he and Minocchi were laymen. On Murri's scholasticism, see Loisy, *Mémoires*, II, 520, 561, 570, III, 95; la Piana, *loc. cit.* p. 367.   [2] Rivière, *op. cit.* p. 89.

[3] *Histoire du modernisme catholique*, p. 108.

The other periodicals, *e.g. Il Rinnovamento* and *Nova et vetera*, which became a prominent, though transitory, feature of Italian modernism, and to which Tyrrell contributed articles, did not begin publication till 1907 or after. These were controlled by groups of younger men, who if they had more zeal had also less discretion and less solid learning than Minocchi and Semeria. These younger Italian modernists were prone to hasty generalizations; their restatements of Catholicism were too facile to be of much enduring worth. They were prone also to quarrel among themselves.[1]

Meanwhile, the most important accession to the ranks of the Italian modernists was that of Senator Antonio Fogazzaro (1842–1911), the famous novelist and poet, who was said to be 'the leading Catholic layman in Italy'.[2] Fogazzaro's conversion to modernism was not sudden, for he had always been a liberal Catholic. In his youth, when he had abandoned the practice of religion, it was Gratry's *La philosophie du Credo* that brought him back (1873). From an early period he had been a student and adherent of Darwin's theory of evolution.[3] But his chief master was Rosmini.[4]

No decree issued at Rome (he wrote in 1883) will ever persuade me that certain books, such as Antonio Rosmini's *The five wounds of the Church*, are evil....I detest all intolerance, that petty formalism in which many would imprison the religious sentiment.[5]

Antonio Rosmini...one of the most powerful philosophers of our century, and who is still held in veneration by that portion of the clergy which is not jesuitical, wrote of the ills of the Church, but failed to enumerate them all....But does the fact that the Church is ill constitute a good reason for forsaking her?[6]

[1] Cp. Loisy, *Mémoires*, III, 137; Buonaiuti, *op. cit.* pp. 109f.
[2] In the introduction (unsigned) to *The Saint* (1906), p. v.
[3] T. Gallarati-Scotti, *The life of Antonio Fogazzaro* (n.d.), pp. 44, 118; on this book see Loisy, *Mémoires*, III, 241, 404.
[4] *Life of Fogazzaro*, pp. 167ff.   [5] *Ibid.* p. 74.   [6] *Ibid.* p. 75.

Again, in 1893, he wrote to a correspondent:

I feel bound to entreat you to re-examine your opinions concerning the immovability of Catholicism; to examine whether within Catholicism itself not dogma but the interpretation of dogma be not undergoing a continuous process of evolution; I must beg you to ascertain whether within Catholicism itself there be not, besides the force that tends to preserve ancient forms, a force that tends to produce new ones...whether this absolute immovability be not merely the tendency, the programme of a party in the Church.[1]

Here obviously was fertile soil in which the seed of modernism would flourish. It was Semeria, Fogazzaro says, who finally made clear to him 'that a knowledge of Biblical criticism is indispensable'.[2] He was largely influenced too by the writings of Blondel, Laberthonnière, Loisy, Houtin, and Tyrrell.[3]

The immense success of *Il Santo* (1905) brought him to the forefront of the modernist movement. This novel was translated into French, English, and German; it was put on the Index (April, 1906), but this only had the effect of increasing its sales.[4] *Il Santo*[5] is an appeal for a comprehensive reform of the Roman Church from within. It has been said that it puts 'into our hands a résumé of what is essential in the thought of Blondel, Laberthonnière, Loisy, Newman and Tyrrell'.[6] Such a statement must not be taken *au pied de la lettre*, but it truly indicates that Fogazzaro sought to constitute himself the mouthpiece of all the manifold reformist tendencies which were at work in the Church.

In a typical passage a group of young men address the Saint as follows:

We were educated in the Catholic faith, and on attaining manhood we—by an act of our own free will—accepted its most

---

[1] *Life of Fogazzaro*, p. 137.   [2] *Ibid*. p. 205.
[3] *Ibid*. pp. 200f., 205, 216.   [4] J. Rivière, *op. cit.* pp. 307f.
[5] Reference is here made to the Eng. trans. published by Hodder and Stoughton in 1906.
[6] Quoted by Houtin, *op. cit.* p. 136.

arduous mysteries; we have laboured in the faith, both in the administrative and social field (*sic*); but now another mystery rises in our way, and our faith falters before it. The Catholic Church, calling herself the fountain of truth, to-day opposes the search after truth when her foundations, the sacred books, the formulae of her dogmas, her alleged infallibility, become objects of research. To us this signifies that she no longer has faith in herself. The Catholic Church, which proclaims herself the channel of life, to-day fetters and stifles all that is youthful within her, to-day seeks to prop up all that is tottering and aged within her. To us these things mean death, distant, but inevitable death (p. 242).

The Saint, keenly alive to these aspirations for a regeneration of Catholicism, has a dramatic interview with the pope, whom he tells that the life of the Church is corrupted by four evil spirits, viz. (1) falsehood, (2) domination of the clergy, (3) avarice, and (4) immovability (pp. 281 ff.).

The pope, an idealized, if not sentimentalized, figure, is represented as sympathizing with the Saint's ideas, but as too old and too uncertain to undertake any general policy of reform. In his reply to the Saint he says:

You...have to deal with the Lord alone; I have to deal also with the men the Lord has placed round me, among whom I have to steer my course according to charity and prudence, and above all, I must adapt my counsels, my commands, to the different capacities, the different states of mind of so many millions of men. I am like a poor school-master who, out of seventy scholars, has twenty who are below the average, forty of ordinary ability, and only ten who are really brilliant. He cannot carry on the school for the benefit of the ten brilliant pupils alone, and I cannot govern the Church for you alone or for those who are like you... (p. 291).

Fogazzaro here shrewdly recognizes the difficulties which even a well-disposed pope, *i.e.* one who was personally favourable to the movement for reform or for the toleration of progressive tendencies, would have to overcome if he tried to carry his personal sympathies into practical effect.

Still, like von Hügel,[1] like Lamennais,[2] like Dante and Roger Bacon, he dreamed of a *papa angelico*, who in God's good time would arise and do the seemingly impossible (cp. p. 64).

It is evident that Fogazzaro's modernism was in quality much more like Tyrrell's than Loisy's. It included in its scope a reinterpretation of dogma and a full acceptance of historical and biblical criticism, but it was primarily the prophecy of a great spiritual revival of the Franciscan kind and it was inspired by a mystical fervour. Fogazzaro was not a *savant*, and he was incapable of being dispassionately intellectual.[3]

Loisy has reproduced the following terse entry from his journal: '13th December, 1905. Fogazzaro has sent me his *Santo*. Very interesting. More orthodox than I'.[4] Later, in 1910, Fogazzaro returned the compliment by publicly dissociating himself from Loisy; he went so far as to say that there was no common ground for discussion between them.[5] But this was after the condemnation of modernism, when Loisy had definitely abandoned Catholicism. Fogazzaro, on the other hand, although he deplored the repressive policy of the Vatican,[6] wanted, like Tyrrell, and more submissively than Tyrrell, to remain a Catholic, and therefore his repudiation of Loisy, if not generous, was at least diplomatic.

Among the literary products of Italian modernism, after *Il Santo*, it was *Il programma dei modernisti*, published on October 28th, 1907, that attracted most attention.[7] Its authorship was anonymous, and it affected to be the reply of an important group of modernists to the encyclical

---

[1] *Eternal life* (1912), p. 363.
[2] Cp. Hon. W. Gibson, *The abbé de Lamennais etc.* (1896), p. 206.
[3] Cp. *Life of Fogazzaro*, pp. 269, 292, 313.
[4] *Mémoires*, II, 457.   [5] Houtin, *op. cit.* p. 317.
[6] See *Life of Fogazzaro*, pp. 277, 290 f.
[7] Eng. trans. *The programme of modernism* (1908), with an introduction by A. L. Lilley, to which reference is here made. Translations were also published in France, America, and Germany.

Pascendi. According to Houtin,[1] it 'was the work of two priests who had received no mandate from their *confrères* and who, consequently, engaged no one but themselves'. As early as 1912, J. Schnitzer attributed it to E. Buonaiuti, who may since be taken to have implicitly acknowledged the truth of this supposition.[2] It may therefore be regarded as chiefly his work and, in spite of its ambitious title, as not necessarily expressing more than his personal opinions. At the same time, it derives a certain representative character from the facts that it was Tyrrell who translated it into English,[3] and that Loisy has expressed his approval of it.[4]

The main contention of the book is that not philosophy but criticism was the presupposition of modernism, a contention which the present writer has already shown that he regards as in the main justified. The modernists had been trained in the traditional scholastic orthodoxy; they had become dissatisfied with this (*a*) because, in its received form, it was incompatible with the assured results of the criticism of the Bible and of the history of Christianity,[5] and (*b*) because as a method of apologetic for Catholicism it was quite unintelligible and unacceptable to men of modern culture.

---

[1] *Histoire du modernisme catholique*, p. 283.

[2] Rivière, *op. cit.* p. 405. It may also be observed that R. Murri in an article in the *Hibbert Journal* (July, 1926, p. 664) says that it is highly probable that Buonaiuti in collaboration with others produced *The programme of modernism.*

[3] The translation was the work not of Lilley, as H. P. V. Nunn (*What is modernism?*, p. 9) and C. Harris (*Creeds or no creeds*, p. 7) assert, but of Tyrrell; see his *Life*, II, 356.

[4] 'L'esprit de ce livre était à peu près le même que celui de mes *Réflexions*' (*Mémoires*, II, 623).

[5] A considerable part of *The programme of modernism* (pp. 27–109) is taken up with an exposition of these 'assured results'. This is, on the whole, a fair and moderate statement of which later research would require only slight modification. There is no trace of the wild and extravagant critical conclusions, which are sometimes attributed to the modernists, and to which Tyrrell refers in a note on p. 141.

In so far as modernists have put forward a fresh philosophical synthesis, they have done so only tentatively: this has not been their first interest. Their main object has been to insist that Catholicism can and must accept the scientific and critical methods, and only as a consequence of this have they suggested a restatement of apologetic.

That the modernist restatement is in a sense 'immanentist' is admitted, but not in the sense of the encyclical. It is certainly impossible for modernists 'to conceive a purely intellectual and speculative faculty, immune from all influence of the will and the emotions', which can demonstrate the existence of God, but they maintain 'that from the knowledge of itself and its own inward experiences...the human spirit in its entirety (including reason, will and feeling), can naturally arrive at a living certainty of the existence of God' (p. 128). Modernists are immanentist (cp. p. 109) in the sense that their apologetic is based on human knowledge and human experience of the supernatural, but they do not deny the ontological reality of the supernatural.

Thus when they distinguish 'the Christ of faith' from 'the Christ of history' they do not suppose 'that from an ontological point of view the historical Christ did not include those ethical values and those religious meanings which Christian experience, by living the Gospel life, has slowly become aware of....Religious facts include mysterious meanings which pure science misses. Faith, with its peculiar power, penetrates to these meanings and feeds on them. It does not create them; it finds them' (pp. 138f.). Modernists therefore are not agnostics; God and the supernatural order are not for them 'the Unknowable'. On the contrary, through the distinction which they draw between 'different orders of knowledge—phenomenal, scientific, philosophic, religious—' they 'contrive to give an enormous expansion to the region of "the knowable"' (pp. 113, 115).

As a reply to the misrepresentations contained in the

encyclical *Pascendi*, *The programme of modernism* is of great interest and value. As a constructive restatement of an apologetic for Catholicism it is too immature and too general to be more than suggestive. It is also marked by an excessive zeal to present Christianity in a form which would be acceptable to men of strictly contemporary culture and of democratic enthusiasms.

It was this excessive zeal, provoked further and further by the extreme rigour of the Church's *non possumus* attitude, which drove many of the Italian modernists into a position that was humanitarian and only vaguely Christian, if not definitely secularist and anti-clerical.

Chapter XXIII

IN GERMANY

The 'virulence' of modernism in Italy is admitted by every-one; in Germany its very existence is a matter of dispute. When the encyclical *Pascendi* was published the German bishops, as well as the Catholic press, denied that it had any relevance to their country.[1] And even in retrospect it has been possible to point to only one 'symptom of doctrinal modernism' prior to 1907.[2] On the other hand, there is the paradoxical fact that nowhere was the opposition to the papal repression of modernism more vigorous than in Germany. It is true that this is not to say very much; but there, and nowhere else, can it be said that this opposition met with a measure of positive success. Various circumstances explain the peculiar characteristics of the movement in Germany.

(1) In the first instance, it is important to recognize that the Roman Catholic Church in Germany has for several reasons an ethos of its own, much more distinctive than that of the Church in other European countries. The Church in France during the nineteenth century ceased to be Gallican and became purely ultramontane. De Maistre, the father of modern ultramontanism, was a Frenchman, and no one did more than Lamennais, the founder of liberal Catholicism, to

[1] Rivière, *op. cit.* pp. 73, 417. On modernism in Germany, see also Houtin, *Histoire du modernisme catholique, passim*; J. Schnitzer, *Der katholische Modernismus* (1912), pp. 7ff., 24–64; E. Buonaiuti, *Le modernisme catholique*, pp. 151–65.

[2] Rivière, *op. cit.* p. 82: 'Comme symptôme de modernisme doctrinal avant 1907, tout juste a-t-on pu relever une conférence sur la notion de foi, prononcée à Munich, en 1905, par le Dr K. Gebert'. Cp. Loisy, *L'Église et la France* (1925), p. 101: 'En Allemagne il y eut quelques modernistes isolés, mais le mouvement n'y atteignit pas, comme en France et en Italie, une partie notable du clergé'.

kill Gallicanism. Catholicism in Germany did not undergo so complete a transformation.

Although early in the century the new ultramontanism had been fashionable, and after the Vatican council it became an essential part of Catholicism, yet it never reached so far in Germany as in France. The Church in Germany, more than elsewhere, succeeded in retaining some of its national and relatively independent character, and there was a strong vein of resistance to any further extension of the papal prerogatives and powers. The defection of the 'Old Catholics' and the career of Döllinger were extreme instances of this resistance; but the general submission to the Vatican decrees did not by any means imply that extreme ultramontane tendencies had free course. German Catholicism was not only politically less ultramontane, but theologically less so as well. Neither the old nor the new scholasticism was able to dominate and monopolize the theological schools, as was the case elsewhere.

This was largely due to the existence of the Catholic universities alongside the Protestant ones. Catholic scholars here were, by force of circumstances, in much closer connexion with the general development of modern culture than they were in France, Italy or England. If they were not pioneers in criticism, they had at least to adapt themselves to critical methods. Their apologetic, while not modernist, had to be related to modern needs. Nor must we ignore the natural tendency of Teutonic pride to regard its Catholicism, which thus happened to be a comparatively liberal Catholicism, as superior to that of the Latin races.[1]

(2) These distinctive tendencies in German Catholicism found from time to time expression in the work of some

---

[1] The interesting, but too facile, generalization of A. Fawkes, *Studies in modernism*, p. 375, should be noticed: 'Modernism proper is a movement of the Latin mind.... Its home is in the Latin countries—France and Italy; and at the head of every department of its activity stands a man of Latin race'.

influential teacher; and at the turn of the century there were two noteworthy instances of this. Fr.-X. Kraus (1840–1901), a distinguished ecclesiastical historian, attacked political ultramontanism, the papal absolutism and the increasing centralization of power in the Roman Curia. H. Schell (1850–1906)[1] was an original, although obscure, philosopher and theologian, some of whose writings were put on the Index in 1898. His 'errors' were concerned with such matters as original sin and everlasting punishment; it does not appear that he desired a revision of dogma in general or of the traditional Christology in particular. The teaching of Kraus and Schell inspired the *Reformkatholizismus* movement. This 'reformist Catholicism' was not substantially different from the liberal Catholic movements of the nineteenth century, and it had none of the characteristic features of modernism. In fact, just because Catholicism in Germany was less retrograde than elsewhere, and less in need of drastic revision, there was less disposition to adopt the radical apologetic of modernism. In theology, the intelligent moderate conservative is less likely than the obscurantist to become a radical. The *Reformkatholizismus* movement did, however, provide conditions in which a lively interest was taken in the modernist movement in other countries, and those few German Catholics, who subsequently became declared modernists, had no doubt been influenced by the teaching of Kraus and Schell.

(3) If then *Lamentabili* and *Pascendi* were coldly received in Germany, it was not because German bishops or theologians felt that their own teaching had been condemned, but because they saw that the papal acts, through their extreme conservatism in regard to biblical and historical criticism and the glorification of scholasticism as the only philosophy that was worthy of the name, played straight into the hands of

[1] See J. B. Pett, *Revue du clergé français* (January 15th, 1898), pp. 310–26: 'Un théologien novateur en Allemagne'.

Protestants and of unbelievers. How could Catholic professors any longer claim to exercise a proper liberty of research in their studies or perfect candour in their teaching? And most objectionable of all were the practical measures proposed by the encyclical, *e.g.* the institution of 'councils of vigilance' in every diocese and the régime of delation which such an institution implied. So strong was the feeling in Germany on this point that the holy see did not dare to enforce the prescriptions of the encyclical.[1]

The German opposition to the anti-modernist oath is to be understood in a similar sense. It does not mean that the university professors, who were dispensed from taking the oath, were modernists, but that they were unwilling to be humiliated before their Protestant colleagues and to have their position as scholars hampered and restricted by the extravagant demands of the papacy. Those scholars, who after 1907 had declared themselves as modernists, *e.g.* J. Schnitzer and T. Engert, had been excommunicated before 1910, and therefore were not qualified to take advantage of the dispensation from the oath. Nor need they detain us; in no case were they men of the first rank or of any marked originality. It may be true that modern theological movements have usually originated in Germany, but this was not true of Catholic modernism. The statement that it did originate there, which has sometimes been made, is the result either of confusing Catholic modernism with liberal Protestantism, or of the curious supposition that since no good thing can come out of Germany all evils must originate there.

Germany produced no modernist of the stature of Loisy, Tyrrell, Le Roy, or Fogazzaro. After the excitement of the crisis had died down, German Catholicism proceeded on its way, affected by the repression of modernism somewhat less than other countries, just as it had been little affected by the movement itself.

[1] Houtin, *Histoire du modernisme catholique*, p. 229.

Chapter XXIV

IN ENGLAND

It is remarkable that of the two modernists in England, who played a part of first importance in the movement—Tyrrell and von Hügel—neither was of English birth. And of the two others, who became at all conspicuous—Miss Petre and Alfred Fawkes—the latter was not so much a modernist as a liberal Protestant.

Baron Friedrich von Hügel (1852–1925)[1] was, as Miss Petre has said, in the early stages of the movement 'not only a leader, but an arch-leader'.[2] Later events tended, in England at least, to obscure his career as a modernist and he came to be regarded, not inaccurately, as a broad-minded, but in the last resort an orthodox and submissive, Roman Catholic. This was partly because his own major writings,[3] his best known and most influential writings, were mainly concerned with subjects that were not directly involved in the modernist controversy. But the obscuring of von Hügel's modernism was also due to the modification which, from

---

[1] See B. Holland's memoir prefixed to *Selected letters* (1927); the writer of this memoir was evidently more in sympathy with von Hügel's later, than with his earlier, attitude to the modernist movement. It should also be noticed (p. 67) that he does not profess to give a full or representative selection of the Baron's modernist correspondence. For a more understanding, though briefer, treatment of his relation to the modernist movement, see Miss Petre's article in the *Hibbert Journal* for October, 1925. Von Hügel's correspondence with Loisy, published in the latter's *Mémoires*, is also of great importance.

[2] *Hibbert Journal, loc. cit.*

[3] *The mystical element of religion* (1908), *Eternal life* (1912), *Essays and addresses* (two series, 1921 and 1926).

about 1907 onwards, it did in fact undergo.[1] Nevertheless, even in the latter period, he did not abandon, however much he ceased to emphasize, what had been a primary object of the modernist movement, viz. that 'Catholics...should claim and obtain full freedom in all regions of history and science, and fearlessly face and adopt the fully demonstrated results of such research'.[2]

Von Hügel's parentage and upbringing[3] had been such as to fit him for a life of European activity. He had thrown himself with zest into the wide stream of modern culture, scientific, historical, philosophical, and both in reading and writing he was at ease with English, French, German, and Italian. His intellectual gifts were massive rather than brilliant. 'The Baron's mind', wrote his biographer, in a style not unlike the Baron's own, 'was laborious, many-side regarding, fully weighing, slow-moving, deep-ploughing. He thought and wrote slowly and with difficulty, writing and rewriting, and again rewriting, and qualifying, because so anxious not to overstate or understate his case, and to see what could be said both for and against every position, with the aim of arriving at the most exact possible truth.'[4]

His spiritual gifts were not less massive than his intellectual gifts. During his early manhood he had passed through a severe crisis, spiritual and moral as well as intellectual. But

[1] His reputation has been so redeemed that a Jesuit reviewer in *The Month* (June, 1933, p. 563) is able to write: '*Although the Baron always opposed Modernism*, there was yet within him a sneaking regard for some of its showy claims....Despite his aberrations and his mistakes, he showed by his action no less than by his written and spoken word that he regarded authority and submission to it to be the essence of any true religion' (italics ours).

[2] B. Holland, *op. cit.* p. 30.

[3] For details see B. Holland, as also for an account of those persons and books which specially influenced him.

[4] B. Holland, *op. cit.* p. 13.

through this crisis his faith passed on[1] to that ever-increasing richness of assurance which is typical of Catholic sanctity and mysticism in all ages. It was quite unlike the easy and narrow intellectual assurance which is often exhibited by Catholic, and not only by Catholic, theologians. Von Hügel's faith and spiritual life were inextricably bound up with devoted allegiance to the Roman Church, and, however stringently he criticized the Church's human limitations and corruptions,[2] he could never forget that it was—at least for him and all those within it—the God-given agency through which there was mediated to man the experience of that supernatural world which is his eternal home. Thus, he was never able, like Loisy, to regard the service of truth as ultimately separable from the service of the Church.

From about 1890 onwards he began to enter, through personal intercourse and correspondence, into close contact with all the leading modernists, although they were not yet of course known by that name. He made it his business to encourage the special work of each, to introduce them to the work of each other, to criticize where he detected timidity or superficiality, to suggest fresh lines of thought and wider ranges of study. We have seen how important in this way was the encouragement that he gave to Loisy and Tyrrell, and these instances could easily be multiplied. Such slight cohesion as the modernist movement had was largely derived from his co-ordinating activity.[3] Nor did he limit himself to stimulating and co-ordinating the work of others. From time

[1] He was specially indebted to the saintly Parisian director of souls, the abbé Huvelin, who was also a liberal thinker. See his advice to von Hügel in 1886 (*Selected letters*, pp. 58–63), and cp. Loisy's comments thereon, *Mémoires*, I, 286 f.

[2] E.g. *Eternal life* (1912), pp. 344 f., 354, 357 ff., 362 f.

[3] Paul Sabatier, the Protestant pastor, who had an unbounded enthusiasm for the modernist movement, exercised to some extent a similar co-ordinating influence.

to time he himself made specialist contributions to the development of the movement.

Thus at the international Catholic congress at Freiburg in 1897 von Hügel, in a paper which was read on his behalf by Semeria, gave an erudite exposition of modern critical views as to the composition of the Hexateuch.[1] Traditional beliefs about Mosaic authorship and strict historicity were frankly discarded in favour of the new views of Wellhausen, etc. This, the first important manifestation of incipient modernism after 1893, was intended to be, and was taken to be, a challenge to the conservative attitude to biblical questions and to the *prima facie* interpretation of the encyclical *Providentissimus*.[2]

Again, at a still more crucial period, when in 1904 Maurice Blondel published some articles[3] in which he advocated a *via media* between what he called 'l'extrinsécisme', *i.e.* the traditional, scholastic apologetic, and 'l'historicisme', *i.e.* the claim that a Catholic ought to treat historical criticism as a completely autonomous science, it was von Hügel who came forward to espouse the latter cause and to disallow the possibility of any compromise.[4] Blondel had in effect argued, with regard to Christology, that, if historical criticism did not by itself yield an account of the historic Christ that was sufficient to justify the faith and experience of the Church, it was legitimate to regard this faith and experience as giving a supplementary knowledge of the historic facts. Thus, if the historical character of the fourth gospel could not be demonstrated by criticism alone, tradition, being the expression of the perpetuated experience of Christ,

---

[1] See A. Houtin, *La Question biblique au XIXe siècle*[2], pp. 253 ff.; Loisy, *Études bibliques*, pp. 195–210; *Mémoires*, I, 478 ff.

[2] Cp. A. Fawkes, *Studies in modernism*, pp. 56 f.

[3] Published afterwards in book form, *Histoire et dogme* (1904).

[4] See A. Houtin, *La Question biblique au XXe siècle*[2], pp. 180 f.; Rivière, *op. cit.* pp. 241 ff.; A. L. Lilley, *Modernism*, pp. 112–20; Loisy, *Mémoires*, II, 335–8, 391–4.

could be held to provide additional, retrospective evidence of what actually happened, although it was not fully observed at the time of happening. Against what seemed to him a subtle attempt to provide a new defence for the accepted implications of the traditional Christology, von Hügel championed the autonomy of criticism, and stoutly denied that there is any supplementary method available for determining what were or were not the facts of history. Christian experience of the eternal Christ rightly assists us to determine the significance which attaches to the life of the historic Christ, but it can neither add to, nor detract from, our knowledge of the actual events of His life.

In the former of these instances von Hügel placed himself in the vanguard of the modernist movement, and in the latter on its left wing. On purely critical questions he was in fact practically at one with Loisy. See his article on the fourth gospel in the *Encyclopaedia Britannica*. It was just in so far as modernist apologetic impinged on metaphysics, just in so far as it ignored or treated with indifference the ontological reality of the supernatural world and the objectivity and transcendence of God, that von Hügel became ill at ease. With the method of immanence, as taught by the philosophy of action, *i.e.* as a method of showing the necessity and reality of the supernatural, he had no quarrel; on the contrary, he keenly appreciated it, and wished to extend its use. But when in the later stages of the movement some modernists, chiefly, as it seemed to him, Loisy, but also Tyrrell to a less extent and some of the Italians to a greater extent, stressed the immanent and subjective aspects of religious experience in such a way as to imply agnosticism as to the nature of the ultimate reality of its object, then he was moved more and more to dissociate himself from them.

Von Hügel, both by the bent of his mind and by his own wide and profound study of philosophy, was never able to regard metaphysical problems as unimportant or as of secondary interest. Loisy,[1] on the other hand, found himself constitutionally incapable of regarding such questions as the personality of God or the immortality of the soul as of any real moment. Such an attitude was utterly unintelligible to von Hügel with his mystical sense of the absolute reality of God and with his aptitude for metaphysical speculation and discrimination. In the years which succeeded the condemnation of modernism he was increasingly preoccupied with emphasizing the ontological transcendence of God and with discriminating his own position from every form of 'immanentism'. Loisy not unnaturally came to the conclusion that this preoccupation was a more or less pathological obsession. Miss Petre, who is not a partisan either of immanence or of transcendence, writes (in 1925): '(Von Hügel's) repugnance for sheer immanentism was so pronounced that he did, I think, in the latter days of the modernist crisis, often suspect its presence where it did not exist, and it made him, at times, mistrustful of friends and fellow-workers who greatly needed his full confidence.'[2]

Alfred Fawkes (1849–1930)[3] was a type of modernist very different from von Hügel; his career was perhaps unique.[4] Like Tyrrell, he was a convert to Roman Catholicism from High Anglicanism, and he became similarly disillusioned. But although he was on terms of close friendship with Tyrrell during the years of the modernist crisis, he does not appear ever to have had any real faith in the reforming

[1] See an important passage in the *Mémoires*, III, 23 f.

[2] *Hibbert Journal* (October, 1925), p. 85.

[3] Prefixed to a volume of Fawkes's sermons (*The Church a necessary evil* (1932)—an expressive title) is a memoir of him by Dr H. D. A. Major, but little or nothing is said about his career in the Roman Church or about his attitude during the modernist movement.

[4] Rivière, *Le modernisme dans l'Église*, p. 397, writes as though Fawkes was one of a number of converts from Anglicanism who after the condemnation of modernism returned to the Church of England. Who were the others?

movement in the Church of Rome, and in 1909 he quietly
returned to the Church of England.[1] Here he became
associated with the school of Modern Churchmen. He found
their liberal Protestantism congenial (see pp. 245 f. below),
and his attitude to Christianity had in fact, even while he
remained a Roman Catholic, been far more that of Harnack
than of Loisy or Tyrrell.[2] 'Ce brave Fawkes est bon et
intelligent,' wrote von Hügel in 1905 with reference to an
article of his, 'mais je me demande souvent où précisément
réside son catholicisme. Je n'en trouve que diablement peu
ici.'[3]

Fawkes, like Houtin in France, was a *rapporteur*, rather
than an actual adherent, of the movement.[4] He published
a number of articles on various aspects of it in English
periodicals, which were assembled in his *Studies in modernism*
(1913). He wrote in a lucid and epigrammatic style, not
unlike that of Houtin; but when he finally left the Roman
Church, he did not, like Houtin, become a pure sceptic.
While he had learned by experience as well as by a wide
study of history the inherent defects and dangers of all
institutional religion, he was yet realist enough to see that
Christianity cannot dispense with an institutional embodiment. But he wanted this to be as large and inclusive, and as
nationally representative, as possible; he came to feel most at
home in the Latitudinarian and Erastian tradition of Anglicanism. Thus, although in the strict sense he is hardly to be

[1] It is said that J. E. C. Bodley persuaded Fawkes to return to the
Church of England, and 'brought his talents to the notice of the Anglican
episcopate', *i.e.* of Dr Percival of Hereford; see Shane Leslie, *Memoir of
J. E. C. Bodley* (1930), pp. 412 ff.

[2] See Loisy, *Mémoires*, II, 418, 426; Petre, *Life of Tyrrell*, II, 374 f., 399;
and a letter from Miss Petre in *The Church a necessary evil*, pp. 15 f. Cp.
Fawkes, *Studies in modernism*, p. 292.

[3] Part of a letter to Loisy; *Mémoires*, II, 425.

[4] Houtin (*Une vie de prêtre*[2], pp. 432 f.) records that Fawkes intended to
write a history of modernism, but, after the appearance of Houtin's own
work, abandoned the project.

reckoned as a modernist, his case is interesting as an instance
of those who were *in*, but not *of*, the movement. Miss Petre
records a shrewd remark made by a French friend of hers:
'We had in Fawkes, Loisy, and Tyrrell three typical attitudes
in the case of ecclesiastical condemnation. Fawkes said: "I
am not wanted, I will go". Loisy said: "I will go when I am
put out". Tyrrell said: "You cannot put me out, I stay".'[1]

Miss Petre herself, with a singular and undeviating consistency, adopted, and continues to adopt, the last of these
three attitudes. Tyrrell's friend and adherent during his life
time, his literary executor and biographer after his death, she
has been faithful to his general position with a firm and
lonely courage which must excite the admiration even of
those who have little sympathy with its object. Twice at
least the ecclesiastical authorities tried in vain to make her
subscribe to what was in effect the anti-modernist oath.
After the latter of these occasions, she published in *The
Times*[2] an 'Open letter to my fellow Catholics', which was
an eloquent protest against the tyrannical methods that the
authorities were using in order to suppress modernism. She
quoted her own letter to the bishop of Southwark, in which
she had asked that, before she solemnly subscribed to the
decree *Lamentabili* and to the encyclical *Pascendi*, she might
be informed precisely in what sense she was required to do so.
There were, she said, three possible ways of subscribing.
(1) To treat such an act of submission as one of blind
obedience, which implies nothing as to the personal beliefs or
convictions of whoever makes it. (2) To treat the docu-

[1] See *The Church a necessary evil*, p. 16.
[2] November 2nd, 1910. On the same day *The Times* has a leading
article, in which the papal condemnation of modernism is deplored, and
which ends with these words: 'When one thinks of what a really progressive Pope might accomplish among the millions of people now longing
for a faith in harmony with knowledge and life, the sight of this attitude
of blind reaction is one that cannot be too deeply deplored'.

ments, to which submission is made, after the customary manner of theologians, *i.e.* to regard their meaning as matter for explanation, qualification, and subtle distinctions, in much the same way as Anglicans sometimes treat the XXXIX Articles.[1] (3) To accept the documents in their plain sense, both in their spirit and in their letter, according to the clear intention of the pope. For herself, only the third manner of subscription seemed honest and sincere; but would the bishop kindly assure her that each condemnation or proposition contained in these two documents without a single exception was, and would always in the same sense continue to be, *de fide*? Ought she to accept them in such a way that, if necessary, she should be ready to face torture in defence of their least word? Were they to be regarded as articles of faith like the Apostles' creed?

The bishop, in accordance, it may be presumed, with the directions of his superiors, omitted to reply to Miss Petre's letter. There are questions which it is safest for an infallible Church to evade or ignore. As he wanted if possible to avoid publicly excommunicating a lady who belonged to one of the most ancient and faithful Roman Catholic families in England, he contented himself with privately ordering his clergy to refuse her the sacraments in his diocese.[2] Loisy's final comment on Miss Petre's letter is as follows: 'Si tous ceux que l'on contraignait à prêter le serment antimoderniste avaient été capables de tenir un pareil langage, Rome eût été bien forcée d'en suspendre l'application. Mais le catholicisme romain ne forme pas les consciences à un si grand respect d'elles-mêmes'.[3]

---

[1] Loisy (*Mémoires*, III, 209) observes with regard to this point: 'Ainsi avions-nous procédé, du temps de Léon XIII, avec l'encyclique *Providentissimus*, pour y trouver un sens raisonnable. C'était beaucoup moins facile pour *Lamentabili* et *Pascendi*'.

[2] Houtin, *Histoire du modernisme catholique*, p. 329.

[3] *Mémoires*, III, 209f.

Chapter xxv

SUMMARY OBSERVATIONS

Outside France, Italy, Germany, and England, there was no modernism, or at least none that calls for attention here. Of other countries, the U.S.A. is the one where some manifestation of it might have been expected, for thence the preliminary heresy, known as 'Americanism', took at least its name and such semblance of existence as it had.[1] American Catholics do not seem to have been much troubled by doctrinal difficulties; absorption in 'practical Christianity' was their besetting weakness. No one pretends to throw any of the responsibility for the modernist movement across the Atlantic. 'I cannot understand America...', Tyrrell is reported to have said less than a year before his death, 'Modernism has produced there hardly an echo. The Church in America is asleep; and I can conceive nothing that will awaken it, but the production of some book native to the soil'.[2] In 1910 an anonymous writer tried to supply this need, but his book[3] does not seem to have had the desired effect.

The only countries in which the modernist movement attained to any considerable proportions were France and Italy and, to a much smaller extent, England; but it is quite

[1] 'The phantom heresy', of which 'no one has ever been able to discover, either in the old world or the new, an avowed supporter' (Loisy, *Mémoires*, II, 253). Cp. W. Barry, *Memories and opinions* (1926), pp. 221 f.; E. Renard, *Le cardinal Mathieu* (1925), p. 295. On the whole subject see Houtin's *L'Américanisme* (1904).

[2] *Letters to His Holiness Pope Pius X* by a Modernist (1910), p. xiii.

[3] The book referred to in the preceding note. Rivière, *op. cit.* p. 400, says that its authorship was attributed to an American priest named Sullivan. C. Harris (*Creeds or no creeds*, p. 373) attributes it to Tyrrell, but gives no reasons for doing so.

impossible to give any exact account of what these proportions were.[1] The movement had no organization, and nothing that remotely resembled a roll of membership. There was never any reliable means of ascertaining how many adherents it had, whether closely or loosely attached, nor is there ever likely to be. Fantastic suggestions as to the number of modernist priests were at one time in circulation.[2] Thus Salomon Reinach gave credence to the conjecture that there were 15,000 among the French clergy, to which Loisy replied that he doubted if there were 1500. Enthusiastic propagandists of the movement, like Paul Sabatier, were also given to gross exaggerations.

All that can be said with safety is that the works of Loisy, Tyrrell and of the other modernists, to whom reference has been made in the foregoing Chapters, excited lively interest and varying degrees of sympathy among many of the more intelligent priests and seminarists in France and Italy. The Catholic laity, especially in Italy, even where comparatively cultured, was as a whole uninterested in theological questions, and the movement received only the most meagre support from that direction. If it had been able to enlist a large number of lay supporters of the standing of von Hügel, Le Roy, and Fogazzaro, its outcome might have been different. But these were isolated instances. The papacy had the whip-hand of the clergy, and the laity had neither the interest nor the courage to protest.

[1] Cp. L. de Grandmaison, *Études* (September 20th, 1923), p. 644: 'Sur l'importance numérique de ceux qui y ont adhéré, il ne semble pas possible d'arriver à des précisions satisfaisantes'.

[2] See Houtin, *Histoire du modernisme catholique*, pp. 268–73; Rivière, *op. cit.* pp. 323–7.

PART V

THE OUTCOME OF THE MODERNIST MOVEMENT

The primary outcome of the modernist movement was the completeness of its defeat. The papal acts of condemnation and suppression that it provoked not only affected the modernists themselves, but they imposed on the whole Roman Church conditions which have added to the restrictions on the intellectual freedom of its members, and which have retarded the development of its theology. These effects of the movement, and the attempts that are being made to neutralize them, are the subject of Chapter Twenty-six.

The movement was not only defeated; it was killed, it came to an end. It did not continue as a movement outside the Roman Church, when it had been suppressed inside. It had no schismatic outcome. If it can be said to have survived at all, it is only in the sense that the writings of the modernists have had some influence outside the Roman Church, and especially upon certain High Anglican theologians. It would be misleading to say that the movement became re-incarnate in High Anglicanism, but the necessary qualification of this statement leads to a recognition of what may be regarded as its most considerable outcome. These results of the movement, outside the Roman Church, are the subject of Chapter Twenty-seven.

Chapter XXVI

WITHIN THE ROMAN CHURCH

The chief acts by which the holy see condemned and suppressed the modernist movement were as follows:

(1) The decree *Lamentabili* (July 3rd, 1907)[1], commonly
known as the syllabus, condemns sixty-five propositions,
'errors' concerning 'the interpretation of Sacred Scripture'
and 'the principal mysteries of the faith'. There is no reference
by name to those who are supposed to have maintained these
errors; but most of them are extracted, although not exactly
quoted, from Loisy's writings; others have a more general
reference.[2] The propositions may be divided into two classes:
(*a*) those which reiterate the previously defined teaching of
the Church and of the holy see, and (*b*) those which condemn
errors which had not hitherto been singled out for special
condemnation. To the latter category belong, for instance,
the propositions which relate to the integral truth of the
gospels (13–15) and to the historical character of the fourth
gospel in particular (16–18).[3] The general effect of the decree
is to deny that 'the progress of science' can require any
reformation or modification of Christian doctrine and to
prohibit Catholics from the free use of the methods of
historical and biblical criticism. A Catholic, who wants to
be a critic, may be one only on condition that he reaches the
conclusions which are prescribed by the Church. The conclusions here prescribed are of a rigorously conservative kind.

(2) The encyclical *Pascendi* (September 8th, 1907) contains,
as we have already observed (see pp. 1 ff. above), an elaborate

[1] There is an Eng. trans. of the decree in P. Sabatier's *Modernism* (1908),
pp. 217–30.
[2] Loisy in his *Simples réflexions* discusses the probable source of each
proposition.
[3] Cp. J. Rivière, *Le modernisme dans l'Église*, pp. 340 f.

systematization of the so-called 'doctrines of the modernists'. The abstract and artificial character of this systematization will have become more and more apparent during the course of this essay. The composition of a logically coherent system out of the heterogeneous materials provided in the writings of the modernists was undeniably a skilful undertaking; but if it was an attempt to give a just and accurate account of what the modernists had in fact taught, it must be pronounced a failure, and an inevitable failure. They had all, it is true, in various ways desired some reform of the Church's teaching, but not one of them had desired the kind of system which the encyclical attributes to them, nor could any of them admit that their teaching implied such a system.

It would, however, be a mistake to suppose that the object of the encyclical was to give a just and accurate account of what the modernists had in fact taught. Its object was to condemn every attempt to introduce a reform of the Church's traditional teaching, and the method of the *Pascendi* was recommended not by any desire to do justice to the modernists, but by its convenience. It was easier to canonize the scholastic system of philosophy and theology, when it appeared as the only alternative to an innovating system which was nothing less than 'the synthesis of all the heresies'.

But the encyclical was more than a theoretical condemnation of the modernist movement; it also ordained practical measures for its suppression. Thus, for instance, 'anyone who in any way is found to be tainted with modernism is to be excluded without compunction' from offices, whether of government or of teaching, in seminaries and Catholic universities. 'The same policy is to be adopted towards those who openly or secretly lend countenance to modernism either by extolling the modernists and excusing their culpable conduct, or by carping at scholasticism, and the Fathers, and the magisterium of the Church, or by refusing obedience to ecclesiastical authority in any of its depositaries;

and towards those who show a love of novelty in history, archaeology, biblical exegesis... Equal diligence and severity are to be used in examining and selecting candidates for Holy Orders.'[1] And again, bishops are to exercise the strictest possible vigilance over Catholic publications, rules of censorship are to be rigidly enforced, and each diocese is to have a 'vigilance committee' to see that the papal prescriptions are observed. Its members will be 'bound to secrecy as to their deliberations and decisions'. Diocesan bishops and the heads of religious orders are to make triennial reports to the holy see.

(3) Three years later, these practical measures were supplemented and crowned by the imposition of the anti-modernist oath (motu proprio *Sacrorum antistitum*, September 1st, 1910).[2] It must be taken by all clerics who are to be promoted to major orders, and by all clergy who exercise any ministerial function. The oath includes, in addition to a complete submission to the decree *Lamentabili* and the encyclical *Pascendi*, a declaration that the existence of God can certainly be demonstrated by the light of natural reason, an admission of external proofs of revelation, in particular miracles and prophecies, as most convincing signs of the divine origin of the Christian religion, a declaration that the Church was immediately and directly instituted by Christ during His life on earth, etc.

The oath was subscribed by the clergy without any opposition, except in Germany, where the university professors were dispensed from taking it (see p. 203 above). 'With the anti-modernist oath', says J. Rivière, 'ends the history of the doctrinal crisis which had raged for about ten years. From this moment, everything in fact justifies the view that modernism had disappeared.'[3] This statement can hardly be

[1] Sabatier, *op. cit.* pp. 328 f.
[2] Eng. trans. in Petre, *Modernism*, pp. 241–6
[3] *Le modernisme dans l'Église*, p. 538.

questioned, for subsequent manifestations of modernism were so insignificant and isolated as only to confirm its truth.

The condemnation of the modernist movement in 1907 did not come as a surprise to those who had closely followed the policy of Pius X, whether approvingly or disapprovingly. The attitude and intentions of the Curia had been evident from 1903 onwards, from which time the issue of a new syllabus of errors had been anticipated.[1] We have seen how Loisy in his retirement had discerned what the issue of the movement must be, so far as he was himself concerned. Others may have been more hopeful, but during these years there was little to justify their hopes and plenty to damp them.

Still less does the condemnation of the movement seem surprising to those who at the present time study its history dispassionately and in relation to the development of Roman Catholicism during the previous century. Every liberal and progressive movement in the Church had sooner or later been condemned or frustrated. Absolutist and conservative principles had become steadily predominant. The centralizing of power in the holy see had made immense strides. The papacy, which was thus able to control the whole Church more effectively than ever before, was plainly committed to strict traditionalism in theology and to the utmost possible resistance of all innovation. In these circumstances, any further attempt to give Roman Catholicism a modern orientation would have seemed futile, had it not been for the illusions which were fostered by the pseudo-liberal policy of Leo XIII. The aims of the modernists, which were in one way or another to give their religion such an orientation, were born of these illusions. Under Pius X, who did not even try to disguise his horror of everything that was distinctively modern, the condemnation of the movement was a

[1] See Rivière, *op. cit.* pp. 329–37. It seems evident that the first draft of the syllabus was prepared as early as 1903; cp. p. 138 above.

foregone conclusion. The decree *Lamentabili* and the encyclical *Pascendi* were the natural sequel to the *Providentissimus*
of Leo XIII, to the syllabus and *Quanta cura* of Pius IX, and to
the *Mirari vos* of Gregory XVI.

Nevertheless, although the condemnation of modernism
seems natural and inevitable when seen in its historical
perspective, yet the terms of its condemnation and the sup-
pressive measures which accompanied it appeared at the
time, as they appear still, surprisingly extravagant. The
former condemnations of liberal Catholicism, severe as they
had been, had still, whether by design or accident, left room
for evasion. Liberalism had been able to survive in the
Church although, to use Renan's famous metaphor, its wings
had been clipped. Lacordaire and Montalembert continued
the pursuit of liberty in spite of the *Mirari vos*. Dupanloup
had been permitted to explain away the *prima facie* meaning
of the syllabus of 1864. The modernists themselves had found
loopholes in the encyclical *Providentissimus*. It was far less
easy for any liberal-minded Catholic to give even a formal
assent to the acts of Pius X, and in any case the prescriptions
of a practical order made evasion perilous. The anti-modernist
oath made it impossible.[1]

This does not of course mean that the whole of the Roman
Catholic clergy, who subscribed to the anti-modernist oath
in 1910 and have since continued to do so, were really convinced of the truth of all that it contained and implied.
Many must have subscribed to it who inwardly deplored the
necessity of doing so. They realized, however, that subscription was the only condition on which they could
remain in the Church. Any scruples they had, or any

---

[1] Cp. M.-J. Lagrange, *Revue biblique* (1924), XXXIII, 159: 'Le modernisme supposait une certaine dose d'illusion qui n'est plus possible depuis
que Pie X a déchiré les voiles. On pourra encore sortir de l'Église, on ne
pourra plus y rester en caressant le dessein d'en changer les doctrines
essentielles'.

modernist tendencies however slight, they had to keep to themselves, for the anti-modernist campaign rendered the least disclosure of them liable to denunciation. 'A priest is more afraid of being called a modernist', wrote Miss Petre in 1914, 'than of being accused of negligence in his sacerdotal obligations and duties.... He has the diocesan council of vigilance, instituted by the *Pascendi* for the extirpation of modernism, ever in mind; he is like a shepherd who should be too much afraid of being bitten by the sheep-dogs to have time to look after the sheep; his pastoral solicitude is transformed into anti-modernist zeal.'[1] No one was safe, for the papal policy definitely encouraged private delation.[2] It is not then difficult to see why modernism disappeared with the anti-modernist oath.

The movement had indeed been routed already. Before 1910 Loisy had finally broken with Catholicism, and Tyrrell was dead. The modernist phase of von Hügel's career was over. Most of the other prominent modernists had either been driven out of the Church or decided to submit and remain. As a movement within the Roman Church it was flickering out; the anti-modernist oath completed a process that was already nearly complete. For a time some said that the movement had been only driven underground and would reappear. Nothing has happened to justify this expectation. So far as we can ascertain, the only two original modernists, who continue to profess themselves as such, are Miss Petre and E. Buonaiuti; the latter was excommunicated in 1924. Miss Petre described herself in 1922 as 'a solitary marooned passenger; the sole living representative of what has come to be regarded as a lost cause—the cause of modernism in the Roman Catholic Church'.[3] L. de Grandmaison apparently

---

[1] *Modernism*, pp. 194f.

[2] For particulars of an actual instance of delation (before 1910), see von Hügel's article in the *Hibbert Journal* (January, 1910), p. 247.

[3] *Hibbert Journal* (April, 1922), p. 401.

forgot Miss Petre when in 1927 he described Buonaiuti as 'perhaps the only faithful remaining adherent of the movement'.[1]

The direct outcome of the modernist movement was therefore exactly opposite to what those who had promoted it had intended. They had hoped to make the Roman Church more habitable for men of modern culture, especially for those who wanted their faith to be compatible with the results of an unbiased criticism of the Bible and of history, and who were not willing to regard scholasticism as the one and only way of arriving at, and of presenting, theological truth. In the event the movement itself became as though it had never been, and it left the Church more decisively committed to an intransigent position than it had been before. After the anti-modernist acts of Pius X it was more difficult for a Roman Catholic to make even a restricted use of modern critical methods than it'had been before, and the rule of scholasticism was not less, but more, exclusive and secure. The new *Codex Juris Canonici* (1917) confirmed and completed the process by which all power in the Church was centralized in the papacy.[2]

It was not only the modernists themselves who were victimized, but also professedly orthodox scholars like Mgr Batiffol (1861–1929) and Père M.-J. Lagrange (b. 1855), who had used critical methods in such a way as to support the traditional dogmatic teaching of the Church, who had been among the first to dissociate themselves from the modernists, and who had assiduously attacked them. If they had hoped thereby to put their own reputation for orthodoxy beyond question, they were deceived. Thus Batiffol claimed that in 1900 he had himself enunciated in anticipation the program of the *Pascendi*; none the less, 'in the wave of reaction which

[1] Quoted by Rivière, *op. cit.* p. xxv.
[2] Cp. F. Heiler, *Der Katholizismus*, pp. 305–11.

followed the condemnation of modernism, its most per-severing and most perspicacious adversary had the para-doxical misfortune to be himself overwhelmed'.[1] In 1907 his book, *L'Eucharistie*, was placed on the Index, and he was removed from the rectorship of the Institut Catholique of Toulouse which he had held since 1898.

The Dominican order, of which Père Lagrange is a member, was powerful enough at Rome to prevent his condemnation, but he was in constant difficulties with the ecclesiastical authorities.[2] Since the decree of the biblical commission with regard to the Mosaic authorship of the Pentateuch, it is understood that he has found it impossible to publish his commentary on the book of Genesis.[3] His vast erudition and the great value of his critical work on all matters, where there are no dogmatic interests at stake, are generally acknowledged, but his published conclusions have necessarily to be in conformity with the prescriptions of the holy see. It may be observed that he begins the introduction of his commentary on the fourth gospel as follows:

L'Église catholique a rangé parmi les livres canoniques les évangiles selon Matthieu, Marc, Luc et Jean. Le quatrième évangile a donc été écrit sous l'inspiration de l'Esprit-Saint. Pour nous c'est un dogme, ce n'est pas une question.

Ce n'est pas non plus une question de savoir s'il a eu pour auteur le disciple bien-aimé, Jean, fils de Zébédée. Ce point est fixé par la tradition ecclésiastique.[4]

It is patently difficult to reconcile this approach to one of the most notoriously disputable questions which arise from the critical study of the New Testament with the full and free use of critical methods. 'Obviously a Catholic theologian',

[1] J. Rivière, *Monseigneur Batiffol* (1929), pp. 56ff. Cp. Loisy, *Mémoires*, II, 602–5.

[2] Cp. Loisy, *Mémoires*, I, 539, II, 435, III, 252f., 555; von Hügel's *Selected letters*, p. 197; E. Barbier, *Histoire du catholicisme libéral* (1924), v, 263.   [3] Loisy, *op. cit.* III, 254–5.

[4] *Évangile selon saint Jean* (1925), p. vi.

writes Lagrange elsewhere, 'will not even dream of revising the decisions of the Church in matters of dogma and morals'.[1] For practical purposes at least, these decisions include those of the biblical commission. There may be a touch of bitterness in Loisy's remark that Lagrange 'has spent the best part of his life in spreading over the biblical texts a layer of erudition sufficiently thick to prevent the difficulties which they create for the official theology from being seen'[2]—but it is not devoid of truth.

An illustration of the procedure followed by those who wished to combine the use of critical methods with perfect loyalty to the holy see is provided by Mgr Barry's *The tradition of Scripture*. The first edition of this was published in 1906. The aim of the author is to give a description of what moderate or conservative critics teach about the Bible, while committing himself as little as possible to any particular critical conclusions. It is, however, evident that his own sympathies lay with the school of Lagrange and Batiffol, and not with either the pure traditionalists or the modernists. In 1908 a second edition was published, which had been revised in the light of the recent decisions of the biblical commission and of the papal condemnation of modernism.

A close comparison between the two editions is instructive, and shows how in the latter edition the author found it necessary to modify and safeguard even the modest concessions to criticism the desirability of which he had tentatively implied in the former. This is particularly manifest in the part of the book which deals with the Pentateuch, where a large number of minor but significant alterations have been made.[3] The following is a typical instance.[4] The first sentence which is identical in both editions is succeeded by a paragraph in which we italicize the variations between the two editions.

---

[1] *M. Loisy et le modernisme* (1932), p. 74.   [2] *Mémoires*, II, 99.

[3] *E.g.* see *op. cit.* pp. 40, 44, 47, 51, 52, 54, 57, 61. The pagination of both editions is the same.   [4] *Ibid.* p. 55.

(Both editions)

So far as its materials are pre-Mosaic, there is no reason why Moses himself should not have dealt with them in writings on which the Pentateuch has drawn; still more so in its legal chapters, which cannot fail to incorporate the leading enactments, or to reproduce the institutions, whereby the greatest of the Prophets literally created Israel.

(1st edition: 1906)	*(2nd edition: 1908)*
Moses *Virtual* Author.—To what extent these Mosaic *contributions* are traceable in a work so frequently edited is another question. But *allowing* them to be present, we see that a *virtual* authorship — *suppose of* the 'Book of the Covenant'— need not be incompatible with recensions that belong to *a much later period.* 'The early Hebrew historians did not affix their names to their works; they had, indeed, no idea of authorship.' Codes of law are, by necessity, subject to continual changes and additions; but they keep certain names as titles, *e.g.* Theodosius or Napoleon, however much revised. From all which considerations it is apparent that Moses might be held to have originated the Pentateuch, though not responsible for its *historic shape*, and be termed its author, since it embodied the work of writers who obeyed his inspiration, *direct or remote.*	Moses *Original* Author.—To what extent these Mosaic *foundations* are traceable in a work so frequently edited is another question. But *affirming* them to be present, we see that an *original* authorship—*far beyond* the 'Book of the Covenant'— need not be incompatible with recensions that belong to *different periods.* 'The early Hebrew historians did not affix their names to their works; they had, indeed, no idea of authorship.' Codes of law are, by necessity, subject to continual changes and additions; but they keep certain names as titles, *e.g.* Theodosius or Napoleon, however much revised. From all which considerations it is apparent that Moses might be held to have originated the Pentateuch, though not responsible for its *every line*, and be termed its author, since it embodied the work of writers who obeyed his inspiration.

Even so, Mgr Barry must have considered that such judicious modifications as these in his account of critical views were insufficient to prevent him from being suspected of heterodoxy, for he prefixed to the second edition an 'advertisement' in the course of which occurs the following statement:

All that follows here must be construed in the light of these authoritative documents (*i.e.* the decisions of the biblical commission, the decree *Lamentabili*, and the encyclical *Pascendi*) to which every Catholic owes submission. The writer would lay stress yet again on his attitude towards the opinions reported, as being purely that of one who describes them without interposing his private judgment, or taking on him the responsibility which those have to sustain that put them forward. Outside the directions of the Holy See it has been neither his wish nor his purpose to travel. Accordingly, he professes in particular no views regarding authorship, composition, dates, or contents of any part of Scripture which go beyond what has been laid down in the Church's teaching, whether in Conciliar decrees or in Papal and Roman utterances. The rest, in what way soever quoted, is merely *ad eruditionem*; it is matter for learning, not the subject of assent.[1]

In the light of the foregoing, the same author's remark in his *Memories and opinions* (1926, p. 278), that in no single instance has he been requested by Catholic authority to change or withdraw what he had set out in print, appears to be slightly disingenuous, although we do not of course question its accuracy. The same may be said of the reminiscence which he has recorded in connexion with his signing of the anti-modernist oath. 'When we were signing the Papal declaration against (modernism), Dr McIntyre...was standing beside me. He remarked with a smile how redundant was our signature, considering that in our lectures we had refuted year by year the Kantian philosophy, of

[1] *Op. cit.* pp. xxi f.

which Modernism was just an application to Gospel, Creed, and Catholic dogma.'[1]

The wave of reaction which followed the condemnation of modernism abated somewhat with the death of Pius X and the distraction of the great war. But under his successors there has been no material change in the policy of the holy see. The most remarkable illustration during the present pontificate of what this policy is has probably been the putting on the Index of the *Manuel biblique* of Saint-Sulpice, originally compiled by Vigouroux and Bacuez, and subsequently edited by Brassac and Ducher.[2] This book, which was placed on the Index on December 12th, 1923, had been published with the *imprimatur* of the archbishops of Paris and had been widely used for about forty years by seminaries in France and elsewhere. It was scrupulously and sincerely orthodox; it accepted, for instance, the traditional view of the miraculous experiences of Joshua and Jonah. At the same time, while thus perfectly loyal to tradition, it ventured to give a cautious but fair indication of some modern critical theories. The imparting of such information to seminarists was apparently, and it may be supposed correctly, regarded as dangerous by the papal authorities, and consequently the *Manuel biblique*, in spite of its close connexion with the venerable society of Saint-Sulpice, was condemned.

It is still impossible for a Roman Catholic theologian to put forward opinions that are clearly discordant with *Lamentabili* and *Pascendi* or with the decisions of the biblical commission. But are there yet any signs that these pronouncements and decisions are being less rigorously applied, or that attempts to neutralize them indirectly are being tolerated? While it can hardly be doubted that in the course of time they will be emptied of their worst meaning, and

[1] *Memories and opinions*, p. 279.
[2] See Loisy, *L'Église et la France* (1925), pp. 151 ff., 173 ff.

that new knowledge about the Bible and Christian origins will become acclimatized even in the Vatican, it cannot be said that there is any evidence that this is likely to happen soon. The process of neutralizing the anti-modernist excesses will be a long and delicate one.

There are, however, already signs that some less purely traditionalist writings are now receiving toleration.[1] Thus it is improbable that Dr Karl Adam, German though he be, would have been suffered to publish his *The spirit of Catholicism* (1929) or *Christ our Brother* (1931) in the years which immediately succeeded the condemnation of modernism. The reviewer of the latter book in *Irénikon* (x, 16) observes with regard to Dr Adam's works that there are some who 'y soulignaient des imprudences de langage'; and we can well believe it. Dr Adam, like Möhler a century ago, is a professor at Tübingen, and his work seems to bear the impress of Möhler's influence. He emphasizes strongly the organic life of the Church and the dynamic aspects of faith. His apologetic is far removed in tone and ethos[2] from the cold and rigid intellectualism or the sentimental piety that are more familiar. In particular, he protests against 'the one-sided prominence given to Christ's divinity and the obscuration of His humanity'[3] in traditional orthodoxy as commonly interpreted. The tendency of his own Christology, if we may judge rather from what he leaves unsaid than

---

[1] Cp. M. D. Petre, *Hibbert Journal* (April, 1922), p. 401.

[2] Dr Adam's works are in striking contrast, for instance, with A. M. Lépicier's *De stabilitate et progressu dogmatis* (1910) or with H. Felder's thoroughly cavalier refutation of the critics and re-assertion of the most challenging features of the traditional Christology. See his *Christ and the critics* (1924). Yet even he comes dangerously near to contradicting the 12th proposition of the decree *Lamentabili* (*q.v.*), when he declares that the Catholic apologist must 'pay no attention to the alleged inspired character of the Bible' and must 'see in the sacred books of the New Testament merely historical documents': see *op. cit.* I, 14.

[3] *Christ our Brother*, p. 43.

from what he says, seems to be towards a position that is equivalent to, though formally distinct from, a kenotic theory of the Incarnation.[1] If this is so, it might be fair to say that the most advanced Roman Catholic theologians are now being permitted to approach a point which High Anglican theology reached in 1889 with the publication of *Lux Mundi*.

A similar tendency may perhaps be remarked in the two posthumously published volumes by Léonce de Grandmaison (1868–1927)[2], entitled *Jesus Christ: His Person, His message, His credentials* (Eng. trans. of vol. I in 1930, of vol. II in 1932). This professes to be a work of purely historical criticism, and the author was a New Testament scholar of the first rank. His critical conclusions are, as we should expect, strictly conservative (*e.g.* he regards John, son of Zebedee, as author of both the fourth gospel and the apocalypse), but they are for the most part finely and freely reasoned. Sometimes he tries bravely to escape from the fetters imposed by the decisions of the biblical commission. Thus, for instance, while he is bound to maintain the priority of St Matthew's gospel to St Mark's, he does so in such a way as to minimize the discrepancy between this theory and the now generally accepted solution of the synoptic problem which contradicts it (I, 114–17).[3] In regard to Christology, he concludes that the Chalcedonian definition must be regarded as finally satisfying, nor will he grant the propriety of anything in the nature of a kenotic theory of the Incarnation (II, 315, 317). Nevertheless, he approaches the Christ of the gospels from

[1] *E.g. Christ our Brother*, pp. 59 f.; he does not say that Christ during His life on earth was omniscient. See also Dr Adam's more recent book, *Jesus Christus*, Eng. trans. *The Son of God* (1934).

[2] See J. Lebreton, *Le Père Léonce de Grandmaison* (1932).

[3] H. Felder, on the other hand, displays no such ingenuity. He roundly rebukes those Catholic critics, *e.g.* Lagrange and Batiffol, who, before the condemnation of modernism, had acknowledged 'the priority of Mark's Gospel and the dependency of Matthew and Luke on the second Synoptist'. *Op. cit.* I, 103.

the standpoint of historical realism, refrains from reading back into them all the implications of traditional dogma, and emphasizes the genuine humanity of Jesus (*e.g.* II, 230). Significant too is the respect which he shows for non-Catholic critics, a respect that is very different from the disdain which is inculcated by the *Pascendi*.

Still more significant is Dr Adam's manner of referring to the encyclical *Pascendi*. Does this suggest how it will ultimately be explained away or reinterpreted?

The Church cannot possibly be an enemy to sober criticism (he writes), least of all to the so-called 'historico-critical' method. Even the much-attacked anti-modernist encyclical of Pope Pius X (*Pascendi*) and the anti-modernist oath, do not forbid this method, but rather presuppose it. What they forbid is simply this, that men should make the affirmation of supernatural faith dependent exclusively on the results of this method, thereby subjecting it wholly to philologers and historians, and to profane science. Our faith does not rest upon dead documents, but upon the living witness of that stream of tradition which has brought its doctrines down from Christ through the apostles and the apostolical succession of bishops to the present day. Christianity is not a religion of dead documents and fragmentary records, but a life in the Holy Spirit preserved from generation to generation by the apostolical succession of commissioned preachers. The historico-critical method, if it would not lose itself in extravagant and unlimited criticism, must adjust itself to this life which pulsates through the heritage of revealed truth. That was what the papal encyclical meant when it declared—in words that have been so much misunderstood—that holy Scripture and the Fathers are not to be interpreted 'merely by the principles of science'.... So the Church does not quarrel with the historico-critical method, or dispute the right and the duty of scientific research. What she does is to guard against the abuse of these things, to prevent the neglect of that living element in Christianity wherein these methods should find their final norm and standard.[1]

---

[1] *The spirit of Catholicism*, pp. 218 f.; cp. pp. 156 f., and also a passage on p. 137 which sounds like a clear echo of Tyrrell's voice.

It seems that it may ultimately become possible to allege that the anti-modernist acts of Pius X meant something very different from what at the time they were taken to mean.[1]

Meanwhile, however, the strength of the Roman Church, so far as dogma in concerned, will continue to reside, not in any compatibility of its theology with modern knowledge, but in its claim to be the infallible repository of traditional Christian orthodoxy. In a time of intellectual uncertainty and of spiritual and moral unrest, the appeal of a Church, which can plausibly claim to provide both certainty and peace, is inevitably considerable. Those who are attracted by Catholicism as a religion, by the Catholic ideal of spirituality, and who do not appreciate the difficulties that are inherent in the official theology of Romanism, tend naturally to gravitate towards such a Church. If their intellectual interests[2] lie in fields which are remote from, or only indirectly connected with, ecclesiastical dogma, they do not necessarily find the theological obscurantism of the Church a burden to their faith. On the contrary, they may be glad to escape from the necessity of thinking for themselves in the sphere of theology. Those who have no special intellectual interests—and the majority of the faithful belong to this class—find a Church where awkward problems are settled,

[1] For other ways in which revisions of traditional orthodoxy are being advanced even by conservative theologians, see an article by G. la Piana in the *Harvard Theological Review* (July, 1922), 'Recent tendencies in Roman Catholic theology'. It is also significant that Roman Catholic writers are at last being allowed to accept the scientific theory of evolution; see *The Modern Churchman* (May, 1933), pp. 59–62. At the same time, the official teaching of the Church—according to Cardinal Gasparri, *The Catholic Catechism* (1932), p. 81—is still that 'the prevalent notions that man was originally in a purely savage condition, or that he has evolved from an ape and so arrived at his present more perfect state... will be instinctively repudiated by those imbued with Catholic faith'.

[2] It is needless to remark that the Roman Church numbers in its ranks many scholars who are leading authorities in different branches of learning as well as many brilliant men of letters.

or suppressed, by authority, more imposing than one which does not affect to possess any short-cut to truth. The general anathema is a labour-saving device and it will always be popular.

As an example of this kind of attractiveness some remarks of Bernard Holland, the biographer of von Hügel, may be cited from his book, *Belief and freedom* (1923):

Catholics who understand what faith means, and are firmly founded upon the rock of authority, should have advantage even in the affairs of this world. They can be light-hearted. They need not waste their time by discussing, *ab initio*, questions of faith and morals. They can go serenely about their business with minds free from disturbance and questionings, and with certain settled *ab extra* rules of conduct. Having a fixed point of view, they can live boldly and cheerfully. So a man on a highroad can move freely on, thinking about what he likes, without asking himself at every moment, 'am I on the right way?' (p. 177).

Chapter XXVII

OUTSIDE THE ROMAN CHURCH

The modernist movement, when it was extirpated within the Roman Church, was extirpated altogether. It did not become a schism, nor did it ally itself with any other existing Church or group within a Church. As a movement it disappeared. Those who had taken part in it either submitted and remained within the Roman Church or else each pursued his own course independently outside. So far as the modernists were concerned, the attempt to initiate a revision of Roman Catholic orthodoxy was over. The movement therefore had no direct outcome elsewhere.

As a projected revision of Roman Catholic orthodoxy it had, however, attracted the attention of non-Roman theologians who were conscious of the need of forwarding in their own communions a revision of traditional teaching. This was especially so in the Church of England. In the purely Protestant communions it won only a slight degree of sympathy, such sympathy as is naturally felt for any movement which can be represented as a rebellion against the power of the papacy. But the supposition that modernism was a movement in the direction of Protestantism was due only to misunderstanding; there was never any tangible evidence to show for it. Thus when the excitement caused by the condemnation of the movement died down, it ceased to be an object of interest in Protestant circles, and it had no noticeable influence there.

Modernism was essentially a Catholic movement. Its object was to revise and revive Catholic, not Protestant, theology. The modernists were firmly attached to Catholicism as a living religion and as a social institution; they were attached to the idea of the Church as a supernatural society, to the traditional orders of the ministry, to the sacramental system, to the Catholic ideals of devotion, sanctity and asceticism. Their quarrel was not with the religion of the Roman Church, but with its theological rationalism and with the papal autocracy which suppressed any attempt at its modification. Moreover, the movement, so far from being congruous with, had been consistently opposed to, liberal Protestantism. Loisy had not tried to adapt Harnack's theology in a Catholic sense, but had attacked it root and branch. To the modernists liberal Protestantism had seemed a reduced Christianity, an emaciated religion, which was supported by a prejudiced criticism of Christian origins and by a mistaken reading of history. It was therefore hardly to be expected that modernism, when recognized in its true colours, would commend itself to Protestants, whether orthodox or liberal.

On the other hand, it might seem antecedently probable that the failure of the movement within the Roman Church would have led to a reinforcement of the 'Old Catholic' Churches. The *raison d'être* of these bodies, most of which came into existence as a result of the Vatican council,[1] was the endeavour to maintain in living reality a Catholicism which rejected the absolutist claims of the papacy. Was not this what the modernists desired, since papal absolutism was the rock on which their movement had foundered? The Old Catholics certainly appear for a time to have looked upon the modernists as fellow-workers with themselves, and, when the movement was condemned, to have hoped that their special work of destroying the papacy in its present form would be strengthened.[2] Tyrrell did indeed for a short

---

[1] All in fact except the Church of Utrecht, which broke with Rome early in the eighteenth century. See *Northern Catholicism*, edited by Williams and Harris (1933), pp. 531–50.

[2] See *e.g.* the *Revue internationale de théologie* (the organ of the Old Catholics), 1907, p. 62, and 1908, p. 208.

period (in 1908)—much to the surprise and regret of the staunchly Roman von Hügel[1]—look favourably towards the Old Catholics and entertain the idea of co-operating with them.[2] But nothing came of this; nor did they receive either then or later any influx of modernists.

But it is not difficult to account for this. In the first place, the Old Catholic Churches were tiny and struggling. They did not constitute an imposing or formidable institution. Regarded as a challenge to the power and prestige of the papacy, *Alt-Katholizismus* had failure written across it. Whatever degree of sympathy or admiration might be felt for those who initiated and sustained it, it was scarcely possible to suppose that it had any large or promising future before it. Then, again, the Old Catholic Churches were sectarian and schismatic, whereas the modernists had stedfastly refused to contemplate the formation of a sect in schism from the Roman Church. It had been their object to carry through reforms within the Great Church—that or nothing. And thirdly, while the Old Catholics were doctrinally free from the bondage of the papal autocracy, and while they had a due regard for the importance of sound learning, yet there was little that was specifically modern about their theology. It might in fact be said that the fundamental and constant theme of their apologetic was essentially retrogressive. The Vincentian Canon—*quod ubique, quod semper, quod ab omnibus creditum est*—was their basic formula— one might say without impropriety, their 'slogan'. Thus they boasted that they had been foremost in refuting 'Newman-ism'.[3] They perceived truly that even Newman's theory of development was subversive of their own position, as indeed Newman himself had by implication pointed out.[4]

---

[1] *Hibbert Journal* (January, 1910), pp. 247f., 251.
[2] Petre, *Life of Tyrrell*, ch. XIX.
[3] *Revue internationale de théologie* (1908), p. 203.
[4] See p. 55 above.

A fortiori, there was little affinity between their attitude to dogma and that of the modernists.

The fact that Dr Friedrich Heiler, when he left the Roman Church, became not an Old Catholic but a High Church Lutheran is in this connexion instructive. He is also one of the few continental theologians, perhaps the only one, on whom the modernist movement has left an authentic impress. Heiler was born in 1892, and was brought up as a Roman Catholic.[1] He came under the influence of modernism about 1910, that is, when the movement was already virtually finished. But for him it had a message full of inspiration. The influence of modernism, combined with that of the Protestant biblical critics, and especially with that of Nathan Söderblom, afterwards archbishop of Upsala, contributed to Heiler's noble conception of a living, growing synthesis between historical Catholicism and historical Protestantism, a synthesis which should be genuinely liberal, progressive and inclusive in its theology. Of such a synthesis he became, and continues to be, an apostle. He realized that it was impossible, for him at least, to work fruitfully for this ideal within the Roman Church under the conditions which at present prevail there; in 1919 he left it, and in the following year was nominated to a professorship in the Lutheran faculty of theology at Marburg. He has remained incurably Catholic in his religious sympathies, and it is therefore significant that he threw in his lot not with the Old Catholics, but with the Lutheran Church, that he regarded the incipient *Hochkirche* movement in that Church as a more promising field for his life's work.

The manner in which he was influenced by modernism can be gathered from his great book, *Der Katholizismus*,[2]

[1] See Dr G. K. A. Bell's foreword to Heiler's *The spirit of worship* (1926); and also an article by B. E. Meland in *The Journal of Religion* (1933), XIII, 139–49.
[2] This was an expansion of the much briefer *Das Wesen des Katholizismus*, published in 1920.

published in 1923. He there suggests that his book is the most comprehensive *Programmschrift* of Catholic modernism that had so far appeared. It is all conceived, he says, in the spirit of Tyrrell, except that it differs from him and other modernists by its high esteem and love for the pure evangelical Christianity.[1] The modernism which appealed to Heiler most was certainly not that of Loisy, but that of Tyrrell, the great revolutionary protest and prophecy of *Medievalism* and *Christianity at the cross roads.* He will not even allow that Loisy was a real modernist, since he lacked religious power and passion.[2] But this is a purely arbitrary and subjective judgment. What it means is that the modernism which captured Heiler's imagination and contributed to his ideal of the evangelical Catholic Church of the future was the modernism which represented itself to him as moving in the direction of a great spiritual revival rather than as a current of critical knowledge.

Nevertheless, Heiler's indebtedness to Loisy is greater than he acknowledges or, maybe, than he is aware. For his account of Christian origins and of their relation to Catholic development closely follows the lines of *L'Évangile et l'Église*, as reproduced by Tyrrell in *Christianity at the cross roads.* The recognition of the eschatological character of the gospel of Jesus is for Heiler the *kopernikanische* fact of modern theology, which by itself overthrows the traditional dogmatic system of the Roman Church.[3] Yet, while from an historical point of view it is impossible to attribute the institution of Catholicism to the conscious and deliberate purpose of Jesus, it is true that the Catholicizing of Christianity began directly after His death. Pentecost was the birthday of the Catholic Church, which was founded, not by the Man Jesus, but by the Kyrios Christos and His Pneuma.[4] This does not, however, invalidate the Catholic position, for the historical

---

[1] *Der Katholizismus*, pp. xxxi f.   [2] *Ibid*. p. 648.
[3] *Ibid*. p. 3.   [4] *Ibid*. p. 43.

genesis of a phenomenon does not determine its inner value.[1]

Heiler's defence of Catholicism is in effect even more anti-intellectualist and pragmatist than Tyrrell's. He constantly emphasizes the irrational character of religious life and truth.[2] But while in these ways he reproduces much typically modernist thought, he differs from the modernists in that (1) he is not attempting to work from within the Roman Church, and (2) it is not so much a revision of Roman Catholic orthodoxy at which he is aiming as the growth of a new organic incorporation of Catholicism with Protestantism. The practical achievement of this object is as yet small in its proportions, even if it is magnificent in its aspirations; but whatever be its prospects, the modernist movement was one of the factors which led to its conception. Among the outstanding continental divines Heiler's position is at present unique; there are not, so far as we can ascertain, any others who are avowedly trying to carry on the work of the modernists.

But there is one other suggested instance of modernist influence on individual theologians outside England which perhaps ought to be noticed here because of the source whence the suggestion proceeds. Dr W. R. Inge, but apparently no one else, has affirmed that Drs Kirsopp Lake and Foakes-Jackson, the editors and, for the most part, the authors of the first volume of *The beginnings of Christianity* (1920), were disciples of Loisy, and that the kind of Christianity they were seeking to commend was similar to that

---

[1] *Der Katholizismus*, p. 4.

[2] 'Die wirkliche Frömmigkeit ist das Kriterium aller theologischen Anschauungen und Doktrinen. Der lebendige Gottesumgang der Seelen muss Ausgangs- und Endpunkt aller theologischen Spekulation sein' (*ibid.* p. 367). 'Das innere Frömmigkeitsleben des Katholizismus zeigt ein ganz anderes Bild als seine äussere Organisation; in ihm offenbart sich der ganz Irrationalismus der lebendigen Religion' (*Ibid.* pp. 373 f.; cp. pp. 355, 361, 368–72).

which it was the object of *L'Évangile et l'Église* to commend.[1] These affirmations, however, rest on a misapprehension, at least so far as Dr Lake is concerned, and it remains to be shown that there is any more justification for them in the case of Dr Foakes-Jackson.[2] It is true that, writing as historians, they implied that the classical liberal Protestant account of Christian origins, *e.g.* Harnack's, was mistaken,[3] and in this they agreed with what Loisy had said nearly twenty years before. *L'Évangile et l'Église* may admittedly have been the first effective refutation of the liberal Protestant thesis, but, especially after the work of Schweitzer, the eschatological view of the original gospel had become part of the general heritage of critical scholarship, and its acceptance is not in itself a reason for supposing discipleship of Loisy. There is no evidence in *The beginnings of Christianity* of any special indebtedness to him. Indeed Dr Lake has since made this point clear. 'I certainly am not a disciple of Loisy, as that scholar would not be slow to state'.[4]

It is not less erroneous to suppose that the kind of religion which Dr Lake himself seeks to commend[5] can by any stretch of the imagination be described as a modernized

---

[1] *Outspoken essays*, 2nd series (1922), pp. 51 ff. Dr Inge does not mention Drs Lake and Foakes-Jackson by name, but there can be no doubt as to the reference. 'Some of Loisy's disciples (he writes) still claim their right to remain ministers of the Gospel, and two of them, Anglo-Americans and priests of the Episcopal Church, have recently written a history of the Christian origins from this point of view.'

[2] But see pp. 245 f. below; Dr Foakes-Jackson's criticism of the Anglican Modern Churchmen that is reproduced there does not show that he was in any specific sense influenced by Loisy, still less that his own religious convictions are an outcome of the modernist movement.

[3] *E.g. op. cit.* pp. 265, 395, 401 *et passim.*

[4] *The religion of yesterday and to-morrow* (1925), pp. 141 f.

[5] *The beginnings of Christianity* does not aim at commending any particular religious convictions; it professes to be not an apologetic, but a purely historical, work. For Lake's own religious opinions see the book referred to in the preceding note.

Catholicism. His 'religion of to-morrow' involves a more complete break with historical Christianity than was ever contemplated by the modernists as either practicable or desirable. If he admits that Catholicism is the religion of the New Testament, he does not for that reason nor for any other regard it as true or as likely to be the religion of the future. He does indeed admire certain features of contemporary Catholicism, *e.g.* the aesthetic appeal of its liturgy and the supra-national character of the Roman Church, and he says that formerly he was hopeful as to the outcome of the modernist movement, *i.e.* presumably before its suppression. But there is nothing here that is definite enough to justify Dr Inge's suggestion.

It is to the Church of England that we must turn if we are to discover, apart from the case of Heiler, any definite and conscious attempt to continue what the modernists tried in vain to do. The Church of England, as is often pointed out by its friends and its foes, occupies an unique position among Christian denominations. When at the Reformation Western Christendom broke into two parts, Catholic and Protestant—the former represented by the Roman Church, the latter by the Lutheran and Calvinistic Churches and by the various sects—the Church of England adopted a middle course and attempted to combine the two forces which elsewhere were regarded as incompatible. Amid the shifting fortunes of history it has continued to pursue this course and to make this attempt. Its historical formularies, as well as its subsequent and recent official pronouncements, are generally marked by a studied ambiguity, which is evidently designed to be interpreted in an inclusive sense, although partisan Anglicans, whether Catholic or Protestant, are prone to claim that the exclusive interpretations which appeal to them respectively are alone legitimate. The consequence of its singular history is that Catholicism and Protestantism have each maintained a position within the Church of England as living religions, and at the same time neither has officially and finally been bound up with a hard and narrow theological system. The latitude of Anglican theology has been wider than that of any other Christian Church,[1] and room has been found for those who are broadly attached to Christianity but not to Catholicism or Protestantism in particular. Hence the threefold division of the Anglican tradition into High Church, Low Church, and Broad Church, or Catholic, Protestant, and Latitudinarian.

During the nineteenth century the Low Church party, in spite of the fact that it had been reinforced as a result of the evangelical revival, tended to lose ground. This was partly due to the incapacity of a theology which was based on biblical infallibility to withstand the impact of modern knowledge, but still more to the effects of the Catholic revival within the Church of England. The Oxford movement, which was largely occasioned by the same forces as gave rise to the Catholic revival on the continent, in spite of secessions to Rome and the hostility of the Anglican hierarchy, made steady progress throughout the century. In theology the leaders of the movement were at first content to revive traditional Catholic orthodoxy, and their appeal was to 'that primitive Christianity which was delivered for all time by the early teachers of the church, and which was registered and attested in the Anglican formularies and by the Anglican

---

[1] An interesting testimony to this is that of a recent Unitarian writer: 'It is easier to be heretical inside the English Church than outside it. So long as the forms are observed, the thought may be free, but if the forms are given up the thought is more strictly watched, more quickly suspected, and more severely condemned. It is as true now as it was in the times of Elizabeth or James that Anglican thought may wander widely, while a Dissenter may not look over the hedge. Unitarian thought in an Anglican clergyman is often attractive; in a Unitarian minister it is treated with hostility or contempt' (Henry Gow, *The Unitarians* (1928), pp. 26f.).

divines', especially by the divines of the seventeenth century.[1] But the publication of *Lux Mundi* in 1889 marked a new departure on the part of a fresh generation of High Churchmen; it was the first considerable attempt to adapt Catholic teaching in its Anglican form to the requirements of modern knowledge. Meanwhile, the Latitudinarian theology, which had been dominant in the eighteenth century, had been superseded by a newer type of Broad Church thought that owed much to the influence of Coleridge. One stream of this liberal theology, notably in the case of F. D. Maurice, flowed into the Catholic movement, and contributed to the development of the *Lux Mundi* position to which reference has just been made.[2] In another direction it issued in a kind of Broad Church theology that was not unlike the continental liberal Protestantism which culminated in Harnack and Sabatier.

It is no part of our purpose to consider in detail the tenets, or to weigh the merits and defects, of these three parties or 'schools of thought' as, with perhaps a measure of euphemism, they are often described, any more than it is to enter into the controversies which separate the Anglican Church from the Roman. We are only concerned to discover where, if anywhere, the modernist movement influenced Anglicanism.

Professor E. Buonaiuti, in his *Le modernisme catholique* (1927), assumes that it is in the Broad Church party that we should see the counterpart, if not a continuation, of the modernist movement. From one point of view the Anglican Modern Churchmen may certainly be regarded as a counterpart of the Roman modernists. The Churchmen's Union was founded in 1898; its members, and those who were in sympathy with them, later became known as 'Modern

[1] Newman, *Apologia* (Everyman's edition), p. 63.
[2] Cp. W. L. Knox and A. R. Vidler, *The development of modern Catholicism* (1933), part I, chs. V and VI *et passim*.

Churchmen' or as 'Anglican modernists',[1] and they succeeded to the place of the older Latitudinarian or Broad Church school. There can be no doubt that Modern Churchmen in the twentieth century, like Broad Churchmen in the nineteenth, have most conspicuously advocated the need of bringing Christianity into closer relation with modern thought, and herein lies one point of resemblance to the modernists. There is also some similarity between certain restatements of Christian doctrine which Modern Churchmen have proposed and those which the modernists proposed. But it has not been demonstrated that there was direct affinity between the two movements, or that Modern Churchmen were to any considerable extent indebted to the modernists. It should be recognized that the general preference of Modern Churchmen for Protestantism as against Catholicism was calculated to make them regard so inherently Catholic a movement as modernism as an ally of doubtful value.

That they took over the word 'modernism' from the Roman Catholic movement is admitted, and it may be this that misled Buonaiuti; it remains to be shown that they took over much more than the word. It does not appear that they were directly influenced by the movement, or that they appropriated and made their own its distinctive spirit, whether in its Catholic or critical aspects.[2] Modern Churchmen, says Dr Major, 'are the lineal and legitimate descendants of the Old Broad Churchmen and Liberal Churchmen of the nineteenth century'[3]; and he adds that in so far as they were

[1] In order to avoid confusion, they will be referred to here by the former title.

[2] Thus C. W. Emmet in his article on 'The Modernist movement in the Church of England' (*Journal of Religion*, November, 1922, pp. 561–76) says nothing to suggest that the Anglican Modern Churchmen derived anything more than the name 'modernist' from the Roman movement.

[3] H. D. A. Major, *English modernism* (1927), p. 24.

influenced by Roman modernism it was 'mainly through the Anglo-Catholic school'. 'Modernism in the Church of England', says a writer in *The Modern Churchman* (April, 1933), 'has been predominantly Protestant in tone and spirit....But this must not blind us to the fact that the Catholic idea, free of Ultramontanism, and in sane and capable hands, has a real place in English Christian thought and life. There are those who, under Anglican conditions, are doing what Tyrrell tried and failed to do in the Church of Rome, and from a point of view very like his own'.[1] The latter reference is to the High Anglican theologians whom we shall be considering directly.

Dr Major considers that until about 1908 liberal Protestantism of the Harnack-Sabatier type was the dominant note of English liberal Churchmanship,[2] but that more recently liberal Catholicism has been gaining ground at the expense of liberal Protestantism.[3] However this may be, liberal Protestantism certainly seems so far to have been the dominant note of Modern Churchmanship. During recent years *The Modern Churchman* has given the weight of its support to Bishop E. W. Barnes, the most consistent and courageous opponent of the whole Catholic revival in the Church of England. And again, most of the papers read at the conferences of the Churchmen's Union show much closer affinity to liberal Protestantism than to Catholic modernism. After the conference at Girton in 1921 this was pointed out by Dr Foakes-Jackson in an article in the *Hibbert Journal*.

Modernism in England (he wrote) has presented a non-miraculous, non-mysterious, easily understood, non-sectarian, and popular religion. The only question is whether this is Christianity. At the head is placed the human Jesus of history, a gifted teacher of the Fatherhood of God and the brotherhood of

[1] *Op. cit.* p. 24; the writer is Mr R. Gardner.
[2] *English modernism*, pp. 24, 28.
[3] *Ibid.* p. 24; cp. *The Modern Churchman* (December, 1932), pp. 484-7.

man, and, to quote Dr Barnes, one 'gifted with rare psychical strength. His power to cure disease was remarkable.' This Jesus is credited with being accurately reported as regards His words and many of His acts by the Synoptists, and, when convenient to His admirers, by St John....He is presented as a Teacher rather than as a Saviour....So wonderful is the portrait of Jesus preserved in Christian tradition, that it is possible to construct an ideal in Jesus of all that man should be. Yet this worship of the ideal man is not Christianity, which is the acceptance of salvation through Christ alone; nor is the figure that of the Jesus of history.

Modernist Churchmanship in England fails in two respects. It is too rational and also too unscientific. In its desire to save Protestantism it has protested against the catholicism in the Anglican community, whilst its anxiety for the future of the Church has made its leaders repudiate those who are determined to follow criticism to the full....

The modern Churchman has set up a figure of which the Catholic says, 'This is not the Christ I worship'; and the critic, 'This is not the Jesus of history.'[1]

Modern Churchmanship is a much more complex movement than this quotation may suggest, nor should we allow that there is more than a broad element of truth in these criticisms. But it should be observed that, *mutatis mutandis*, they are precisely the criticisms which the Roman modernists levelled against the liberal Protestantism of Harnack and Sabatier; and in the present instance they appear to be equally to the point. Modern Churchmen have, it would seem, been reluctant to learn some of the lessons that Loisy might have taught them. They have not altogether escaped the danger of presupposing that those parts of traditional Christianity which happened to appeal to them must be the essence of the Christian revelation, and then in their historical criticism of proceeding to discover that it was just this essence of which the Jesus of history was the unique teacher and embodiment. This may be the reason why Modern

[1] *Hibbert Journal* (January, 1922), pp. 204 ff.

Churchmen as a whole have tended to discount the eschatological element in the original gospel, and have deprecated the more radical conclusions of New Testament criticism.

Dr Major, however, may well be right in considering that the affinities of Modern Churchmanship to liberal Protestantism are now growing less; and if it is true that the liberal Catholic element in the Churchmen's Union is growing stronger, it seems probable that Modern Churchmanship will ultimately coalesce with that school of High Church theology which, as we shall now observe, has consciously been attempting to continue and develop within the Church of England the kind of doctrinal revision that the Roman modernists proposed for their Church, but that failed to secure toleration there.

We may then narrow our field of inquiry to the professedly Catholic section of the Church of England. Even here, there is no reason to suppose that the modernist movement has influenced, or was followed with sympathetic approval by, the High Church party as a whole. Some High Churchmen were and have remained as opposed to modernism as Pius X himself. None of the three sections of the Church of England—High Church, Low Church, or Broad Church—is a closely knit, compact unit. There is no clear-cut division between them; and among High Churchmen at least it is certain that there are considerable differences of belief and practice. There are, for instance, differences as to the extent to which the Book of Common Prayer is regarded as a fully satisfactory medium for Catholic worship and sacramental life. And cutting across these ritual differences, as they may be called, are theological differences, which are more relevant to our present inquiry.

High Anglican theology during the present century appears to fall into three main divisions. The classification is of course a rough one, but it is a necessary background for an understanding of the influence of the modernist movement on Anglican Catholicism. It is in the third of the following classes that direct traces of this influence can be discerned.

(1) There is a small group of High Churchmen whose theology is hardly distinguishable from modern Roman Catholic orthodoxy, and who in particular applaud the attitude of the papacy to all forms of religious liberalism. The document, entitled 'A centenary manifesto', which was issued in October, 1932, and which attracted some slight attention in the press at the time, may be taken to represent the position of this group. The chief purposes of the manifesto seemed to be (i) to protest against the 'modernistic' tendencies of many High Churchmen, and (ii) to urge that 'the real and essential goal' of the 'Anglo-Catholic' movement was 'reunion with the Apostolic See of Rome'. It may seem surprising that Anglicans who think thus do not become Roman Catholics; some of them do. Needless to say, there is no question here of modernist influence.

(2) A second type of theology, which may probably be regarded as that of the majority of the High Church party, is what may be described as that of the *Lux Mundi* school. We do not mean that *Lux Mundi* is treated with precisely the same degree of veneration as, for instance, the *Summa* of Aquinas is treated by scholastics, but that the general position of *Lux Mundi* is taken to represent the largest concessions which traditional orthodoxy can safely make to modern thought. This is in fact an attempt to determine a new and more liberal standard of orthodoxy. It is liberal, but liberal within limits.

Lux Mundi did indeed in its time represent a considerable, and even a sensational, modification of traditional Catholic orthodoxy, as compared for instance with the standard set in Liddon's Bampton lectures. It accepted in principle the free application of critical methods to the Bible, and definitely abandoned the older views of the Old Testament. In regard to the New Testament, however, it admitted in practice the results only of a conservative criticism, *e.g.* it retained the Johannine authorship and historical character of the fourth gospel.[1] The most striking innovation of the *Lux Mundi* school was a theory of kenotic Christology which allowed the admission that Our Lord may have held the erroneous opinions of his time on literary matters, *e.g.* the authorship of the psalms; but this admission was not regarded as impairing His infallible authority as a teacher of religion and morals.

The test of doctrinal authority is, broadly speaking, found by this school to consist in an application of the Vincentian Canon. Belief in papal infallibility is of course rejected, but belief in the infallibility of the Church is retained, generally in the sense that the definitions of the Undivided Church are to be accepted as statements of finally revealed truth and that the creeds are irreformable. The historical statements in the latter, *e.g. re* the Virgin Birth or the Resurrection, are to be regarded as historically certain, and as a necessary part of the Catholic faith. An element of symbolism can be admitted only in regard to statements concerning matters that lie entirely outside the range of human experience, *e.g.* the descent into hell. It is held that the historical propositions in the creed can be verified by the ordinary methods of historical inquiry.

This school[2] has little in common with modernism, and indeed much to render it antipathetic thereto. For the *Lux Mundi* position is closely bound up with the belief that the criticism of the New Testament can be relied on to yield

[1] It may be observed that according to von Hügel (in 1901) the question of the fourth gospel was the touchstone by which one could tell those who accepted *sérieusement et définitivement* the application of critical methods to religious history. See Loisy, *Mémoires*, II, 62.

[2] What is said here is intended to represent the general position of many High Anglican theologians; but there are of course considerable variations. The distinction we have in mind is similar to that noticed by Dr E. G. Selwyn in his *The approach to Christianity*, pp. 244 f., where he distinguishes between the 'historical' and the 'analytical' schools.

conservative results, results sufficiently cogent, that is, to maintain the argument to the truth of Catholic dogma from the history of Christian origins. The modernists, on the other hand, thought that it was a mistake to make the truth of Catholicism depend on this belief, and they themselves were for the most part prepared, if necessary, to accept the most radical results of criticism. In particular, they were not at all disconcerted by the eschatological view of the original gospel, which the *Lux Mundi* school has never been able to assimilate.

The critical conservatism of High Anglicans was in fact deplored by the modernists.[1] Equally, the 'relativism' and the appeal to religious experience as a whole instead of to a final and historical revelation in the past, which characterized much modernist apologetic, could not meet with the approval of those who wanted in effect to stabilize the modification of orthodoxy at the *Lux Mundi* level. If therefore they regretted the intransigent manner in which Pius X condemned modernism, they none the less regarded the condemnation itself as justified and salutary. And in the second decade of the century Bishops Gore and Talbot, two of the founders of the *Lux Mundi* school, took a prominent part in the attempt to suppress theological liberalism among the Anglican clergy.[2]

(3) But there were also from the beginning of the century and onwards some High Anglicans who recognized that the conservative or moderate critical position on which *Lux Mundi* depended was insecure, and also that there was need for a more thoroughgoing reinterpretation of Catholic theology which would take fuller account of the relation between dogma and religious experience. These followed the modernist movement with close and sympathetic attention,

---

[1] *E.g.* by von Hügel, see Loisy, *Mémoires*, II, 104, 517, and by Tyrrell, see *George Tyrrell's letters*, p. 132; but the last two of these references are to the Anglican Romanizers and not to the *Lux Mundi* school.

[2] See C. W. Emmet, *Conscience, creeds and critics* (1918).

and realized that the writings of the modernists contained much that they might with profit read, mark, learn, and inwardly digest. They were not of course prepared to follow blindly at the heels of Loisy or Tyrrell or Le Roy. How should they be? Modernism was an attempt to justify Roman and not Anglican Catholicism. But it was an attempt to do something of which both forms of Catholicism stood in pressing need. There are two main directions in which modernist influence can be traced: (i) in the claim that biblical criticism must be an autonomous science and that the Catholic critic must be allowed the same freedom as other critics; and (ii) in the development of the argument from religious experience to the truth of Catholic dogma.[1]

One of the High Anglicans who from the beginning followed the movement with sympathetic interest was G. C. Rawlinson (1868–1922),[2] who was a personal friend of Loisy and visited him more than once in France.[3] As a

---

[1] Dr W. R. Matthews writes in *The Green Quarterly* (April, 1933), p. 71: 'Anglo-Catholic theologians have been and are among the most distinguished and sometimes the most drastic of Biblical critics; and the Modernism of Loisy and Tyrrell, driven underground in the Roman Church, has found a congenial home in Anglo-Catholic theology'.

[2] For Rawlinson's interest in, and attitude to, modernism see his article in *The Church Times* (January 1st, 1904) on 'The abbé Loisy and his books', his *Recent French tendencies* (1917), ch. II, and *An Anglo-Catholic's thoughts on religion* (edited by W. J. Sparrow Simpson, 1924), *passim*. For the interest in, and sympathy with, the modernist movement shown by *The Church Times*, for which both Rawlinson and Lacey wrote, see W. L. Knox and A. R. Vidler, *The development of modern Catholicism* (1933), pp. 194–8.

[3] Dr Sparrow Simpson in his memoir of Rawlinson appears to have confused two visits. He says (*An Anglo-Catholic's thoughts on religion*, p. xxiv) that R. visited Loisy in 1908 and stayed with him several days, when he was living at a small place near Dereux (*sic*), *i.e.* Garnay. But Loisy was not living at Garnay in 1908, but at Ceffonds where in fact R. himself (*ibid.*, p. 115) says that he spent a day 'not long after (Loisy's) excommunication'. It was on the occasion of his visit to France in 1908, that R. also had an interview with Mgr Mignot.

writer for *The Church Times* he was partly responsible for disseminating information about, and arousing interest in, Roman Catholic modernism. Shortly before his death in 1922, when the movement had long been dead and buried, Rawlinson said to von Hügel: 'What Loisy originally intended and in part executed was right. It is still what we require.'[1]

A better-known representative of this attitude was T. A. Lacey (1853–1931), who in 1904 published a pamphlet, entitled *Harnack and Loisy*,[2] in which he welcomed Loisy's refutation of liberal Protestantism and with slight reservations adopted the same position. When this pamphlet was attacked by Dr W. R. Inge,[3] whose criticism of the modernist movement from what is more or less a liberal Protestant standpoint has from the outset been uniformly and persistently hostile, Lacey replied with a small volume, *The historic Christ* (1905). Here he makes his own the argument of *L'Évangile et l'Église* and of *Autour d'un petit livre* with regard to the supposed essence of Christianity and the character of the primitive gospel. He stresses too the distinction between the facts of history which are matter for critical investigation and the spiritual interpretation of history which is matter for faith, although he thinks that Loisy has over-emphasized the distinction. He does not commit himself to such advanced critical conclusions as Loisy, who, it must be remembered,

---

[1] *Church Times* (February 9th, 1923), p. 158. Von Hügel also emphasizes, while he regrets, Rawlinson's keen and persistent appreciation of Bergson. This further illustrates R.'s affinity to the modernists.

[2] Lord Halifax (1839–1934), who for more than one generation was the most revered of High Anglican laymen, contributed an introductory letter, in which he said that, while he did not himself agree with Loisy's critical conclusions, he hoped that the papacy would not, by excommunicating him, repeat the mistake it made in the case of Galileo. He also deplored the attack which had recently been made on Loisy by Mgr Batiffol. Cp. *George Tyrrell's letters*, pp. 130f.

[3] See *Faith and knowledge* (1904), pp. 281–92.

has always been, both in his Catholic days and still more since his break with Catholicism, on the left wing of biblical critics.[1] Thus Lacey does not deny altogether the historical character of the fourth gospel, but at the same time he maintains that such denial is perfectly compatible with orthodoxy (pp. 74f.). He is prepared to accept the view that Our Lord regarded the coming of the Kingdom as imminent.[2] Miracles, which traditionalists defend to the uttermost and liberal Protestants try to explain away, Lacey regards as unimportant. 'Miracles do not mean much for us, and the doubts and difficulties which their narration once raised are also coming to be of little consequence' (pp. 54f.). 'Extraordinary events are continually occurring, nor do we allow them to affect our spiritual convictions' (p. 113). He himself regards the evidence for the empty tomb as convincing, but it is a matter for historical investigation. The Resurrection as an object of faith does not depend on it. 'Certitude of faith may coincide with the extreme of scientific scepticism' (p. 121).

There is no reason to suppose that Lacey ever shared Loisy's indifference to the ultimate metaphysical problems which are implicit in all theology. The argument of *L'Évangile et l'Église* and *Autour d'un petit livre* assumed rather than asserted Christian theism as its background.[3] It was only after the condemnation of his books and when he was already on the margin of the Church that Loisy came to call in question the metaphysical aspect of Christian theology. The final result was that he ceased to believe in a personal God Who is distinct from, as well as immanent in, the universe. But his later religious philosophy was no part of his modernist

[1] *I.e.* if we leave out of account the Christ-myth theories, which are hardly to be reckoned as within the range of serious criticism. Loisy has always been a resolute opponent of these theories.

[2] For a more explicit statement of Lacey's acceptance of this view, see an article which he contributed to *The Church Times* (April 16th, 1908), quoted by Knox and Vidler, *op. cit.* pp. 198f.

[3] Cp. p. 125 above.

apologetic, nor was it postulated thereby. So far as we know, no High Anglican has ever followed him in this direction.

It is, however, through the writings of Tyrrell and Le Roy rather than of Loisy that Roman modernism has had a more far-reaching influence on Anglican theology.[1] The nature of dogma, its authority, and its relation to religious experience, are problems which during the last twenty years have largely engaged the attention of a new generation of High Church theologians. Here again, they have not taken over *en bloc* the theories of the modernists, but rather from the modernists they learned to ask the questions which they have themselves been trying to answer in what they regard as a more adequate way.

It was the merit of the modernists that they were men of their own time; along fresh lines they had proposed a re-conciliation of Catholicism with contemporary thought. This made their work suggestive for all who desired such a fresh reconciliation; but also their proposals had by force of circumstances their limitations. In particular they shared the defects which were common to most contemporary thought during the period. For the modernist movement approxi-mately coincided in time with the rise and fashionable vogue of pragmatism, Bergsonianism, and philosophical anti-intel-lectualism; and, although the movement was primarily concerned not with philosophy but with history and criti-cism, this circumstance did not fail to impose limitations on

---

[1] Doubtless, the writings of von Hügel have been as widely read by Anglicans as those of any other modernist; but it is not *qua* modernist that he has exercised his own distinctive and enduring influence. Cp. p. 204 above. The leading part which he took in the modernist movement was not a literary one, and the books through which his thought has influenced Anglicans belong to the non-modernist or post-modernist phase of his career. They are no more to be regarded as modernist literature than *e.g.* M. Loisy's second series of 'petits livres rouges'. Von Hügel's influence on Anglican theology, considerable as it has been, lies therefore beyond the scope of the present essay.

its apologetic. Thus the modernists tended in general to emphasize out of due proportion the doctrine of divine immanence, the purely evolutionary aspects of religion, and the practical and empirical aspects of dogma. This emphasis was indeed in some ways the strength of the movement, in so far as it marked a wholesome reaction from the scholastic rationalism which erred in the other direction and to which it was opposed, but it also gave it the weakness which is inherent in every reaction. The Anglican theologians whose work we are now considering were in a position to utilize the modernist lines of apologetic, and at the same time to redress the balance of its emphasis. They were careful to avoid the dangerous anti-intellectualism which seemed to be involved in Tyrrell's and Le Roy's theories of dogma. If dogma is rightly to be regarded as in the first instance a rationalization of religious experience, theology must also show the reasonableness of believing in the ultimate reality of the object of this experience.

In confirmation of what has just been said, we may notice first a small book by Dr A. E. J. Rawlinson, entitled *Dogma, fact and experience*, which was published in 1915. It consists of five distinct essays, all of which illustrate to some extent the effect of modernism on High Anglican theology. But most significant is chapter II; this is devoted to a discussion of the relation between dogma and history in the form in which the problem had been raised by the modernist controversy. After expounding Le Roy's view of dogma as primarily 'une prescription d'ordre pratique' and as having only a negative intellectual function,[1] Dr Rawlinson says: 'If we consider it purely as a philosophy of the significance and function of dogma in the life of a Churchman, I am disposed personally to accept this view. It does not, however, go to the root of the question of truth; it merely raises it and leaves it unanswered. "*Dogma interpreted as a rule of conduct involves*

[1] See p. 189 above.

the implicit affirmation that ultimate Reality is such as to justify the conduct prescribed." Precisely: there the whole problem resides. How much or how little need those words imply?' (pp. 36f.).

It is admitted that one who is already a practising churchman 'might continue to be such upon the basis of a very considerable agnosticism as to ultimate questions.' But on such a basis how could the Church make the appeal to those outside its fold which as a matter of history it has made? That appeal has always assumed the existence of a personal God for communion with Whom man was created. Man's fallen condition prevents him from attaining to this. The Church's gospel has ever consisted in the proclamation that God in Christ, by a definite historic act, was reconciling the world unto Himself. To the objective reality of such an act and its abiding consequences Christian religious experience bears evidence, and to nothing less. Dr Rawlinson here appeals against Le Roy to Laberthonnière, although he seems to overlook the fact that he too was a modernist.[1] Laberthonnière had shown that 'Christianity, in so far as it is doctrinal,...is an apprehension of the inner significance of certain events past and present in which God is pre-eminently operative and active. In brief, it tells *how God came and how God comes to man.*'

Assuming that Laberthonnière has correctly formulated the essential Christian position (continues Dr Rawlinson), it is immediately obvious that a Gospel so conceived cannot possibly be independent of all imaginable conclusions, either of historical science on the one hand or of philosophical speculation on the other. Philosophically, for example, it will be in conflict with any metaphysical school which is unable to concede the validity of its implied conception of God; while on the side of history, though not indeed necessitating *a priori* any particular order of

[1] Laberthonnière's book, *Le réalisme chrétien et l'idéalisme grec,* to which Rawlinson refers, was put on the Index on April 4th, 1906.

events, or prescribing beforehand to historical criticism the conclusions at which it shall arrive...it is yet inconsistent with the acceptance of any such reconstruction of the external order of events as would render inadmissible their interpretation *as from within* in terms of the doctrine that 'God was in Christ reconciling the world unto Himself' (pp. 46 f.).

Many questions may be left open, for example, 'questions with regard to specific events in the ministry...or even... what it felt like to be Messiah, and how much our Lord knew about it at the time.'

In a further essay Dr Rawlinson definitely accepts the eschatological interpretation of Our Lord's teaching and consciousness, and maintains that this is compatible with the orthodox doctrine of the Incarnation, although not with that doctrine as it has been generally interpreted by tradition.

Dr Rawlinson in his later writings does not appear to have laid the work of the Roman modernists under direct contribution. He has been one of those chiefly responsible[1] for the development of a type of High Anglican theology which claims to retain the essential truth of the gospel of the Incarnation while it definitely abandons the idea of ecclesiastical infallibility. It is consonant with intellectual freedom, because it disclaims absolute truth or finality for dogmatic formulas, whether scriptural, credal, or conciliar. The authority of the Church is conceived to rest 'upon the broad basis of continuous verification in reason and experience. The true authority is that which is able to flourish and to maintain itself, not simply under a *régime* of intellectual repression, but in an atmosphere of intellectual and religious freedom.'[2] It is reasonable to infer that modernism was at least one of the

[1] See his *Studies in historical Christianity* (1922), *Authority and freedom* (1924), *The New Testament doctrine of Christ* (1926), and also his essay on 'Authority' in *Essays Catholic and critical* (1926). He contributed a less mature essay on the same subject to *Foundations* (1912).

[2] *Essays Catholic and critical*, p. 95.

forces which gave an initial impetus to Dr Rawlinson's line of thought, but not that he owes to it any sustained guidance.[1]

This is probably true also of Mr Will Spens (now Master of Corpus Christi College, Cambridge), whose book *Belief and practice*[2] may be regarded as the most definite initiation of the newer type of High Anglican theology. Mr Spens was one of a group of young High Churchmen at Cambridge who in November, 1907, wrote a joint letter to Tyrrell, in which they expressed their sympathy with him in his difficulties and their gratitude for 'much that he had written'.[3] In October, 1908, he contributed to the *Journal of Theological Studies* a review of A. L. Lilley's *Modernism: a record and review*. A few extracts from this review will best indicate the nature of Mr Spens's debt to and sympathy with the modernist movement.

In this country, and not least within Mr Lilley's own communion, many are trying to understand the Modernist movement, and to discriminate between the different tendencies of which it is made up, and the various conclusions to which it seems to point...

Probably many who have followed the controversy will feel that, however considerable their substantial agreement with the Modernists, the Vatican is not without claim on their sympathy; and they may feel that not the least value of Mr Lilley's volume is the opportunity it gives for concentration of attention on possible dangers in the position of the Modernists....

---

[1] Cp. *Essays Catholic and critical*, p. 92. Rawlinson refers to Tyrrell's argument from the pragmatic value of religious experience, and remarks that it 'is of value as far as it goes....But the argument of Tyrrell, while suggesting that in every spiritually vital religious tradition there is *some element* of truth, of which account must be taken, does not obviously justify the intellectual acceptance at face value of the *prima facie* claims of any and every tradition, as such.'

[2] First published in 1915; second edition, 1917, to which reference is here made.

[3] See Petre, *Life of Tyrrell*, II, 371.

It is of course obvious that we cannot be called upon to accept unreservedly all the beliefs of former ages: the question arises as to what credentials a belief must have that its prevalence in the past may command our acceptance in the present. Here, not least, the views advanced by some of the Modernists are peculiarly suggestive....

It would be unnecessary as well as impertinent to praise M. le Roy's discussion of dogma,...and I can only express my own admiration and acknowledge a real personal debt; nor is the least part of that debt a greater realization that the questions which most concern the spiritual life are those the answers to which directly affect our action, demanding that we should follow one course not another; that in consequence dogmas embody truths which have most relation to such questions. But there seems at least a danger in the direction indicated (*i.e.* that the Catholic faith is only a successful code for self-suggestion) when the intellectual value of dogma is subordinated to the practical....

The review concludes as follows:

Some attempt has been made to indicate two possible dangers in Modernism—exaltation of the outlook of our own age, and minimizing of the intellectual value of dogma. If, however, there are these and other dangers, they arise from what constitutes the great value of the movement—a close connexion with modern thought inseparable from some touch of its weakness. It is this close connexion and the sympathy underlying it that lead many to hope for much from that new apologetic which Modernism is endeavouring to provide.[1]

In *Belief and practice* Mr Spens elaborates a new system of apologetic for Catholicism, which may be taken to be the outcome of his own study of modernism and of its possible dangers. It must however be pointed out that he now uses the terms 'modernism' and 'modernist' in an abstract sense of his own, *i.e.* to denote a 'synthesis' from which he wishes to differentiate his own position. The procedure may be

[1] *Op. cit.* x. 148–53.

legitimate for its purpose,[1] but it must be recognized that
what Mr Spens now means by modernism is not the actual
movement in all its concrete and complex variety and incoherence, but a system of thought and in particular a theory
of the Incarnation towards which he supposes that the movement was tending and which, if it had been allowed free
course, it would have developed.[2] It is a procedure that
would be liable to obscure the extent to which his own
position represents a departure from traditional orthodoxy,
were it not that he himself explicitly allows, and even
emphasizes, the fact of this departure (*e.g.* p. 71). There can
be no doubt that, if *Belief and practice* had been written by a
Roman Catholic, it would have been regarded as a dangerously modernist work and as certainly falling under the
condemnation of the encyclical *Pascendi* as, for instance,
L'Évangile et l'Église, *Through Scylla and Charybdis*, or *Dogme
et critique*, and that its author, if he had been a priest, would
have been compelled to recant or, failing that, would have
been excommunicated.

What Mr Spens does is to use the methods that had been
used by some of the modernists, in particular by Tyrrell,
who is the only one to whom he refers by name,[3] and
to show that they lead in some respects to different conclusions, to conclusions that are less evidently subversive
of traditional orthodoxy. Thus his apologetic is based not
on any metaphysical structure, nor on an appeal to the

---

[1] It has been adopted by other Anglican theologians for similar
reasons, *e.g.* by Canon O. C. Quick (see his *Liberalism, modernism and
tradition*, 1922, ch. 11) and by Professor A. E. Taylor (see p. 264 below).
In any case it is less likely to lead to misapprehension than the more
popular usage which treats 'modernism' as practically synonymous with
'liberal Protestantism'.

[2] He expressly allows (see p. 23) this point with regard to Tyrrell; *a
fortiori* it applies to the modernist movement as a whole.

[3] See also his article on Tyrrell in the *Expository Times* (March,
1929).

New Testament as by itself justifying a supernatural Christology, but to the whole stream of Christian experience[1] as requiring the theology, which is its intellectual expression, as the most adequate means of explaining and co-ordinating that experience. Religious experience, not a body of information or a series of propositions which were once upon a time revealed *ab extra*, constitutes the data of theology.

The purpose of every branch of science is to explain and mediate the experience which is its own proper subject, and the wider the range of facts which it succeeds in relating the greater is its claim to acceptance; this is also the purpose of, and the case with, theology. But there can be no absolute finality in any science. No more can be claimed for theology than that it is 'the expression of a growing insight into ultimate reality' (p. 62). Mr Spens goes further than Tyrrell, and in so doing safeguards his position from the charge of pragmatism in a way that Tyrrell failed to do. He points out that a scientific theory, to be successful, must not only explain the particular facts with which it is directly concerned but also it must produce 'a sound general outlook', *i.e.* it must be compatible with a general philosophy of the universe. And he claims that Christian theology, which is the rationalization of Christian religious experience, does stand this test. Thus, for instance, while the main ground for belief in the existence of God is religious experience, the general value of this belief as a philosophical conception is attested by the metaphysical arguments for theism, and it receives thereby at least partial verification.

The central doctrine of historical Christianity is the In-carnation, and the crux of every method of apologetic lies in its attempt to defend this doctrine. Having dismissed the liberal Protestant theory on the grounds that it 'involves a

[1] For an important elucidation of what is meant by religious experience, see *op. cit.* p. 254.

fundamental rejection of the facts of experience' and also that it 'is in collision with modern emphasis on the eschatological element in the Gospels', Mr Spens holds that there remain two possible doctrines of the Incarnation.

(i) There is what he calls an 'improved form of Modernism' —'the conception of a diffused incarnation.'

It can accept the whole Christian doctrine of the body and members of Christ, and can regard the historic Jesus as the head in that body; but it would urge that, just as in natural physiology we had to alter our views, and regard the life as dwelling in the body as a whole rather than as drawn from the head, so we must make a similar change of view in regard to our conceptions of the mystical body. It would be urged that, although Jesus of Nazareth was the head of the body, the life of the body dwelt in the body as a whole, and simply in Him as its supreme and most important member; that it was not drawn from Him or through Him....

Ultimately the decision as between such a Modernist synthesis, and more traditional conceptions, must rest on the full consideration of that view, and on its final adoption or rejection by thought which fully allows both for Christian experience and for the literary relics of the initial period, regarded in the light of that experience (pp. 90 f.).

(ii) Mr Spens allows that modernism, so regarded, can build up a theology 'which appears to cover the great bulk of Catholic experience', but he argues that it 'involves grave and fatal defects' as compared with his own re-interpretation of the traditional theology. It gives a less adequate explanation of the evidence which the New Testament yields as to the life and consciousness of Our Lord. A more serious defect is its failure to do justice to Christian experience, which has been 'led more and more to a very strong instinct in favour of the view that our spiritual life is drawn from (or through) one person, at once human and divine', and in particular to 'the whole type of experience which is associated with the doctrines of Atonement and Redemption.' This experience 'appears to be very directly dependent on the conception of an Incarnation in the person of Jesus' (pp. 97 f.). Mr Spens therefore holds that the traditional Christology, which regards God as having become incarnate in the Jesus of history, has greater claims to acceptance.

He proceeds to a discussion of the difficulties that are raised by the view which he favours. In the course of this he sets out what is in effect a modification of the traditional interpretation of orthodox Christology. He urges, for instance, that the notion that Our Lord during His human life was omniscient must be definitely abandoned. He admits too that the acceptance of '"miracle" was carried much too far, made reaction inevitable, and makes modification necessary' (p. 132). 'While it seems probable that truth will lie in a development, not of Modernism, but of traditional Christology, we must expect to find that any adequate solution is far richer and more complex than past conceptions of that doctrine' (p. 134).

There has in fact since the great war been a considerable development of High Anglican theology along the lines anticipated by Mr Spens in *Belief and practice*. The theology, which we have described as that of the *Lux Mundi* school, has indeed continued to be advocated by distinguished representatives, not least by Bishop Gore himself until his death in 1932. The type of thought, which Mr Spens described as modernism, *i.e.* the modernism from which he differentiated his own position, has not, so far as we can ascertain, been advocated by any responsible High Anglican theologian. But there has been a steady succession of High Anglican writings which, whether consciously or not, illustrate or develop the newer type of apologetic for Catholicism which in the cases already noticed derived an impetus and important suggestions from Roman modernism. But it does not seem possible to show that the later writings alluded to[1] have directly made use of the work of the modernists to any noteworthy extent.

Professor A. E. Taylor's *The faith of a moralist* (1930) is perhaps a partial exception to this. He discusses the relation of Christianity to historical *credenda* in a wider context than Mr Spens, but his position, and in particular his manner of referring to the modernist movement, are much the same. Thus the modernism, from which he differentiates his own position, is of an extreme or, as he himself expresses it, of an 'unqualified' form, a modernism for which 'the spiritual value of a religion is *wholly* independent of beliefs about historical fact' (ii, 116; italics in the original). He quotes a saying of Tyrrell's which is representative not of Tyrrell's modernism but rather of the scepticism to which in certain moods he was reduced by its failure. Professor Taylor is entitled for his own purposes to define modernism as the 'tendency to dispense with the historical element in religion' (ii, 134), but such a definition would be a caricature if it were intended to be objective and comprehensive. The modernists as a whole, including Loisy and Tyrrell, would surely have accepted Professor Taylor's description of his own position as a not improper description of theirs.

The appeal to history (he writes) by the success or failure of which Christianity, or any other faith, may fairly be judged has very little to do with what are known as the 'historical evidences' of a religion; it is the application to religion of the Gospel

[1] *E.g.* W. L. Knox, *The Catholic movement in the Church of England* (1923); R. H. Thouless, *An introduction to the psychology of religion* (1923); *Essays Catholic and critical* (1926), edited by E. G. Selwyn, though these essays also include work which stands rather in the *Lux Mundi* tradition; L. S. Thornton, *The Incarnate Lord* (1928); E. Milner-White and W. L. Knox, *One God and Father of all* (1929); E. O. James, *The Christian faith in the modern world* (1930); W. L. Knox and A. R. Vidler, *The development of modern Catholicism* (1933), where the influence of modernism on High Anglican theology is specifically admitted and illustrated. See also A. E. J. Rawlinson's books referred to above, p. 257n.

maxim 'by their fruits ye shall know them'. The vital question is not how much or little of the chronicled detail of the Founder's life can be authenticated in a way which will satisfy the exacting historical critic, or how far his certainly genuine utterances can be made into a code of 'categorical imperatives'; it is whether he has brought, and continues to bring, a new quality of spiritual life into humanity, or not (II, 131).

Professor Taylor appears, like Mr Spens, to have regarded the modernist movement with keen, if critical, sympathy,[1] but it is unlikely that the influence of its literature upon his intellectual development was so considerable. However, he certainly had a very high regard for Tyrrell as a thinker, as is illustrated by the fact that, in 1914, he expressed the wish that Tyrrell, if he had lived, might have been appointed as a Gifford lecturer.[2]

It should also be observed that Professor Taylor, again like Mr Spens, differentiates his position not only from 'unqualified' modernism, but also from what we have called the *Lux Mundi* theology. Thus he criticizes Gore's attempt to allow a symbolical interpretation of some articles in the creed, *e.g.* the Ascension, while rigidly insisting on a literal interpretation of others, *e.g.* the Virgin Birth. 'What I dispute', writes Professor Taylor, 'is the right of any man, or body of men, to claim once and for all to limit the right to recognize the presence of the symbolic element to the case of certain specified articles and to exclude from active participation in the devotional life of the Christian community those who do not make the same precise restriction'.[3]

The evidence, which has been adduced, is sufficient to justify the conclusion that the modernist movement contributed substantially, if only in its initial stages, to the development within the Church of England of a new

---

[1] *The faith of a moralist*, II, 131.
[2] Von Hügel, *Selected letters*, p. 211.
[3] *The faith of a moralist*, II, 142, cp. p. 113.

apologetic for Catholicism that is intended to meet modern thought on its own ground and to evade none of the assured results of historical and biblical criticism. The revival in the Church of England during the last hundred years of Catholicism as a living religious system, whatever may be thought of its legitimacy, has certainly been remarkable, and this revival continues steadily to extend its influence. The newer type of theology, in which it is now expressing itself, may be held to support the suggestion that what the Roman modernists, in various ways but entirely unsuccessfully, aspired after is likely to be realized, in part at least, in Anglicanism, *i.e.* a development of the historic Catholic religion whose theology will take full account of the progress of human knowledge.

It is interesting to recall that towards the end of his life Tyrrell, although he had decided that it was his own vocation not to return to the Church of England but instead to live and die as a professedly Roman Catholic who protested against 'the Vatican heresies', expressed the hope that what the modernists had vainly sought to achieve in the Church of Rome might come to pass in or through the Church of England. At the time however the hope seemed very uncertain because Anglican Catholicism still appeared to be predominantly traditionalist in outlook. On January 13th, 1909, he wrote to Arthur Boutwood (Hakluyt Egerton) as follows:

Possibly the Church of England may be able to accept the results of history, and yet retain the substance of her Catholicism, *i.e.* she may have room for Modernism. I *hope* so. But my growing impression is that the instinct of the Athelstane Riley, Spencer-Jones, and Halifax schools is like that of Pius X, wise in its generation.... My own sympathies are not with Spencer-Jones but with those who seek an *entente* with science on the one hand and with the historical Catholicism of the East and the Alt-Katholicismus on the other.... If Modernism fails in the Church of England (and by Modernism I always mean a synthesis of Catholicism and Science—not the supremacy of the latter) it may be abandoned as a noble dream. In the Roman Church it has not a fair chance because the other term of synthesis there is not Catholicism, but Ultramontanism, which is a species of Protestantism. My own work—which I regard as done—has been to raise a question which I have failed to answer. I am not so conceited as to conclude that it is therefore unanswerable. And I think that it may be the destiny of the Church of England to answer it.[1]

In 1909 Tyrrell's misgivings were justified; the hope he thus expressed is being realized to an extent which could hardly then have been foreseen. To Anglicans this realization,

---

[1] *George Tyrrell's letters* (1920), pp. 118f; cp. a letter to the same effect written to Mrs Dowson in 1907, *ibid.* pp. 132ff.; also Petre, *Life of Tyrrell*, II, 368. It is curious to find this hope—that what had failed in the Roman Church would succeed in the Anglican—reflected in a very different and somewhat unexpected quarter. Thomas Hardy, in the 'apology' which is prefixed to his *Late lyrics and earlier* (1922), spoke of his fear that 'we seem threatened with a new Dark Age', and of his hope that a progressive religious movement might do much to counteract the dissolvent forces in our civilization. Since the failure of the modernist movement in the Roman Church, he thought that the Anglican Church appeared to be the most likely field—so far at least as England was concerned—for a religious movement which, while preserving what was good in tradition, would be willing to 'remove those things that are shaken'. Thus he wrote: 'Since the historic and august hierarchy of Rome some generation ago lost its chance of being the religion of the future by doing otherwise, and throwing over the little band of New Catholics who were making a struggle for continuity by applying the principle of evolution to their own faith, joining hands with modern science, and outflanking the hesitating English instinct towards liturgical restatement (a flank march which I at the time quite expected to witness, with the gathering of many millions of waiting agnostics into its fold); since then, one may ask, what other purely English establishment than the Church of England, of sufficient dignity and footing, with sufficient strength of old association, such scope for transmutability, such architectural spell, is left in this country to keep the shreds of morality together?' (*op. cit.* pp. xvif.).

and its future prospects, may seem to be the most directly interesting, and even the most important, outcome of the modernist movement. At the same time the complete failure of the movement within the Roman communion and the manner in which all the forces opposed to it there have consolidated themselves ought not to be regarded with indifference by anyone who takes a large view of the future of European civilization and of Christianity as a world-religion. The Church of England is only one among several, indeed among many, institutions upon which the future of Christendom depends; it depends not least upon the Church of Rome.

There must be many non-Roman Christians who will subscribe to the words of a recent Anglican writer: 'The condemnation of this liberal movement in the Roman Catholic Church by Pius X was one of the greatest theological misfortunes of modern times; and the words *Pascendi* and *Lamentabili* will for long continue to evoke feelings of regret in the minds of those who look forward to a world-wide Catholicism with its arms open to modern intellectual and cultural needs.... Upon the development and success of a second Modernist Movement in the Roman Catholic Church, the ultimate future of Christian culture in Western Europe, humanly speaking, depends.'[1]

It has not been possible to point to any signs that a second modernist movement is likely to develop shortly or that, if it did develop shortly, its fate would be much different from that of the first. Ultimately, no doubt, the Roman Church will be unable to maintain its intransigent attitude to all that conflicts with its traditional teaching. The story of Galileo will in one form or another repeat itself. Sooner or later the doctrinal and disciplinary absolutism, in which ultramontanism has issued, will have to undergo radical change.

[1] Dr F. L. Cross in the *Church Quarterly Review* (April, 1933), pp. 147 f.

Those who believe that the truth ultimately prevails will believe also that the truths, for which the modernist movement was an attempt to win acceptance, mingled there as they inevitably were with error, are bound to triumph in the end. The history of the movement, however, prompts the reflection that certain parts of the truth are at present likely to prevail in the Roman Church much later than elsewhere.

Appendix I

ON THE USE OF THE TERMS 'MODERNISM', 'MODERNIST'

The most careful and complete examination of the use of the terms 'modernism' and 'modernist' (in their various linguistic forms), prior to their definitive adoption in the encyclical *Pascendi*, is that of M. J. Rivière, *Le modernisme dans l'Église* (1929), pp. 13–34. The words had a longer and more interesting history behind them than was at first supposed. The adjective at least has been used since the sixteenth century, although with various shades of meaning and in widely different contexts. The first instance appears to be its application to the nominalists by Luther in 1524.

The origin of its application to the Roman Catholics, who were condemned by the pope in 1907, is still somewhat obscure. But, as Rivière points out (*op. cit.* pp. 25 f.), there is no evidence to justify Dr H. D. A. Major's assertion that 'the word *Modernisti* began to be used ecclesiastically during the pontificate of Pope Leo XIII whose policy encouraged it if it did not actually originate it'.[1] The earliest instance of its use, or rather of the use of *modernismo*, by any ecclesiastical authority occurs in a pastoral letter from the bishops of the provinces of Turin and Verceil, which was published on Christmas day, 1905. The first instance of its use in Italy by anyone at all is in an article by a priest named Umberto Benigni, published in January, 1904. It is uncertain whether

[1] *English modernism* (1927), p. 19; cp. *Ency. Brit.* 14th ed. (1929), xv, 637: 'The word Modernism had been used on the Continent during the pontificate of Leo XIII as the designation of a neo-scholastic (!) movement in the Roman Catholic Church which was condemned by the Encyclical *Pascendi* in 1907'.

the use of the terms in France arose independently or was derived from Italy. In any case it was not until about the beginning of 1906 that 'loisysme' and 'loisyste' gave way to 'modernisme' and 'moderniste'.[1]

[1] Rivière does not notice the use of the word 'modernism' by Tyrrell in two of his published letters (one written in August, 1901, the other in November, 1903) in a sense which, so far as can be judged from the context, approximates closely to that which it later acquired. See *Life of Tyrrell*, II, 52; *George Tyrrell's letters*, p. 132. Even so, this use of the word in private correspondence may do no more than confirm Rivière's hypothesis of 'une génération spontanée dans des milieux différents' (*op. cit.* p. 30).

LAMENNAIS ON THE NEED OF DOCTRINAL RENOVATION

F. de La Mennais, *Des progrès de la révolution et de la guerre contre l'Église* (1829).

Pp. 276 ff. Ne craignons point de l'avouer, la théologie, si belle par elle-même, si attachante, si vaste, n'est aujourd'hui, telle qu'on l'enseigne dans la plupart des séminaires, qu'une scolastique mesquine et dégénérée, dont la sécheresse rebute les élèves, et qui ne leur donne aucune idée de l'ensemble de la Religion, ni de ses rapports merveilleux avec tout ce qui intéresse l'homme, avec tout ce qui peut être l'objet de sa pensée. Ce n'étoit pas ainsi que la concevoit saint Thomas, lui qui, dans ses ouvrages immortels, en a fait le centre de toutes les connoissances de son temps. Empruntez de lui cette méthode admirable qui coordonne et généralise, et joignez-y ces vues profondes, ces hautes contemplations, cette chaleur, cette vie, qui caractérisent les anciens Pères: alors disparoîtra ce pesant ennui, qui éteint parmi les jeunes gens destinés au sacerdoce, le goût de l'étude et même le talent. Retranchez de vos cours tant de vaines questions qui les fatiguent sans fruit, et leur enlèvent un temps précieux, qu'ils emploieroient bien plus utilement à s'instruire de choses applicables au siècle où ils vivent, et au monde sur lequel ils doivent agir. Tout a changé autour de vous; les idées ont pris et continuent de prendre incessamment des directions nouvelles; institutions, lois, mœurs, opinions, rien ne ressemble à ce que virent nos pères. A quoi serviroit le zèle le plus vif, sans la connoissance de la société au milieu de laquelle il doit s'exercer. Il est nécessaire d'apprendre autrement, et d'apprendre davantage: autrement, pour mieux entendre; davantage, pour ne pas rester en arrière de ceux qu'on est chargé de guider. Ce n'est point par ce qu'ils savent, que les ennemis du christianisme sont forts, mais par ce qu'ignorent ses défenseurs naturels. Cette espèce d'infériorité, résultat, comme nous l'avons dit, de circonstances passagères, affoiblit singulièrement l'influence du Clergé sur les classes instruites, et nuit beaucoup à la Religion dans un siècle vain de ses prétendues lumières, et où l'éducation, les journaux, les recueils périodiques de tout genre, les livres plus multipliés que jamais, mettent certaines notions générales à la portée d'un grand nombre de gens sottement fiers de ce mince avantage.

Mais il ne suffit pas de perfectionner les premières études cléricales; on doit étendre plus loin ses regards, et se proposer un but plus élevé. Long-temps l'Église tint en sa main le sceptre des sciences, et ce fut une des causes de l'ascendant qu'elle acquit sur les esprits. Ce moyen d'action seroit maintenant plus puissant qu'à nulle autre époque, et l'on feroit ainsi tourner à l'avantage des hommes ces connoissances indifférentes en soi au bien et au mal, mais qui produisent infailliblement plus de mal que de bien quand le principe religieux ne préside pas à leur développement.

D'immenses travaux ont été entrepris depuis trente ans, et sont poursuivis avec ardeur par les savants de tous les pays. Il est temps que la science catholique vienne recueillir la riche moisson qu'on lui a préparée....

BIBLIOGRAPHY

Note. This is not intended to be a complete bibliography of the modernist movement, still less of its origins and outcome. The fullest existing bibliography of the movement itself will be found in Rivière's *Le modernisme dans l'Église*, pp. xiii–xxix. The following is a list of books which have been used by the writer of the present essay; those which have been found most useful and which are regarded as most important are marked with an asterisk.

ACTON, LORD. *History of freedom and other essays* (1907).
— *Letters to Mary Gladstone*, ed. H. Paul (1904).
— *Correspondence*, ed. Figgis and Laurence, vol. I (1917).
ADAM, KARL. *The spirit of Catholicism* (1929).
— *Christ our Brother* (1931).
ARNOLD, MATTHEW. *Literature and dogma* (1873).
BALFOUR, LORD. *The foundations of belief* (1894).
BARBIER, E. *Histoire du catholicisme libéral et du catholicisme social en France, 1870–1914*, 5 vols (1924).
BARRY, W. *The tradition of Scripture* ([1]1906, [2]1908).
— *Memories and opinions* (1926).
BAUDRILLART, A. **Vie de Mgr d'Hulst*, 2 vols ([4]1928).
BAZIN, G. *Vie de Mgr Maret*, 3 vols (1891).
BETHUNE-BAKER, J. F. *The way of modernism* (1927).
BLONDEL, MAURICE. *L'action: essai d'une critique de la vie et d'une science de la pratique* (1893).
— *Histoire et dogme* (1904).
— *Léon Ollé-Laprune: l'achèvement et l'avenir de son œuvre* (1923).
— *Le problème de la philosophie catholique* (1932).
BOURGET, PAUL. *Le démon de midi* ([11]1933).
BRÉMOND, HENRI. *The mystery of Newman* (1907).
— *L'inquiétude religieuse*, 2e série ([4]1921).
BUONAIUTI, E. **Le modernisme catholique* (1927).
CHATEAUBRIAND, F. R. *Le génie du christianisme* (vol. II of *Œuvres complètes*, 1902 edition).
CLÉMENT, M. *Vie du cardinal Richard* ([2]1924).
CROSS, F. L. *John Henry Newman* (1933).

DESJARDINS, PAUL. *Catholicisme et critique* (1905).

D'HABLOVILLE, C. *Grandes figures de l'Église contemporaine* (1925).

DUPONT, E. *Mgr Duchesne chez lui en Bretagne* (1923).

EGERTON, HAKLUYT. *Father Tyrrell's modernism* (1909).

EMMET, C. W. *The eschatological question in the gospels* (1911).

— *Conscience, creeds and critics* (1918).

Essays Catholic and critical, ed. E. G. Selwyn (1926).

FAWKES, ALFRED. **Studies in modernism* (1913).

— *The Church a necessary evil*, ed. H. D. A. Major (1932).

FELDER, H. *Christ and the critics*, 2 vols (1924).

FOGAZZARO, A. **The Saint* (1906).

FORBES, F. A. *Rafael, Cardinal Merry del Val* (1932).

Foundations, by Seven Oxford Men (1912).

GALLARATI-SCOTTI, T. *The life of Antonio Fogazzaro* (n.d.).

GARDNER, PERCY. *Modernism in the English Church* (1926).

GASPARRI, CARDINAL. *The Catholic Catechism* (Eng. trans. 1932).

GASQUET, ABBOT. *Lord Acton and his circle* (1906).

GIBSON, HON. W. *The abbé de Lamennais and the liberal Catholic movement in France* (1896).

GILBERT, K. *Maurice Blondel's philosophy of action* (1924).

GOUT, RAOUL. *L'affaire Tyrrell* (1910).

GRANDMAISON, LÉONCE DE. *Jesus Christ: His Person, His message, His credentials*, 2 vols (Eng. trans. 1930–32).

GUIGNEBERT, CH. *Modernisme et tradition catholique en France* (1908).

— *Le christianisme mediéval et moderne* (1922).

HARNACK, ADOLF. **What is Christianity?* (Eng. trans. 1901).

HARRIS, CHARLES. *Creeds or no creeds* (1922).

HÉBERT, MARCEL. *L'évolution de la foi catholique* (1905).

HEILER, FRIEDRICH. *Der Katholizismus* (1923).

HERMANN, E. *Eucken and Bergson* (²1912).

HOGAN, J. B. *Clerical studies* (1898).

HOLLAND, BERNARD. *Belief and freedom* (1923).

HORTON, W. M. *The philosophy of the abbé Bautain* (1926).

HOUTIN, ALBERT. **La Question biblique chez les catholiques de France au XIX*^e *siècle* (²1902).

— *L'Américanisme* (1904).

— *La Question biblique au XX*^e *siècle* (²1906).

HOUTIN, ALBERT, *La crise du clergé* (^{2}1908).
— *Histoire du modernisme catholique* (1913).
— *Le Père Hyacinthe*, 3 vols (1920–24).
— *Un prêtre symboliste: Marcel Hébert* (1925).
— *Une vie de prêtre* (^{2}1928).
— *Ma vie laïque* (1928).
HÜGEL, BARON F. VON. *The mystical element of religion*, 2 vols (1908).
— *Eternal life* (1912).
— *Essays and addresses*, 2 vols (1921 and 1926).
— *Selected letters*, ed. B. Holland (1927).
INGE, W. R. *Faith and knowledge* (1904).
— *Outspoken essays*, 2nd series (1922).
JAMES, WILLIAM. *The will to believe* (1897).
— *The varieties of religious experience* (1902).
JORDAN, L. H. *Modernism in Italy* (1909).
KNOX, W. L. *The Catholic movement in the Church of England* (1923).
— and A. R. VIDLER. *The development of modern Catholicism* (1933).
KÜBEL, JOHANNES. *Geschichte des katholischen Modernismus* (1909).
LABERTHONNIÈRE, L. *Le réalisme chrétien et l'idéalisme grec* (1904).
LACEY, T. A. *Harnack and Loisy* (1904).
— *The historic Christ* (1905).
LAGRANGE, M.-J. *Historical criticism and the Old Testament* (Eng. trans. 1905).
— *Évangile selon saint Jean* (1925).
— *M. Loisy et le modernisme* (1932).
LAKE, KIRSOPP. *The religion of yesterday and to-morrow* (1925).
LAMENNAIS, F. DE. *Essay on indifference in matters of religion* (Eng. trans. of vol. I, 1895).
— *Des progrès de la révolution et de la guerre contre l'Église* (1829).
LEAR, H. L. S. *Henri Dominique Lacordaire* (1887).
LEBLANC, S. *Un clerc qui n'a pas trahi* (1931).
LEBRETON, J. *Le Père Léonce de Grandmaison* (1932).
LECANUET, E. *La vie de l'Église sous Léon XIII* (1930).
LÉPICIER, A. M. *De stabilitate et progressu dogmatis* (^{2}1910).
LEPIN, M. *Les théories de M. Loisy* (^{2}1908).

LE ROY, E. *Dogme et critique* (1907).
— *Une philosophie nouvelle* (²1913).
LEROY-BEAULIEU, A. *Les catholiques libéraux* (1885).
Letters to His Holiness Pope Pius X, by 'a Modernist' (Chicago, 1910).
LILLEY, A. L. *★Modernism: a record and a review* (1908).
LOISY, A. *Études bibliques* (³1903).
— *★L'Évangile et l'Église* (¹1902, ⁵1929): Eng. trans. *The Gospel and the Church* (²1908).
— *★Autour d'un petit livre* (1903).
— *★Simples réflexions* (²1908).
— *Quelques lettres* (1908).
— *A propos d'histoire des religions* (1911).
— *Choses passées* (1913): American trans. *My duel with the Vatican* (1924).
— *La religion* (²1924).
— *L'Église et la France* (1925).
— *★Mémoires*, 3 vols (1930–31).
— *Y a-t-il deux sources de la religion et de la morale?* (1933).
LOO, VAN. *Kantisme et modernisme* (1917).
Lux Mundi, ed. C. Gore (1889).
MAISTRE, J. DE. *Du pape* (Eng. trans. by A. McD. Dawson, 1850).
MAJOR, H. D. A. *English modernism* (1927).
MAY, J. L. *Father Tyrrell and the modernist movement* (1932).
MERCIER, CARDINAL. *Modernism* (1910).
MILNER-WHITE, E. and W. L. KNOX. *One God and Father of all* (1929).
MÖHLER, J. A. *Symbolism*, Eng. trans. by J. B. Robertson (1894).
MOZLEY, J. K. *Ritschlianism* (1909).
NEWMAN, CARDINAL. *★An essay on the development of Christian doctrine* (²1846).
— *★An essay in aid of a grammar of assent* (1870).
— *Essays critical and historical*, 2 vols (¹⁰1890).
— *Difficulties of Anglicans* (⁵1879).
— *Apologia pro vita sua* (Everyman's edn).
NUNN, H. P. V. *What is modernism?* (1932).
OMAN, J. *The problem of faith and freedom* (1906).
PAGANI, G. B. *The life of Antonio Rosmini-Serbati* (1906).

PETRE, M. D. *Life of George Tyrrell* (1912).
— *Modernism* (1918).
PHILLIPS, C. S. *The Church in France, 1789–1848* (1929).
Programme of modernism, The (1908).
PURCELL, E. S. *Life of Cardinal Manning* ([1]1895).
QUICK, O. C. *Liberalism, modernism and tradition* (1922).
RAWLINSON, A. E. J. *Dogma, fact and experience* (1915).
— *Studies in historical Christianity* (1922).
— *Authority and freedom* (1924).
— *The New Testament doctrine of Christ* (1926).
RAWLINSON, G. C. *Recent French tendencies* (1917).
— *An Anglo-Catholic's thoughts on religion*, ed. W. J. Sparrow Simpson (1924).
RENAN, E. *Vie de Jésus* (33rd edn).
— *Souvenirs d'enfance et de jeunesse* (1883).
RENARD, E. *Le cardinal Mathieu* (1925).
RIVIÈRE, J. *Le modernisme dans l'Église* (1929).
— *Monseigneur Batiffol* (1929).
ROSMINI, A. *Of the five wounds of the holy Church*, Eng. trans. by H. P. Liddon (1883).
SABATIER, AUGUSTE. *Outlines of a philosophy of religion* (1897).
— *The religions of authority and the religion of the Spirit* (1904).
SABATIER, PAUL. *Modernism* (1908).
— *France to-day: its religious orientation* (1913).
SANTAYANA, G. *Winds of doctrine* (1913).
SAROLEA, C. *Cardinal Newman* (1908).
SCHNITZER, J. *Der katholische Modernismus* (1912) in *Die Klassiker der Religion*.
SCHWEITZER, A. *The quest of the historical Jesus* ([2]1911).
SPENS, W. *Belief and practice* ([2]1917).
STEWART, H. L. *Modernism past and present* (1932).
STORR, V. F. *The development of English theology in the nineteenth century* (1913).
TAYLOR, A. E. *The faith of a moralist*, 2 vols (1930).
THORNTON, L. S. *The Incarnate Lord* (1928).
TYRRELL, G. *Nova et vetera* ([4]1905).
— *Hard sayings* ([7]1910).
— *External religion: its use and abuse* ([4]1906).

TYRRELL, G. *The faith of the millions*, 2 vols (²1902).
— *Oil and wine* (²1907).
— *Religion as a factor of life* (1902).
— ★*The Church and the future* (²1910).
— ★*Lex orandi* (²1907).
— *Lex credendi* (²1907).
— ★*A much-abused letter* (1906).
— ★*Through Scylla and Charybdis* (1907).
— ★*Medievalism* (⁴1909).
— ★*Christianity at the cross roads* (²1910).
— ★*Autobiography*, ed. M. D. Petre (1912).
— *Essays on faith and immortality* (1914).
— ★*George Tyrrell's letters*, ed. M. D. Petre (1920).
VERMEIL, E. ★*Jean-Adam Möhler et l'école catholique de Tubingue, 1815–1840* (1913).
WARD, WILFRID. ★*W. G. Ward and the Catholic revival* (²1912).
— *The life and times of Cardinal Wiseman*, 2 vols (1897).
— *The life of John Henry Cardinal Newman*, 2 vols (³1913).
— *Ten personal studies* (1908).
WARD, MRS WILFRID. *Out of due time* (1906).
WEBB, C. C. J. *A history of philosophy* (1915).
— *A study of religious thought in England from 1850* (1933).
WEILL, G. ★*Histoire du catholicisme libéral en France, 1828–1908* (1909).
What we want: an open letter to Pius X, Eng. trans. by A. L. Lilley (1907).

In addition to the above list of books, the files of various periodicals have been consulted with profit, especially *The Home and Foreign Review*, *The Hibbert Journal*, and *The Modern Churchman*. References to these and to others, both English and foreign, will be found in the text or foot-notes of the essay and in the index, as also to works of reference, dictionaries, and encyclopaedias.

INDEX

Acton, 1st Lord, 26, 30, 42, 45–8, 53, 60, 274
Adam, K., 229 ff., 274
Americanism, 213
Annales de philosophie chrétienne, 185
Anti-modernist oath, 203, 219, 221 f.
Arnold, M., 47, 159–62, 274

Balfour, A. J. (Lord), 158 f., 274
Barbier, E., 70, 187, 224, 274
Barnes, E. W., 245 f.
Barry, W., 87, 98, 213, 225–8, 274
Barth, K., 123
Batiffol, P., 126, 128, 223 ff., 230, 252
Baudrillart, A., 27, 71 f., 75, 79, 81 f., 274
Baur, F. C., 33
Bautain, L., 28 f.
Bazin, G., 28, 274
Bell, G. K. A., 237
Benigni, U., 270
Bergson, H., 148, 159, 186, 188
Bertrand, A. N., 93
Bethune-Baker, J. F., 4, 274
Bezzant, J. S., xi
Biblical commission, 96, 128, 134, 138, 224 f., 227
Bickell, G., 65
Biran, Maine de, 188
Blondel, M., 54 f., 126, 148, 162, 165, 185 ff., 194, 207 f., 274
Bodley, J. E. C., 210
Bollandist Fathers, 65
Bonald, L. de, 21, 32
Bossuet, J. B., 16, 20
Bourne, Cardinal, 162
Boutroux, E., 186, 188
Boutwood, A., 266
Brémond, H., 159 f., 274

Broad Church party (Anglican), 159, 210, 242 ff.
Bulletin critique, 71
Buonaiuti, E., xii, 4, 51, 126, 158, 186, 191 ff., 197, 200, 222 f., 243, 274
Burke, E., 43
Butler, J., 54, 143 f.

Cambridge Modern History, 15, 25, 27, 32
Capes, J. M., 45
Carpenter, S. C., xi
Catholic Encyclopaedia, 5
Chateaubriand, F. R., 18 f., 24, 43, 274
Christian democrats, xii, 191 f.
Church, R. W., 52
Church of England, 7, 43 f., 55, 143 ff., 175, 180, 209 f., 212, 241–68
Church Quarterly Review, 57, 268
Church Times, 251 ff.
Churchmen's Union, *see* 'Modern Churchmen, Anglican'
Civiltà cattolica, 42, 96
Clément, M., 135, 137, 274
Codex Juris Canonici (1917), 223
Coleridge, S. T., 43, 243
Collège de France, 73
Comma Johanneum, 94
Contemporary Review, 91
Correspondant, 81
Cross, F. L., 57, 268, 274

Darwin, C., 111, 193
Dawson, A. McD., 21
Desjardins, P., 77, 93, 128 f., 275
d'Habloville, C., 70 f., 77 f., 275

CAMBRIDGE: PRINTED BY W. LEWIS, M.A., AT THE UNIVERSITY PRESS

Date Due

MAR 8 '84			
4-27			
FEB 18 '81			
APR 8 '87			

Demco 293-5